ANALYSIS AND INTERPRETATION OF ETHNOGRAPHIC DATA

ETHNOGRAPHER'S TOOLKIT
Second Edition

Jean J. Schensul, Institute for Community Research, Hartford, Connecticut
Margaret D. LeCompte, University of Colorado, Boulder

PURPOSE OF THE ETHNOGRAPHER'S TOOLKIT

The second edition of the **Ethnographer's Toolkit** is designed with the novice field researcher in mind. In this revised and updated version, the authors of the **Toolkit** take the reader through a series of seven books that spell out the steps involved in doing ethnographic research in community and institutional settings. Using simple, reader-friendly language, the **Toolkit** includes case studies, examples, illustrations, checklists, key points, and additional resources, all designed to help the reader fully understand each and every step of the ethnographic process. Eschewing a formulaic approach, the authors explain how to develop research questions, create research designs and models, decide which data collection methods to use, and how to analyze and interpret data. Two new books take the reader through ethical decision-making and protocols specific for protection of individual and group participants in qualitative research, and ways of applying qualitative and ethnographic research to practical program development, evaluation, and systems change efforts. The **Toolkit** is the perfect starting point for students and faculty in the social sciences, public health, education, environmental studies, allied health, and nursing, who may be new to ethnographic research. It also introduces professionals from diverse fields to the use of observation, assessment, and evaluation for practical ways to improve programs and achieve better service outcomes.

1. *Designing and Conducting Ethnographic Research: An Introduction, Second Edition,* by Margaret D. LeCompte and Jean J. Schensul
2. *Initiating Ethnographic Research: A Mixed Methods Approach,* by Stephen L. Schensul, Jean J. Schensul, and Margaret D. LeCompte
3. *Essential Ethnographic Methods: A Mixed Methods Approach, Second Edition,* by Jean J. Schensul and Margaret D. LeCompte
4. *Specialized Ethnographic Methods: A Mixed Methods Approach,* edited by Jean J. Schensul and Margaret D. LeCompte
5. *Analysis and Interpretation of Ethnographic Data: A Mixed Methods Approach, Second Edition,* by Margaret D. LeCompte and Jean J. Schensul
6. *Ethics in Ethnography: A Mixed Methods Approach,* by Margaret D. LeCompte and Jean J. Schensul
7. *Ethnography in Practice: A Mixed Methods Approach* by Jean J. Schensul and Margaret D. LeCompte

ANALYSIS AND INTERPRETATION OF ETHNOGRAPHIC DATA
A Mixed Methods Approach
Second Edition

Margaret D. LeCompte
and Jean J. Schensul

A division of
ROWMAN & LITTLEFIELD PUBLISHERS, INC.
Lanham • New York • Toronto • Plymouth, UK

Published by AltaMira Press
A division of Rowman & Littlefield Publishers, Inc.
A wholly owned subsidiary of The Rowman & Littlefield Publishing Group, Inc.
4501 Forbes Boulevard, Suite 200, Lanham, Maryland 20706
www.rowman.com

10 Thornbury Road, Plymouth PL6 7PP, United Kingdom

British Library Cataloguing in Publication Information Available

Library of Congress Cataloging-in-Publication Data
LeCompte, Margaret Diane.
  Analysis and interpretation of ethnographic data : a mixed methods approach /
Margaret D. LeCompte and Jean J. Schensul. — 2nd ed.
      p. cm. — (Ethnographer's toolkit ; Book 5)
  Previous title: Analyzing and interpreting ethnographic data
  Includes bibliographical references and index.
  ISBN 978-0-7591-2207-9 (pbk. : alk. paper) — ISBN 978-0-7591-2208-6 (electronic)
  1. Ethnology—Methodology. I. Schensul, Jean J. II. Title.
  GN345.L42 2013
  305.8001—dc23

                                                                                    2012023521

™
∞   The paper used in this publication meets the minimum requirements of American
National Standard for Information Sciences—Permanence of Paper for Printed Library
Materials, ANSI/NISO Z39.48-1992.

Printed in the United States of America

CONTENTS

LIST OF TABLES AND FIGURES

LIST OF EXAMPLES

INTRODUCTION

The *Ethnographer's Toolkit*, a mixed methods approach to ethnography, is a series of texts on how to plan, design, carry out, and use the results of applied ethnographic research. Ethnography, as an approach to research, may be unfamiliar to people accustomed to more traditional forms of research, but we believe that ethnography will prove not only congenial but also essential to many researchers and practitioners. Many of the investigative or evaluative questions that arise in the course of answering basic questions about ongoing events in a community or school setting or in the context of program planning and evaluation cannot be answered very well with other approaches to research, such as controlled experiments or collection of quantifiable data. Often there are no data available to quantify or programs whose effectiveness needs to be assessed! Sometimes the research problem to be addressed is not yet clearly identified and must be discovered. In such cases, ethnographic research provides a valid and important way to find out what *is* happening and to help research-practice teams plan their activities.

NEW IN THE SECOND EDITION OF THE *ETHNOGRAPHER'S TOOLKIT*

In this second edition of the *Toolkit*, we have updated many sections of the books and, based on feedback from our colleagues, we have clarified many of the concepts and techniques. Book 1 of the *Ethnographer's Toolkit* remains an introduction and primer, but it includes new material on data collection, definition, and analysis as well as new chapters on research partnerships and using ethnography for a variety of applied purposes. In Book 1 we define what ethnographic research is, when it should be used, and how it can be used to identify and solve complex social problems, especially those not readily amenable to traditional quantitative or experimental research methods alone. Book 2 now is devoted to the process of developing a conceptual basis for research studies and to more detailed questions of research design and sampling. Books 1 through 4 emphasize the fact that ethnography is a peculiarly human endeavor; many of its practitioners have commented that, unlike other approaches to research, the *researcher* is the primary tool for collecting primary data. As we demonstrate in these books, ethnography's principal database is amassed in the course of human interaction: direct observation, face-to-face interviewing and elicitation, audiovisual recording, and mapping the networks, times, and places in which human interactions occur. Further, the personal characteristics and activities of researchers as human beings and as scientists become salient in ethnography in ways not applicable in research that permits the investigator to maintain more distance from the persons and phenomena under study. Interpretation of ethnographic research results emerges only from the process of engaging researcher understanding with direct, face-to-face field experience.

Book 4, a collection of individually authored chapters, now includes new chapters on cutting-edge approaches to ethnography. Books 6 and 7 also are entirely new to the *Toolkit*. The former provides extensive detail on the burgeoning field of research ethics and the latter approaches the dissemination and application of ethnographic research in new ways.

We have designed the *Toolkit* for educators, service professionals, professors of applied students in the fields of teaching, social and health services, communications, engineering and business, and students working in applied field settings who are interested in field research and mixed methods ethnographic research. The examples we include throughout the books are drawn from these fields as well as our own research projects and those of our colleagues.

INTRODUCTION TO THE SECOND EDITION OF BOOK 5

This book, titled *Analysis and Interpretation of Ethnographic Data: A Mixed Methods Approach, Second Edition*, is the most complete treatment available for showing how researchers transform piles of field notes, observations, audiovisual materials, questionnaires, surveys, documents, maps, and other kinds of data into research results and interpretations that help people to understand their world more fully and facilitate problem solving. Addressing both text and visually based qualitative data as well as quantitative, or enumerated, data, Book 5 discusses methods for organizing, retrieving, rendering manageable, displaying, and interpreting the data collected in ethnographic research. In chapter 1, we discuss what analysis is, what its purposes are, and why it is necessary. We distinguish between qualitative and quantitative data, as well as quantified qualitative data, and we discuss the differences between analysis of data to produce "results" and interpretation of results to render the ethnographic portrait meaningful. Chapter 2 describes the process of recursive analysis, which begins in the field with inscription and head notes, moves through creation of full field notes, and ultimately produces transcription of observations and recordings.

Chapter 3 introduces the reader to an all-important but often forgotten initial stage of analysis, which we have termed "tidying up"; it essentially is a process of winnowing through, organizing, and cataloging data. This stage renders ethnographic data manageable. Ethnographers then begin the process of moving recursively between levels of abstraction, from concrete to abstract and back, creating descriptions of what they have found and generating explanations at levels ranging from local to substantive theories for why what they have found exists. These processes are described in chapter 4. Chapter 5, which is devoted to general and thematic forms of coding, describes the cognitive processes that researchers use to cause themes and codes to "emerge" from the data stream; it also discusses in detail a number of well-known inductive techniques for analyzing coding data.

Chapter 6 addresses issues of specific coding and initial quantification, beginning with ways to aggregate and disaggregate data as well as how to generate codes. We define what specific codes are and how to create and use them, and we discuss how researchers develop and use schemes that are congruent with their own research questions. We describe what codes look like and where they come from, as well as how to handle precoded data. Then, in chapter 7, we discuss what codebooks (records of codes and their definitions) are, how to create them, and how to use them with both qualitative and quantitative ethnographic data. As well, we introduce issues attendant to working in teams of researchers and the particular concerns that exist when multiple researchers in multiple sites handle data; these include procedures for coding verification and team coding. We also present an extended example that illustrates how a researcher not only developed a coding system for a large team project, but used computer software to assist in the process of managing the data.

In chapter 8 we describe how computers can be used to manage and analyze both qualitative and quantitative data. We enumerate all the ways that computers have made the tasks of organizing and analyzing ethnographic data far easier for researchers than in the eras prior to such electronic tools. This is especially true for data-crunching activities that create new composite variables and constructs.

In chapter 9 we first review how ethnographic surveys are built, based on variables defined in formative theoretical models and prior fieldwork. We then present different approaches to quantification of qualitative data. We distinguish between ethnographic survey research and standardized, structured survey research. We make it clear that ethnographic surveys are commonly used by ethnographers, but only after considerable fieldwork has preceded their construction and administration. We hold that while ethnographers make primary use of several types of individual and group interviews, they also employ "mixed-methods" approaches that may include surveys and other forms of quantified data based on concepts and constructs that emerge from prior qualitative inquiry. We call these surveys and other quantified data *ethnographic* because they are specific to the sociocultural settings within which the research is being conducted rather than based on scales and other measures created by others, with different populations and sites. By describing in detail how to go about these basic ethnographic tasks, our goal is to improve the quality of ethnographic research in general. Chapter 9 presents a careful discussion of the most common statistical methods used to describe quantified ethnographic data, as well as ways in which results produced from qualitative and quantitative data can be integrated and differences between such results resolved.

In chapter 10 we discuss how coded data are assembled to create the cultural patterns and structures that constitute the basis of an ethnographic portrayal. This chapter focuses on how to create preliminary results by assembling initial data patterns to create more complex data patterns and explanations. We describe how empirical patterns are grouped within domains to create structures, and how substantive theories emerge to generate explanatory domains and variables related to those structures.

Chapter 11 is devoted to fine-tuning results, beginning the write-up of data and determining how best to display the data collected. We argue that researchers "know" what they can "show" and that showing off data to best advantage requires considerable ingenuity. To aid them, we provide multiple examples of how data can be presented. Ethnographic results are not complete without having been explained or interpreted to ascertain their meaning, both to local participants and to outside audiences. In the final chapter of Book 5, we discuss interpretation of data, helping the reader to understand how to determine what the data really mean and then to present this information to various audiences.

As is the case with all of the books of the *Ethnographer's Toolkit*, we illustrate each chapter with examples drawn from our own research and that of our associates and students. These examples and case studies present ways in which ethnographers have coped with problems and dilemmas found in the field, during their work and over extended periods of time. We believe that these examples can provide guides to best practices for all those wishing to undertake well-grounded ethnographic research.

1

WHY ARE ANALYSIS AND INTERPRETATION NECESSARY?

WHY ARE ANALYSIS AND INTERPRETATION NECESSARY?

As we have noted in Books 1 through 4 of the *Ethnographer's Toolkit*, ethnographers and qualitative researchers have devised many ingenious ways to conceptualize, organize, and collect information, all based on observing and talking to human beings or examining the documents and objects they have created in the past. These information-collecting methods range from very unobtrusive to very obvious and sometimes even intrusive, and from very unstructured to highly structured. Ethnographic and qualitative data collection produces piles and piles of raw data—stacks of interviews, piles of field notes, collections of reports, documents, newspaper clippings, and artifacts, boxes of audio- and video-recordings, and hundreds and hundreds of cards, slips of paper, maps, and photographs and digital materials. This book addresses the problem of what to do with these piles.

"What to do" becomes a critical issue at a point usually about halfway through a research project, when ethnographers begin to notice that their briefcases, offices, closets, hallways, computers, and even their cars have begun to over-

Key point

Definition: Analysis reduces data to a story ethnographers can tell; interpretation tells readers what that story means and why or how it is important.

Definition: Qualitative data are descriptive; they pertain to the "qualities" or characteristics of people, places, events, phenomena, and organizations.

flow with piles of data. While these piles are indeed the raw material for ethnographies, by themselves, they do not create an ethnography. Rather, *ethnographers create ethnography in a sometimes tedious and often exhilarating two-step process of analysis of raw data and interpretation of analyzed data.* **Analysis** reduces data to a story ethnographers can tell; interpretation tells readers what that story means. Without both, ethnographic data is quite literally meaning-*less*.

WHAT ARE QUALITATIVE DATA?

In the first part of this book, we will talk about analysis and interpretation of what is commonly, if awkwardly, called "qualitative" data. **Qualitative data** are descriptive; they pertain to the "qualities" or characteristics of people, places, events, phenomena, and organizations. As Denzin and Lincoln (2003, 13) put it,

> The word *qualitative* implies an emphasis on the qualities of entities and on processes and meanings that are not experimentally examined or measured (if measured at all) in terms of quantity, amount, intensity, or frequency. Qualitative researchers stress the socially constructed nature of reality, the intimate relationship between the researcher and what is studied, and the situational constraints that shape inquiry. . . . They seek answers to questions that stress *how* social experience is created and given meaning.

Qualitative data usually are embodied in audiovisual and text-based records. Sometimes they can be recorded in a manner that is relatively easy to crunch and analyze, such as data collected via systematic interviews or standardized surveys. However, they also can be recorded as very complex and detailed field note descriptions that address complicated issues such as the characteristics of relationships, the origin of events or problems, and the reasons why events transpire as they do.

Qualitative data achieve meaning by being viewed through theoretical or explanatory lenses. They can, therefore, acquire different meanings, depending on the lens being used. For example, data on adolescents who fail to graduate from high school can be interpreted through a psychological lens that blames "dropping out" on characteristics of individual adolescents—perhaps chronic illness, a new baby to care for, or inability to speak and write the school's dominant instructional language. By contrast, a critical lens would look at the same demographic characteristics and interpret the situation as caused by the structure of the school that did not provide special supports for such adolescents to compensate for characteristics that interfered with their ability to meet school timetables, instructional requirements, and financial demands.

Not only do qualitative researchers need to remember that what data mean depends on how they are looked at, but researchers also must recognize that analyzing qualitative data requires a rather different schedule and approach than that usually employed in quantitative or numerical studies. As we indicated in Book 1 of the *Ethnographer's Toolkit*, some research designs that depend exclusively on surveys leave much of the data analysis and interpretation to the final stages of the research process. In such designs, preliminary analysis may occur to see what trends emerge during the initial data collection period, but the final analysis begins when all the data are collected, entered, cleaned, and corrected. In survey research, final data analysis depends on using systematically collected data from a statistically representative sample. In experimental research, where data are collected before and after an intervention takes place, "baseline data" (collected prior to the intervention) can be analyzed, but the effects of the intervention cannot be assessed until all the postintervention data are complete and are ready to be compared with the "baseline" data to see how much change may have taken place. These analyses may even occur long after the researcher has left the field or the laboratory. By contrast, ethnographers begin their analysis almost as soon as they enter the field site.

Because ethnography often is exploratory, researchers always must be alert for possible surprises. Investigations usually begin with some uncertainty about which direction the study might take, the kinds of data which will be most relevant, the specific populations that might be

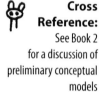

Cross Reference: See Book 2 for a discussion of preliminary conceptual models

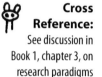

Cross Reference: See discussion in Book 1, chapter 3, on research paradigms

most important to contact, and even which questions are most salient to ask. Studies may begin with an initial set of research questions, a conceptual model or diagram that illustrates the main components of a study at the onset and a desire to explore the origins of a specific social problem, or a hunch that a particular event or phenomenon will facilitate understanding of complex social processes. Often researchers enter with these initial ideas, only to find out when in the field that a different problem or population must be explored, that the event under investigation lacks the dynamics hoped for, or that the original conceptual model for the project must be expanded or even discarded. Likewise, the researcher even may have begun the study informed by a general theoretical paradigm or way of thinking about the world, only to find that this framework does not match with the way people in the field explain their world.

Thus, ethnographic researchers modify their project continually during its entirety. They develop and test initial interpretations of the data as they go along, continuing the process even up to the point at which the final page of the last report is written. The process of analysis, hypothesis creation, and testing persists throughout the data collection process and even into analysis and interpretation of data results. Sometimes, a period of time away from the field is needed in order to help researchers reflect upon and achieve sufficient clarity about what really transpired in the field or to be able to understand the dynamics of the field setting or events that took place during their tenure there.

EXAMPLE 1.1

WHEN THE INSIDER STORY DOES NOT SQUARE WITH THE INITIAL SET OF RESEARCHER QUESTIONS AND CONCEPTS

Carter Middle School is a dual immersion bilingual school with a largely Hispanic and low-income enrollment in a small city in the western United States. Its inner-city building, constructed in the 1930s, was falling apart. It had to be razed and rebuilt, which meant closing the program for eighteen months. School district administrators decided to move the Carter students and teachers into temporary "trailers" on the campus of predominantly white, middle-income, and English-speaking Phillips Middle School, three miles away. Researcher Sarah Staley had hoped to study how the doubling up on one campus affected each school; she anticipated that the renovation plan would provide an opportunity for the two schools to engage in more ethnically integrated activities that could build cross-ethnic contacts. Her initial conceptual framework was built around the idea that contact would improve climate. However, school district administrators had a different set of ideas. They felt that maintaining two completely separate schools—separate entrances, offices, parking lots, instructional programs, and lunch and assembly schedules was "practical" and the only feasible way to run the programs, given that the renovations at Carter began midyear and teachers at neither of the schools had had time to plan for more integrated activities. They made no effort to integrate the two schools' programs, planning only one activity all year—an ice cream social—for the students in both schools (Staley 2010).

⬥—•—⬥—•—⬥

The simple facts of the case did not make sense to Staley. She tried to explore the local explanation—practicality mandated complete separation of the two programs—even though it was not congruent with her original conceptual framework. Ultimately, Staley had to step back to create a new interpretation of the data, one embedded in the dynamics of historical racial and socioeconomic segregation in the community, in order to develop an "outside" interpretation that explained the lack of joint activity—and contradicted the explanations given by administrators. The "outside" interpretation focused on the desire of white and affluent parents to send their children to schools segregated by class, language, and ethnicity, and the desire of administrators to avoid antagonizing those parents.

⬥—•—⬥•—⬥　　　　**EXAMPLE 1.2**

COMPETING VIEWS OF CAUSALITY IN A NAVAJO SCHOOL DISTRICT

During their fieldwork in a Navajo community, LeCompte and her associates found that there were distinct and competing explanations for why so many unfortunate events had happened in the school district they were studying. The gymnasium roof had begun to leak during a sudden rainstorm, flooding the newly installed basketball floor and ruining it. Two faculty members had developed fatal illnesses. Over one-quarter of the students in high school were failing at least one subject. And morale of teachers and staff was so low at the high school that a number of the district's best teachers were planning to leave at the end of the school year. The assistant

superintendent and the researchers attributed the problems to general bad luck, a building boom in the area that had made it difficult to find competent construction workers for the gym roof repairs, and an autocratic new school principal who had alienated students and teachers alike. Teacher turnover always was high in this district, the assistant superintendent explained, because it attracted young white teachers interested in Indians and Indian culture. They soon became disenchanted when they found out just how isolated the community was and that the local Navajos were not very interested in getting to know them. He suggested recruiting teachers who were less naive and more culturally competent and figuring out appropriate grounds to dismiss and replace the high-school principal. By contrast, many of the Indian staff felt that the discord and misfortune in the district resulted from an imbalance between the forces of man, the Holy People, and nature. The disharmony had been caused by some as-yet-unknown transgression; it would be redressed if a traditional healing ceremony to restore harmony were performed on behalf of the district and its personnel. As applied researchers, LeCompte and McLaughlin felt responsible for finding a single "answer" to the many problems. However, the problem was that no single answer could reconcile the multiple ideas about causation afoot in the community (LeCompte and McLaughlin 1994).

In the example above, analysis of results clearly demonstrated major differences between a Western, scientific rationale for events and the more traditional Navajo definition of the problem and its solution. Like Staley's story, the "facts of the case" were clear, but what they meant, and how they should be interpreted, were not. Rather than try to force a consensus between what really were incommensurate explanatory systems, the district used strategies from both the traditional and more bureaucratic perspectives to help identify the origins of the problems and resolve them.

EXAMPLE 1.3

COMPETING EXPLANATIONS FOR THE ORIGINS OF BLINDNESS AMONG CAMBODIAN REFUGEES

A number of refugees who managed to escape the "killing fields" of Cambodia and find their way to California had become blind, though their vision had been unimpaired in Cambodia and they reported no disease or trauma that could have damaged their eyes. Social service personnel arranged medical examinations for the refugees, only to have the doctors say that from a physiological standpoint, nothing was wrong with their eyes. Neurological testing showed that when presented with visual stimuli, the refugees could "see"—as measured by brain waves—even though the people reported that they saw nothing. Convinced that the refugees were not lying or faking, social service personnel probed further and found that all of the people who were blind without apparent cause had witnessed the most horrific acts of savagery, including the murder and torture of their families, entire villages, and thousands of other people by the Khmer Rouge. The social workers reasoned that the refugees simply could not bear to witness any more horrors. Their brains had created some kind of psychological block that prevented visual stimuli from being recognized as sight and rendered them "blind." A remedy for the blindness lay not in medical treatment, but in pyschocultural and perhaps traditional shamanistic therapy for their posttraumatic stress.[1]

◄──●──◄──●──◄

In this case, the usual explanations simply did not fit the case. Careful sleuthing by workers with cultural sensitivity and knowledge of the historical context helped find a reasonable, if unusual, explanation for the blindness of the refugees, one that a modern medical model could not produce.

Another way to look at the idea of poor model fit is illustrated in Example 1.4. In this case, a particular preliminary theoretical model (providing after-school activities popular in their home country to immigrant adolescents will increase their enthusiasm for and attendance at school) provided a catalyst for program planning, but the preliminary model alone proved inadequate in the face of additional data.

◄──●──◄──●──◄ **EXAMPLE 1.4**

WHY LATINA SOCCER PARTICIPANTS WERE DIFFICULT TO RECRUIT

Educators in the high mountain community of Coalville were at a loss to determine ways to build greater enthusiasm for school attendance among Mexican American immigrant girls. Knowing that soccer (football) is a passion among Latin Americans, the high school organized an after-school club for girls to play soccer and anticipated a competition among girls' soccer teams throughout the state of Colorado. Initial enthusiasm was high, but participation among the girls quickly fell off. The disconsolate educators wondered why what they thought was a culturally appropriate activity failed to get off the ground. Had their assumptions been incorrect? A critical analysis by doctoral student (and girls' soccer coach) Erin Alleman showed that while a soccer program was indeed culturally responsive to Mexican American girls' interests, participation in the program was impossible for most of them. The Latino community was physically isolated and socially segregated from the white community and the school that was to serve both. In addition, Latina girls faced insurmountable obstacles of cost, distance, and transportation. Overlaying maps of the physical features of the community (a river bisected it, only one bridge crossed the river) with maps of transportation routes (no public transportation served the trailer parks where Mexican Americans lived) and maps showing income and ethnic distribution in the community made clear that Mexican Americans were located across the river and far upstream from the school and in an impoverished area. Only one bus conveyed Mexican American children to school from their community, and it left school immediately after classes. The distance home was too great to walk or bicycle, and Mexican American girls had no alternative transport. Having to leave with the bus precluded staying for soccer practice, as did required babysitting and chores at home. The solution lay not just in arranging soccer games, but also in providing adequate transportation for soccer practices and other appropriate activities (Alleman 2009).

•◆•◆•◆•

Example 1.4 illustrates exactly why good formative or preliminary fieldwork must precede the implementation of interventions. Had such work been done, the school and its researchers might have initiated their implementation of the soccer program simultaneously with transportation innovations and other interventions so as to produce better outcomes. Similarly, preliminary fieldwork in the neighborhood surrounding Phillips Middle School might have made clear to Sarah Staley that proximity of two very different groups would be insufficient to create a rapprochement between ethnic groups. Ethnographers must realize that if they do not examine critically, or if they remain closed to new ways of formulating and interpreting what they observe in the research site, they may never fully understand or be able to interpret the meaning of the phenomena they observe during their fieldwork. They also must be aware that simply because circumstances *seem* favorable does not mean that enhanced cooperation and problem solving automatically will follow. Fortunately, the three-stage analytic process that characterizes ethnography facilitates openness; it allows researchers to revise original formations, raise different questions, and even come to conclusions far removed from what they originally anticipated. This process is called *recursive analysis*, and it consists of the following:

- Analysis done *in the field* while researchers still are involved in the data collection process
- Analysis *away from the field soon after the data collection is complete* and certainly as soon as one emerges from (if living in and studying an aspect of one's own community) or returns from the field
- Analysis done *after work in the field is complete and at some distance or period of time away* from data collection or analysis of ethnographic data collected by others

Although it may seem counterintuitive to begin analysis while still doing fieldwork and collecting data, the exploratory nature of ethnographic work mandates such a process to identify, clarify, and modify initial impressions and descriptions. Exploratory analysis consists of:

- examining what one has already collected based on initial questions and model;
- making initial comparisons across observations and interviews;
- revisiting the study model and design, determining what has been learned so far, revising as necessary, and formulating the next set of questions to be explored;
- determining what data should be collected to answer them; and then
- collecting those data, examining them, and beginning the process again.

In fact, in some forms of data collection, analysis *must* begin after the very first interview. For example, the narrative interviewing process involves collecting three or four interviews from the same person, each one of which is more targeted and more personal. Later interviews depend on a close review and interpretation of earlier interviews to produce a more nuanced set of questions (Wengraf 2004).

Doing analysis immediately after each stage in data collection assures that the researcher has not missed some important details. Researchers create a summary of the overall broad themes identified in the study and check to make sure that all relevant research questions have been answered—or modified in the light of field realities—and that no information that might still be needed goes uncollected. This process can be facilitated by the use of a data collection matrix or checklist. If done when the bulk of the data are collected and just prior to leaving the field, this stage in the analysis provides an opportunity for researchers to return for one or more short visits so as to collect additional data whose importance was not initially anticipated, to fill gaps where data are missing or were inadvertently not collected, or to examine issues that emerged in the course of data collection and still need further explication. The final stage of analysis is done at some distance in time and space from the field and blends with final interpretation of the data; it gives researchers time to gain perspective on their experiences and the lessons they have learned (LeCompte and Preissle 1993; LeCompte and Schensul 1999; Wengraf 2004).

Cross Reference:
See Book 1, chapter 6 for examples of such matrices

WHAT ARE QUANTITATIVE DATA?

Contrary to some stereotypes, ethnographers use both qualitative *and* quantitative data. In fact, we argue that ethnographers must be able to use both types of data in order to compile a complete and valid portrayal of the events under study. **Quantitative data** are those that can be easily counted and enumerated. Quantitative data include test scores, scaled responses to questions about attitudes, preferences, and reported behaviors, true-false answers, and responses to categorical or demographic questions about age, sex, marital status, racial identification, income, place of residence, and political party affiliation. Even when using very unstructured data collection techniques, ethnographers collect demographic data from each person interviewed or from whom any data are collected, including community experts, and key informants in cultural-level interviews and from semistructured interviews with individuals residing in the study setting about their own experiences. These data can facilitate a search for varia-

Definition:
Quantitative data are those that can be easily counted and enumerated

tion among the population. Further, ethnographers do use semistructured interviews to ask each respondent about the same domains so as to collect generally comparable qualitative information from everyone in the study.

Other quantitative information can be collected in surveys that ask for fixed or closed-ended answers. The questions asked require respondents to choose an option that appropriately describes themselves, their experience, or their perspectives. Ethnographers frequently use such surveys, but only after having done sufficient initial fieldwork to create questions—and possible answers—that make sense for the population and topic under study. Surveys with fixed or closed-ended questions assume that the range of answers already is known and that researchers wish to identify the distribution of responses to specific questions and topics within a given population.

Cross Reference:
See Book 3, chapter 7 for a discussion of the creation of ethnographic surveys

Many researchers do not understand that systematically collected qualitative data always can be quantified for comparative or descriptive statistical analysis. Thus, quantitative data may be collected separately *as* quantitative data, or they may be created by quantifying qualitative data. The "bits" of quantitative data consist of numbers, which are smaller and easier to manipulate, while qualitative data, consisting of chunks of text and artifacts, are larger, lumpier, and more difficult to manipulate; they must be coded and aggregated before they can be enumerated and subjected to statistical procedures. Coding qualitative data numerically (e.g., quantifying these data) can assist in identifying patterns that are then described and interpreted through reference to text or observational data.

Cross Reference:
See chapter 7 in this book for a detailed description of coding procedures

This is done by counting, matching, comparing, contrasting, grouping, and looking for associations and relationships within a qualitative database (Miles and Huberman 1984). Thus, quantifying qualitative data requires researchers to do a great deal of crunching and other manipulation before the data are amenable to enumeration.

Cross Reference:
See chapter 9 in this book for details on the statistical procedures commonly used in data analysis

Mixed Methods

In Book 1 of the *Toolkit*, we considered the ways in which different research designs interact such that both quantita-

Cross Reference:
Tables 4.5 and 4.6 in Book 1, chapter 4 and Book 2, chapter 7 of the *Ethnographer's Toolkit* display how qualitative and quantitative methods may be "mixed" in a given study

Cross Reference:
Books 1, 3, and 4 in this series highlight the many different types of data that can be collected in ethnographic research

 Cross Reference:
See Book 1, chapter 4 for a discussion of mixed-methods designs, Book 2 for ways of designing mixed methods studies, and Book 5, chapters 9 and 10 for ways to quantify and analyze qualitative data

tive and qualitative methods can be combined in a single study. However, the term "mixed methods" in ethnography more or less is a given; all ethnographies make use of various types of data in text, numerical, and audiovisual forms that are collected in a single study and integrated. Pelto and Pelto (1978) were among the first ethnographers to describe clearly the many different ways in which data could be collected at the individual, group, and cultural levels. Most ethnographic studies incorporate some form of text, as well as mapped, elicited, and numerical data. In this sense, most ethnographic research designs employ a mixed-methods approach at the outset because the initial plans call for the collection of both qualitative and numerical data. For example, researchers may know that they lack familiarity with the language uses of the proposed population and need to do initial fieldwork to assure that their survey questions and standardized scales are comprehensible to participants. Or funders may want not only a clear-cut definition of the problem but also to know the actual number of individuals in a community who are affected by the particular problem under investigation. Similarly, census data or standardized survey data may be able to quickly identify the existence of a belief system, social dynamic, or practice in a population but be unable to clearly portray its nuances, participants, or purposes. In such cases ethnographic or qualitative data would be required. Any research design in which multiple forms of data are required should plan for and allow time to address the different kinds of data, making sure that analytic techniques appropriate for more qualitative data are employed and also that appropriate software to assist in the analysis of quantitative data—or quantified qualitative data—is at hand.

The schedule for analyzing the different kinds of data collected in a study depends on the needs of the study and, as well, the story to be told. Sometimes, certain kinds of quantitative data can be analyzed first. For example, if researchers plan to use already existing test score data, student demographic information, and parental satisfaction surveys routinely collected by a school under study, they might analyze these data first. Having a big chunk of data already analyzed can be a morale booster for the researcher. In other cases, conceptual factors dictate analyzing one type of data prior to another, as, for example, when initial exploratory work must be done to identify a population or language style, explain a process, or specify a problem before additional data are collected. Thus, in mixed designs, analysis of qualitative data may be done before analysis of quantitative data so as to contribute to a plan for collection of quantitative data, or both kinds of data may be collected simultaneously, or quantitative data collection may lead to the need for qualitative data collection so as to explicate results. A typical example would be in cases where test results show that a particular educational program did not achieve the desired improvement in student performance. Simple failure usually is insufficient information; qualitative research methods are needed to demonstrate *why, when, and with whom* the program failed. Sometimes failure can be explained not by flaws in the program itself, but in the failure of teachers to understand what they need to teach, the lack of appropriate materials with which to teach, an attitudinal set among teachers that delegitimizes the approach taken, or simply that the program was applied to a different population than that for which it was intended.

In Books 2, 3, and 4 of the *Ethnographer's Toolkit*, we laid out a sequence of basic steps in ethnographic data collection, from review of secondary data to mapping, gathering histories, interviewing gatekeepers and key informants, and doing open ended observations, becoming more focused through semistructured interviewing and observations, and finally, building on these experiences to conduct ethnographic surveys. Such surveys are used to confirm hypotheses and hunches identified through other forms of data collection, with a larger sample of respondents. Book 4 describes many different additional forms of data collection that can be used to supplement these basic steps at any stage. Following this sequence generally requires at least preliminary analysis of earlier data collection to guide next steps. But, of course, other approaches can be used as described above.

WHAT IS ANALYSIS?

What, then, is analysis? And what is its purpose? Sometimes called "data crunching," initial stages in analysis reduce piles

Cross Reference:
See Book 4 for additional forms of data collection including the uses of secondary and archival data

of data to a more manageable form which permits ethnographers to begin "telling a story" about the people or group which is the focus of their research. Harry Wolcott, a noted anthropologist, says that the goal of analysis is to create less data, not more (1990). Wolcott really does not mean that ethnographers lose data when they analyze them; rather, the raw data are examined closely, parsed, coded, counted, tallied, and summarized so that what the ethnographer ends up with are much more concise collections of "crunched" data (LeCompte and Goetz 1982) rather than piles of interviews and file cabinets full of field notes. Crunching data is the first stage in the production of results, which simply are the facts of the case or the story to be told. In practice, several stages of crunching may be necessary before results actually emerge. Michael Patton (1990), an evaluation researcher, says that analysis does three things:

- It brings order to the piles of data an ethnographer has accumulated.
- It turns the big piles of raw data into smaller piles of summarized data.
- It permits the ethnographer to discover patterns and themes in the data and to link them with other patterns and themes.

Qualitative data, then, are coded according to descriptive taxonomies and then grouped using more abstract or conceptual codes that further "crunch" or combine variables. The patterns and themes in qualitative data, then, are aggregated into domains among which relationships can be identified. This process transforms "raw" jottings on scraps of paper, field note entries, recollections, and partial transcripts from raw into "cooked data" or "results." A similar process exists for quantitative data. First, one examines frequencies for all variables/items, then formulates scales or creates composite variables, and finally looks at the relationships among them, first two by two and then in terms of more elaborate models that combine variables in different ways. **Results** constitute the "observed facts" of a study; they are the beginnings of a story worth telling. But just as raw data do not consti-

Definition: Results are constituted of the "observed facts" of a study; they do not constitute an ethnography, or the end product of the analytic process

tute an ethnography, analyzed data do not constitute the end of the process. Analyzed data, as we shall see, must be *interpreted* to produce an ethnography.

Below are some results from a study LeCompte did of the Learning Circle, an after-school program designed to improve the academic achievement and participation in elementary school of American Indian children.

 **EXAMPLE 1.5**

"RESULTS" FROM A STUDY OF THE LEARNING CIRCLE: "RESPECT" FOR NATIVE AMERICAN PARENTS

After reading and rereading daily teacher schedules, transcripts of interviews conducted with teachers, field notes taken while accompanying teachers on home visits, and records of parent conversations made during evening parent meetings, Learning Circle researchers confirmed their initial impression that a consistent style of interaction existed between parents of Learning Circle children and program staff. The researchers had noticed that (a) parents always were contacted by the certified teachers who worked with their children, not by social workers, paraprofessionals, or other lower-status nonacademic personnel (direct communication with a high-status professional, a conceptual code); (b) considerable effort was made to give the parents advance notice of visits (advance notice, a conceptual code); (c) parents (parental engagement—a conceptual code) were provided with many choices (parental input—a conceptual code) in how they worked with the educational materials the teachers left in the homes for child and parent usage; (d) parent meetings always involved a meal or refreshments (ritual significance— a conceptual code)—a practice denoting a significant event in American Indian culture, and (e) (parental input—a conceptual code) parents were encouraged to provide ideas for the curriculum.

The case example above presents what we call stages one and two of the analysis process; these are discussed in more detail below.

WHAT IS INTERPRETATION? HOW RESEARCH RESULTS BECOME COMPLETED ETHNOGRAPHIES

Results such as those presented above do not just speak for themselves. Results have to be *interpreted*, or put into the context of the research questions the researcher is trying to answer. This means giving them meaning that squares with both what makes sense to the research participants and the researcher, and also with what is relevant in both the larger community and the social science disciplines. As well, the meaning of the results must be displayed in a form that conveys their meaning to the people for whom such information is useful. In Example 1.5, LeCompte and her associates (1996) decided that taken together, the activities they documented denoted a pattern of *respect* for American Indian parents and their culture, and perhaps more important, that the pattern differed significantly from the way Indian parents were treated in any other school or social service agency they encountered in the city. Their *interpretation* was corroborated in interviews with parents, who stated repeatedly that they felt respected and as though the Learning Circle was one of the few places in white society where they felt they really belonged. Coming to this set of conclusions constitutes stages one and two of the analysis.

The researchers soon discovered that their interpretation was congruent with patterns of avoidance and disrespect that characterize relationships between white people and many ethnic minority people in the United States in general. Thus, **interpretation** of data involves providing an explanation of the meaning of research results that is grounded in the experience of researchers and research participants, embedded in empirical evidence, and informed by the theories offered by relevant disciplines. If stage one of the process of transforming raw data into an ethnography is the analytic process of data reduction or crunching described above, stage two involves examining relationships and patterns in the data to produce a local interpretation or explanation of what research results mean. This interpretation is grounded in the experience of researchers and research participants. Finally, stage three involves taking the local explanation beyond the specific case and linking it to structural and conceptual understandings of how human behavior operates at a more general level. In the Learning Circle study, this stage occurred when Learning Circle data were found to be linked to patterns of avoidance and discrimination observed in interactions between other minority groups and white people in the United States. While we

Definition: Interpretation of data involves providing an explanation of the meaning of research results that is grounded in the experience of researchers and research participants, embedded in empirical evidence, and informed by the theories offered by relevant disciplines

have explained these as three separate stages, in actual fact, they often take place more or less simultaneously.

At the local level, researchers must answer the following questions:

- What's really going on here?
- What do the data tell me about these people and this site or process?
- What makes sense to me, given my own principles, knowledge, and past experiences?
- How is this related to my research questions?
- How do the local participants explain what is happening?

Assembling the behaviors enumerated in Example 1.5 into a pattern called "respect" produced a "local" explanation, or one that was offered by the Learning Circle parents and children. Extending an interpretation of the results by answering the questions above permitted the Learning Circle ethnographers to describe to a reader what the story means in the context of Native American and white relationships in the public schools. ***Thus, to make sense to all consumers of research, interpretation must produce both an emic and an etic explanation.*** **Emic interpretations** are local; they make the ethnographer's story meaningful to insiders, or the local people who have been studied. They present and privilege participant meanings.

Etic interpretations make the results meaningful to—or translatable for—outsiders. They address the question, "How does what the participants tell me equate with what other researchers or outsiders have said about similar phenomena in the world at large?" Such outsiders can represent many different audiences or constituencies. Interpretations from an etic perspective use the lenses of various theoretical frameworks or disciplinary concepts to explain phenomena and generally are constructed by the researcher.

Etic interpretations can be thought of as "going beyond results." "Going beyond results" involves making an existential leap from the language of concrete, data-grounded patterns and structures to language embedded in theoretical ideas that have no obvious connection to the specific data at

Key point

Definition:
Local or *emic* explanations are those presented by the people being studied; *etic* perspectives are those generated by researchers or other outsiders

hand other than the researcher's logical reasoning and persuasive rhetoric. Linking the Learning Circle results to patterns of disrespect experienced by other minority groups is such an existential leap. For many researchers, going beyond the results is a daunting prospect because it involves taking intellectual risks. Researchers themselves have to figure out what the crunched or "cooked" data mean, or what they say about the persons, groups, or programs the ethnographer has been studying. This involves attaching meaning and significance to the patterns, themes, domains, and connections that the researcher identified during analysis, explaining why they have come to exist, and indicating what implications they might have for future actions. Often, this means that researchers must step outside of the local framework of participants and even contradict what they have been told is going on, as Sarah Staley found out in Example 1.1 in this chapter. Staley learned that the data, the simple "facts of the case" describing *what* happened—two schools were forced to operate on one campus, and they continued to operate completely separately, as if three miles still separated the buildings, not just three or four feet—only told part of the story. Interpretation, using theoretical understandings and a different theoretical vantage point for viewing the data were required to tell the full story. Additional collection of secondary data describing the dynamics of the community was needed to tell *why* events transpired as they did.

Cross reference: See Book 4, chapter 2 for a discussion of secondary data and its uses

Staley examined census data and school enrollment statistics for patterns of racial and income segregation; numerous historical and contemporary accounts also existed documenting the resistance of white parents in the community to having their children attend school with Hispanic and low-income children. Staley also had in the back of her mind the possibility that racial and class discrimination might account for the continued separation of the two schools, both because she had read literature that revealed similar patterns and because she was attuned to the possibility of such differences, given her personal values and experiences. She had only hoped that past practice would not predict current actions in the case of Carter school. In the end, however, she had to entertain such a possible alternative explanation for maintaining a segregated campus and accept that the patterns of discrimination and avoidance in the community outweighed the value of what Staley viewed as a "lost opportunity."

Taken together, the processes of analysis and interpretation can be viewed as a series of stages in which a whole phenomenon is dissected, divided into its components, and then reassembled in terms of definitions or explanations that make the phenomenon understandable to both insiders and outsiders. To understand fully the distinction between analysis and interpretation, it is helpful to return to a figure introduced in Book 1 that displays the *horizontal*—analytic—and *vertical*—interpretive—dimensions involved in making sense of data. In Table 1.1, the horizontal dimension displays how researchers move back and forth between the abstract (the general idea of family dynamics and life achievement and associated phenomena) and the concrete.

Table 1.2 makes this process more concrete, listing types of leisure activities, followed by specific aspects of each activity likely to encourage or discourage people from engaging in that activity, and then made concrete by

TABLE 1.1 Linking Theoretical and Operational Levels in Ethnographic Research

	Structure	*Pattern*	*Unit*	*Fact*
Domain	**Family dynamics** and **life achievement**			
Factor		**Parental discipline** and **job performance**		
Variable			**Modes of parental punishment** and **ability to supervise employees**	
Item				**Frequency of spanking** and frequency of **evaluative feedback to employees**

TABLE 1.2 Empirical/Operational Levels of Research: "Living a Good Life"

Abstract	← Empirical/Operational →		Concrete
Structure	*Patterns*	*Units*	*Item or Fact*
Leisure Activities: Activities that differ from one's work			
	Camping Team Sports Hiking Gardening Building computers Watching movies		
		Positive and negative aspects of work alternatives: Losing weight; Beautifying the yard	
			Yard: weeding, watering, fertilizing; Losing weight: doing exercises, eating less bread, reading motivational books

specifying discrete features of that aspect mentioned by respondents. The *structural* category of "leisure activities" could just have well been "team sports," "gardening," or "building computers," each one with its associated sets of *patterns*, *units*, and *items* or *facts*. Simultaneously with the inductive process of building larger units, patterns, and structures by identifying and then aggregating concrete and discrete items or facts found in the data, researchers also proceed deductively, looking in the database for concrete items or units that match the more abstracted structures and patterns hypothesized to exist or already discovered. For example, a researcher trying to determine what might make individuals loathe the activity of camping could seek in the database mention of items other than the ones in Table 1.2.

In Table 1.3, we display, by contrast, the vertical or interpretive dimension, which illustrates how research-

TABLE 1.3 Theoretical/Conceptual and Empirical Levels of Research: "Living a Good Life"

Local ← **Theoretical/Conceptual** → *Paradigm*	**DOMAIN**	Living a good life			
	FACTOR	Finding activities that differ from one's work	Camping		
	SUBFACTORS	Reasons for avoiding camping even though it can contribute to a healthy life		Discomforts Lack of conveniences	
	VARIABLES	Equipment Food Critters Weather			Tents leak. You have to sleep on the ground. There are bears and mosquitoes and snakes. Freeze-dried food is yucky. I can't have my morning café latte. It usually rains.

ers move between local-level descriptions or explanations of concepts and more paradigmatic descriptions—those rooted in theoretical or conceptual explanations from the social science disciplines or paradigms. Table 1.3 displays interpretive explanations at different levels for a *domain* that might be called "living a good life." One of its components involves seeking a balance in life—a *factor* explaining one aspect of "living a good life" that is supported by research outside the study site or population at hand. It, in turn, leads to other reasons or factors explaining the need to find alternatives to work—to avoid being an unbalanced workaholic—which also could constitute explanations for behavior that are supported by theoretical or conceptual models supporting good health. That factor itself can be differentiated into *subfactors* explaining why particular alternatives to work might be avoided, and the subfactors

can then be disaggregated into *variables* that itemize specific aspects of camping that make it undesirable and give
specific items within those variables that provide a local
interpretation of why camping is to be avoided.

The horizontal dimension in Table 1.2 involves manipulating data items; the vertical dimension in Table 1.3
involves manipulating explanations for or meanings attributed to data items. Another way of thinking of this is that
the horizontal dimension moves between the very concrete
or specific and the very abstract. The vertical dimension
moves between local explanations for phenomena and conceptual or external explanations for phenomena. Together,
these vertical and horizontal processes involve what we have
elsewhere called "playing with ideas."

One also could think in a less linear fashion and use as
an analogy the process of assembling both the "big picture"
and the local details of a jigsaw puzzle. Assembling a jigsaw
puzzle is a similar kind of playing with pieces (or ideas).
The individual pieces of the puzzle represent the horizontal
dimension; as they are matched together, components of
the big picture emerge ("living a good life"). The vertical
dimension is represented not only by the image itself (the
"local explanation" of "why I don't like this or that particular activity") but also by whatever cultural referent or
context that image refers to or is part of (the conceptual
explanation). As we have described elsewhere,

> The edge pieces are located first and assembled
> to provide a frame of reference. Then attention is
> devoted to those more striking aspects of the puzzle
> picture that can be identified readily from the mass
> of pieces and assembled separately. Next [after sneak-
> ing a look at the puzzle picture on the box for hints]
> the puzzle worker places the assembled parts in their
> general position within the frame, and finally locates
> and adds the connecting pieces until no holes remain.
> (LeCompte and Preissle 1993, 237)

Only when the entire puzzle is assembled and the image
is clear (or the horizontal, constitutive level of research is
completed) can one connect that image with whoever cre-

ated it, the era in which it was created, the purpose for its creation, and any other symbolic meaning it might have (completing the vertical or interpretive level of research).

Analysis both creates the chunks of data that are then linked into a portrayal of what the researcher discovered (or, to use the puzzle metaphor, linking together the aggregated edge pieces, the sections of bright blue and black, stippled gold and green, and black puzzle pieces, as well as the beige and gray pieces, to fill in all the blanks) and shows how and why the chunks go together as they do. **Interpretation** of data permits researchers to explain what the picture portrayed is all about, why it was chosen as a puzzle subject, how it might inform human behavior in general, and who might be interested in it. Suppose, for example, the picture that emerges is a reproduction of Van Gogh's iconic painting *Crows over a Wheat Field*. At the most concrete level, the image is a way to facilitate a leisure activity: putting a puzzle together. The finished image also evokes a much-loved painting. However, the image also may have multiple meanings to viewers, ranging from commentaries on the lush nature of the golden wheat field (from a farmer), to the strong brushstrokes (from an artist) or noting the darkening sky, signifying impending night or a storm, to a more sophisticated connection (from a psychologist or art historian) of the darkening sky with the imminent end of the artist's life in suicide. And even that conclusion can be further connected to facts about the life of artists in the nineteenth century, the nature of mental illness, and the vagaries of the art market in Europe at the time.

Thus, interpretation gives answers to some of the most important questions researchers ask. Some of these interpretive questions amplify data that have been obtained with descriptive questions designed simply to map out a phenomenon. Interpretive questions can seek both local and broader explanations. Those seeking local explanations include:

- Why are people acting like this?
- What is the meaning of these activities to them?
- How did this event or condition come to be?
- What congruity between contemporary and historical actors contributes to people's actions?

Definition: Analysis describes what has been found

Definition: Interpretation explains the findings

- What is missing from the picture? What else do we need to know?
- Why are there differences among different groups of people, schools, or other units in how they view this "picture?"
- How can we explain the existence of these differences?
- Why does this (health or other) situation occur in one group but not another?

If the study involves assessing the conduct and progress of an intervention or innovation, questions can include:

- What kind of program or action would be best for us to implement? How do we construct it?
- What's going wrong—or right—with *this* program or course of action?
- Is *this* strategy, course of action, or program effective?
- What are the consequences of implementing *this* program or course of action as opposed to another one?
- What new things have we learned and what new insights have we gained from *this* program or course of action?

Audiences and Purposes

As we will indicate later in this volume, how and which kinds of data are analyzed, interpreted, and presented often depend on the audience to be reached and the purposes for which the study was done. Audiences vary in their interests in and capacity to understand research results, what they mean, and how they were obtained. A study for an academic dissertation, a monograph, a book, or a peer-reviewed paper will need to include considerable detail about how the fieldwork was carried out, what theories informed the work, which of the evidence collected substantiates claims made by the researcher, and how the work links to and enhances knowledge in the discipline. By contrast, a report for program participants may only need to include descriptions of what happened and why. Information supplied to the news media necessarily will differ from that provided to a publisher or dissertation advisory committee, and those will differ considerably from information provided for the use of participants in the study community.

Cross Reference:
See chapter 12 of this book on presentation of results to different audiences; Book 7 of the *Toolkit* details how to present ethnographic data in different settings and how to use ethnographic data for a variety of different purposes

SUMMARY

In this chapter, we have discussed the differences between analysis that produces results and similar processes that produce interpretations, and as well, we have shown how the two are related. We also have cautioned that many researchers leave their work underinterpreted. They give a reader the simple results, or the facts of the case as explained locally, without integrating those results into a web of local and midrange to substantive explanations for the results and what they mean on a variety of levels. Sarah Staley, whose study is described in Example 1.1, could have simply explained the results of her study of the two middle schools as the administrators did: "impracticality" explained the failure to integrate the two programs. However, that she moved on to a third stage of analysis, which linked her results with asymmetrical political and racialized forces in the community, enabled her to provide a deeper and more nuanced portrait not only of the two schools but of their place within a community stratified by inequalities of race and class.

We also have indicated that the processes of analysis and interpretation take place both in the field and after a researcher has completed fieldwork. Finally, we have suggested that data may be interpreted and presented differently, depending on their purposes. In the chapters that follow, we describe how each of these stages is implemented.

NOTE

1. An excellent description of similar miscommunication and total lack of understanding between Hmong/Laotian refugees and medical personnel can be found in Anne Fadiman's *The Spirit Catches You and You Fall Down*.

2

ANALYSIS IN THE FIELD

RECURSIVITY IN ETHNOGRAPHIC RESEARCH AND ANALYSIS

By now, it should be clear that ethnographic research can be envisioned as a spiral process. Ethnographers almost never begin their studies with a single question that remains unaltered throughout the process of fieldwork. As we made clear in Books 1 through 4, ethnographers make many decisions about what should be observed, collected, and asked of people and recorded in people's homes, communities, and workplaces. In the process, they formulate and reformulate hunches—which we also call hypotheses—that help them to figure out why things happen as they do and guide them in deciding what to observe and record next. This spiraling, or **recursive, process of analysis** involves constant questioning, getting answers, asking more refined questions, getting more complete answers, and looking for instances that clarify, modify, or negate the original formulations. The recursive process is the hallmark of ethnographic research. It requires what we call "in-the-field" analysis that permits ethnographers to continually reorder their sense of what is happening, based on "feedback from the field." Sometimes what seemed obviously true at the beginning of a study becomes equally obviously not true in the light of subsequent negative evidence—instances, events, behavior, or other facts that disconfirm what the ethnographers initially found. While it can be all too tempting to discard these cases as anomalies or simply as incorrect, Miles and Huberman (1984) argue that figuring out how negative

Definition:
Recursive
analysis
involves a cyclical
process of raising
questions, collecting
data to answer them,
analyzing the data,
and then reformulating
old or generating new
questions to pursue,
based on the previous
analysis

or disconfirming cases inform the ethnographer's understanding is worthwhile, because these cases sometimes provide the strongest argument for refining or modifying the
research. They also remind researchers that there is considerable variation in the way people go about their business,
conduct daily activities in a community, and interpret what
they mean. The disconfirming instance may be part of a
larger pattern of difference or divisions not noticed up to
that point in the fieldwork.

EXAMPLE 2.1

HOW BIG IS THE SCHOOL DISTRICT? RECURSIVITY AND NEGATIVE EVIDENCE

Pinnacle Independent School District, the Navajo Nation district that LeCompte
studied, had an enrollment of just over two thousand students enrolled in four
schools (an elementary, intermediate, middle, and high school), all located within
easy walking distance of each other. Compared with the other districts LeCompte
had worked with, it was a very tiny district, which she thought should have had
minimal problems with communication and supervision. Administrators, however,
kept attributing their difficulty in implementing curricular reforms to the fact that
the district was "so big." LeCompte puzzled long and hard over this discrepancy
between the actual size of the district and the perception of its size held by the staff.
Only when the superintendent explicitly compared his district with a neighboring
one with fewer than three hundred students did LeCompte understand that perception of size was relative. All of the Navajo districts were extremely isolated physically
and culturally from larger, off-reservation, mainstream districts. This meant that
they compared themselves with each other, rather than with larger districts off the
reservation. Pinnacle school district was, in fact, one of the larger districts in the
Navajo Nation; its administrators were using the even tinier districts around them as
a reference point. By treating the assertions of "bigness" by Pinnacle administrators
as negative evidence, LeCompte not only was able to clear up a puzzling conflict in
perceptions, but to learn more about how the district's isolation was an important
factor in explaining its organizational culture (LeCompte and Wiertelak 1994).

 Key point   *Recursive analysis of the kind described above is done
from the moment an ethnographer enters the field to the
time when the last page of the final report is written.* However, recursive analysis is applied somewhat differently at
different stages of the research process.

INITIAL ANALYSIS IN THE FIELD

The first set of procedures, inscription, transcription, and description (which we describe in the following pages) are done in the field. They require exhaustive and scrupulous attention to details of listening and observing, as well as attention to one's own inner organizational schemes and biases. They also require hours of typing up field notes and a good system for filing or cataloging data.

The second set of procedures involves "tidying up" data right after the fieldwork is completed. Only the third and final stage is what most researchers more commonly recognize as data management and analysis: a laborious process of organizing and "cooking" raw data until it becomes research results. However, we believe it important to emphasize that for ethnographers, analytic processes inform the entire research endeavor.

Cross Reference: See Book 3, chapters 3 and 10 for details of this process

Our discussion of analysis begins with a description of the processes that ethnographers use in the initial stages of fieldwork: inscription, description, and transcription (Clifford 1990). Inscription, description, and transcription create much of the database with which an ethnographer works. A helpful way to think about these processes is to consider how Roger Sanjek (1990), an urban anthropologist, classifies field notes. Sanjek suggests that there are three kinds of notes: *head notes*, *scratch notes*, and *field notes*. **Head notes** are the product of inscription; they can be thought of as memories or mental notes kept in the ethnographer's head or memory until such time as it is possible to actually "write things down." The simple act of storing ideas, observations, and impressions *in one's head* causes them to be organized—and retrieved—according to whatever culturally determined organizational scheme the ethnographer's brain customarily uses for storage and retrieval of information. This is why we emphasize throughout this book the need for all researchers—but especially ethnographers—to be aware of their own ethnocentrisms and the kinds of preconceptions and unconscious biases they bring to the field "with their body" (Metz 1978). These include predispositions constituted by their age, gender, ethnicity, physical size, physical and intellectual ability, social class,

Definition: Head notes are the product of inscription; they consist of mental notes

religious and cultural background, educational level, and personal style. Being aware that such characteristics carry with them specific attitudes toward oneself, events, and other people helps to reduce the degree to which impressions written down are biased by being filtered through the mind of the ethnographer.

INSCRIPTION AND HEAD NOTES

Definition: Inscription is the act of making mental notes prior to writing things down

Inscription is the act of making mental notes prior to writing things down. Some ethnographers write little down and rely mostly on their head notes. However, memory is faulty and subject to constant revision, as subsequent events modify initial impressions. That is why we—and most other methodologists—regard this as a poor field technique that often leads to bad research;[1] we argue that it is critically important to record each impression as soon as possible after it occurs to avoid erosion, modification, and even falsification of the mental record. Deciding what to write and how to write it, however, depends on mental notes taken while observations or informal interviews in the field are going on. Such mental notes might be made during a pause in conversation or a break in activities, as an ethnographer "refers to some prior list of questions, traits or hypotheses" and then jots down a mnemonic word or phrase to help in remembering what he or she wants to investigate (Clifford 1990, 51). Researchers such as Pertti Pelto (1978) refer to this process as "jottings." Jottings on a piece of paper, an envelope, or a small notebook carried in a pocket or purse are the first step in transferring mental notes to field notes. Pelto would argue that no anthropologist should leave the house without a pen or pencil and a small 2-inch × 3-inch spiral-bound notebook kept in a convenient location like a pocket or a front purse flap. Jottings kept in this notebook are dated and consist of words, brief quotes or bits of quotes, as well as small maps or other mnemonic devices that guide the researcher to recall what took place and what to record in greater detail later on.

Sanjek's category of *scratch notes* facilitates this initial stage of inscription. **Scratch notes** consist of jottings and scribblings taken during events, in the field, or immediately after events if taking notes in the presence of research participants is inappropriate. Written on that small notebook, envelopes, file cards, small notebooks, or slips of paper, they are the mnemonics—often in shorthand or codes—that assist one in remembering complete head notes, and they are turned into description, or real field notes, as soon as the ethnographer finds the time and privacy to write everything down.

Making mental and physical "jottings" may seem simple enough, but in the initial stages of an ethnographic study, no ethnographer finds it easy to figure out *what* to write down, what to write *about*, and even *when* to find time to write. Many novice ethnographers have been urged to take care to record "everything"—advice that has led to extreme frustration among the many new field workers who find this impossible. In the first place, although field sites vary in their degree of confusion and complexity, they always are a whirling, buzzing, maelstrom of activity. Does one look at the physical environment? The people? Which specific people? Or all of them? And what if they are doing many different things? Imagine a carnival, a large outdoor market, a clinic waiting room, or a crowded school classroom. Where would one start?

In addition to the impossibility of recording "everything at once" when "everything" is happening at the same time, ethnographers often face the difficult task of simply trying to register what actually is happening in a totally unfamiliar setting. Sometimes ethnographers have difficulty even finding vocabulary to describe events and objects they have never seen before and with which they have had no prior experience (see Clifford 1990). While what the researcher looks at and notices is somewhat organized by the conceptual framework guiding the study, rendering the initial foray into the field manageable requires some form of selective attention and translation.

Definition: Scratch notes are the initial product of description; they are the brief jottings taking during events in the field or immediately afterward

Cross Reference: See Book 3, chapters 2, 3, and 4 on entering the field

All people, including all ethnographers, tend to notice first—and to write down—what they already have learned to notice. We have been trained—consciously and unconsciously—to attend to those items, domains, events, objects, animals, plants, people, and behaviors in our environment that our culture defines as worthy of notice and helpful to our survival. One of the first lessons ethnographers must learn is how to get *outside* of their own heads, or how to go beyond their own ethnocentric frameworks for valuing, noticing, and naming so that they can begin to notice—and to write down information about—items, domains, events, objects, animals, plants, people, and behaviors that have been defined as noteworthy to other, often quite different, people and cultures.

EXAMPLE 2.2

THE IMPORTANCE OF LEARNING WORDS EVEN WHEN THEY ARE NOT IMPORTANT TO YOU

The anthropologist Laura Bohannan described how her initial days in Africa involved a frustrating series of language lessons. She thought it imperative to learn how to ask about acts of daily living and survival: Where is the bathroom? Where does one buy soap? Who is in charge of the village? How does one go shopping? However, the villagers persisted in teaching her the names of objects in the natural world—leaves, stones, plants, types of animals. These were the things that children needed to be taught to survive in a subsistence economy and that were still privileged. Because she was a newcomer to the society, Bohannan was being taught as a newly born child would be. *That* made sense to the villagers. Bohannan's questions made sense to *her* because answers to them were required for survival in a more modern culture, though not the one in which she currently was living. Bohannan had to learn to accommodate to what the villagers thought important for her to learn in order for her also to learn what she wanted to know. The process, however, also revealed much about values and existence in the village (Bowen 1954).

 Key point As Bohannon learned, *the process of inscription involves learning to notice what is important to other people and what one hasn't been trained to see, and then writing it down.* "Writing it down," however, inevitably is done at least to some degree through the lens of the

ethnographer, who writes things down or inscribes them from his or her own frame of reference. Even to notice something is to have some prior idea that it is worth noticing; part of the ethnographic project is first learning what is worth noticing to others and then writing it down in a way that makes sense to those others as well. Thus, while the initial stages of writing things down does in fact involve creating a mental text, it also involves re-creating or modifying a text or set of ideas about that subject that already exists in the mind of the ethnographer. This set of ideas is guided by the earliest phases of the research project, when the researcher creates an initial conceptual or operational model. This model helps the researcher to focus questions, observations, social and geographic mapping operations, and the recording of event sequences more systematically on the research problem.

Cross Reference: Book 2, chapters 3, 4, 5, and 6 discuss a systematic way to formulate an initial working model

Interviews with key informants in the first stages of an ethnographic study also help to frame the exploration process through the eyes of the participants. However, *much of the mental text an ethnographer creates is heavily influenced by his or her past personal experiences and characteristics. What researchers attend to in the field, and hence what they inscribe, also is very much influenced by the research questions they have asked, how they have been trained to think about and conceptualize the world, or what they learned in their prestudy visits to the field.* For example, early anthropologists were trained in functional theories, which stated that every human society had to find ways to carry out basic functions necessary for that society to survive. These included reproduction (carried out by kinship systems and families or sometimes by recruitment of new members), transmission of culture (carried out by families, schools, churches, and other socializing institutions), distribution of resources (carried out in markets, manufacturing agencies, trade organizations, and systems of exchange), aesthetics (exemplified in the practice of the arts, handicrafts, and creative activities), and many other functions. Early fieldwork—and the process of inscription—focused on identifying and describing how these various functions were carried out.

Key point with Cross Reference: See Book 3, chapter 7 on key informant interviews

Cross Reference: Book 1, chapter 2, Book 2, chapters 1–3, and Book 6 discuss how research characteristics and experiences affect what researchers do and can observe in the field

EXAMPLE 2.3

MARGARET MEAD BEGINS HER FIELDWORK

In her early fieldwork, which she described in correspondence with Ruth Benedict, Margaret Mead discussed how she was equipped for the field by Boas and how she began work. Citing specific functional theorists—Radcliffe-Brown, Malinowski, and others—she began by imposing a classificatory scheme on the society she was studying, rather than simply trying inductively to discover what was there. She also felt that her task was to describe an entire culture, which meant covering each of the categories (family and kinship, economics, religion, aesthetics, social organization) outlined by functional theorists as necessary for the survival of a society.

By contrast, contemporary ethnographers focus less often on creating theoretically informed descriptions of a whole society than they do on using theories about specific human processes to identify and explain smaller chunks or aspects of societies. Below we describe how theories about human learning and formation of gender identity helped to structure the inscription process in a study of an educational innovation. We also demonstrate how ethnographers must take care not to miss important elements of the culture under study just because they do not think those elements important at the time.

EXAMPLE 2.4

INSCRIBING INFORMATION ABOUT ARTS INSTRUCTION IN THE ARTS FOCUS STUDY

Even before they began their study of an arts program at Centerline Middle School, LeCompte and Holloway were puzzling over the potential impact that education in the arts might have on the cognitive growth, self-confidence, and identity development of young adolescents. Based on her readings of the sociocultural learning theorist Lev Vygotsky (1978), LeCompte wondered about the degree to which specific strategies in arts instruction could foster higher-level thinking skills such as evaluation, hypothesis testing, and intellectual risk taking. Although LeCompte had had some musical training and Holloway taught creative writing, neither researcher had much experience in visual or performing arts—the two strongest strands in the program. Having read the work of the developmental psychologist Carol Gilligan

(1982, 1990, 1995) and others, Holloway was particularly interested in whether or not arts education would help young women develop less traditional career goals. LeCompte tended to pay particular attention, then, to instructional activities that required students to try on new ideas, engage in critique, "think about unthinkable things," imagine events or activities to be different from what they currently were, or suggest alternatives to how they had always been done. Holloway watched closely for differences between the reactions of boys and girls and for instances when girls took on activities usually reserved for boys. The two researchers tended to watch for these kinds of things during regular classroom instruction because they deemed these activities to be most important. By contrast, the calisthenics, games, and noisemaking that the theater class systematically engaged in at the beginning of each class period did not look very much like instruction to the researchers, except perhaps as a way to help lively children eleven to fifteen years old blow off steam and settle down before "real" instruction began. So they tended to background these activities in their field notes. Even though they "wrote down everything" and had, in fact, made detailed notes on the vigorous pretheater activities, the researchers found that their early field notes primarily were filled with references to ways of thinking and differences between boys and girls as they existed in regular instruction—the original focus of the study and what the researchers thought to be most important. It wasn't until they began to interview theater students and found that students viewed the "warm-ups" done at the beginning of the day to be among the most valuable things they learned that the researchers looked more closely at these calisthenics, games, and vocal exercises—to which they had paid little attention previously. The warm-ups were, in fact, activities that transformed the school experience for students. They helped students relax, reduce stress, and focus their concentration; most important to the study, the students argued that they were useful in their other, nonart classes.

LeCompte and Holloway first mentally inscribed data that were congruent with their initial interests; however, they also tried to make careful note of things that did not make sense to them or that did not fit neatly into their initial model. In this way, they learned to attend to things that, though they were not originally defined as important to researchers, turned out to be very important to the study. As LeCompte and Holloway found out, how one inscribes depends on how the study has been conceived and how the researcher wants to tell its story.

EXAMPLE 2.5

DISCOVERING WHAT REALLY IS IMPORTANT TO TEACH

Bill Fogarty, an anthropologist at the Australian National University, was engaged in a study of aboriginal communities in the far northwestern territories of Australia. His task involved, among other things, trying to figure out how to make the standard text materials used in schools for aboriginal children more engaging. After several years spent watching and recording what children did and how they learned, not only in the school, but also in the community, he decided to depart from studying formal schooled education altogether and instead developed a concept of "education in place." Education in place used as its starting point the environment and natural resources in the local community. Part ecology, part natural science, part studies of language and culture, and part explorations in subsistence agriculture, "education in place" was built on a curriculum whose content was everything about the indigenous community and its physical and spiritual surroundings and whose modes of instruction engaged the children not only in traditional practices, but in culturally congruent ways of learning (Fogarty 2011).

Fogarty's observations finally showed him the utter lack of relevance of the materials teachers had been using to the lives and experiences of indigenous children. Rather than try to force them into "liking" what they were doing, he instead set about developing new materials from information in the local community based on those things for which children already demonstrated an affinity and that they needed to know for themselves and their community to survive.

DESCRIPTION, SCRATCH NOTES, AND FIELD NOTES

 Definition: Description involves writing things down in diaries, logs and field notes (Bernard 1995, 181)

 Key point

Description occurs after inscription. Many ethnographers have written about the urgency of turning head notes and scratch notes into more detailed field notes before they get "cold"—and before the remembered detail in head notes is lost in the onslaught of another day's recollection. *Descriptions are used to create full field notes, which are the "more or less coherent representations of an observed cultural reality"* (Clifford 1990, 51). Assembled narratives of events, behaviors, conversations, activities, interpretations, explanations, and descriptions produce "thick descriptions" (Geertz 1973b); taken together and formulated as what Sanjek calls **full field notes**, these descriptions help to portray the soul and heart of a group, community, organization, or culture. Full field notes are like photographs; they have a "you are there" quality (Clifford (1990, 61) that makes a custom, belief, or practice, its meaning, and its context visible, and at least partly comprehensible, not only to the ethnographer but to outsiders as well. Full field notes go beyond "mere description" or the close-to-the-ground recording of what one sees and hears; they contain the initial interpretation that both simple inscription and transcription lack (see the next section in this chapter).

Going beyond mere description means that the field notes have been written, rewritten, and written over, so that they have ceased to be entirely "raw" data and are already at least partly "cooked"—at least to the extent that all the blanks have been filled in and they are organized in accordance with the conceptual framework informing the study. Full field notes, then, are kept as close to "raw" as possible while still capturing clearly the situation within the photographic frame in all its detail at that particular point in time. In creating full field notes, ethnographers stop the clock; that is, they hold present time constant while they reorder the recent past that they have observed and jotted down. They then systematize the recent past, place it in context with prior events they have learned about in the course of the fieldwork, and turn it into evidence to be assembled into a database from which the full ethnographic account will be created (Clifford 1990, 51–52).

As we have discussed previously, field notes are produced in a quiet place away from the site of observation and interaction with people in the field. They always are dated and contain the name of the site where they occurred and field-worker who produced them. They include descriptions of events and conversations, including maps and other illustrations, and also may include reflections, preliminary analyses, initial interpretations, and new questions and hunches to be answered and tested in the next days and weeks of observation. *Field notes, as we shall see, are organized around those basic conceptual*

Definition:
Full field notes are fleshed out descriptions created from scratch notes, memory, and theoretical insights so as to capture the situation in near-photographic detail

Key point

Cross Reference:
Book 3, chapter 3 discusses how to construct field notes

Key point

frames or questions that structured the study in the first place; they become increasingly focused and "coded" as the research itself progresses and hones in on those features of the cultural scene that become most interesting and as the formative theoretical model emerges. As we have described in Book 3, semistructured data collection (structured open-ended interviews and specifically targeted and timed observations) on selected topics related to the study helps to identify and affirm preliminary hunches and associations that can later be confirmed statistically using structured survey methods.

TRANSCRIPTION, RECORDING, "COPYING," AND SCRIPTING

Transcription usually is considered to be the word-for-word creation of a written text from an audio- or videotaped account given by an informant. However, Clifford (1990) defines the term much more broadly to include any kind of elicitation from an informant. Like description, transcription also creates field notes, but the recording often is a more formal process than recording of naturalistic observations. Transcription activities are more focused and structured and often involve staged activities, such as elicitation techniques (pilesorts, time lines, concept maps, etc.). Transcription involves:

> **Cross Reference:**
> See Books 1 and 3 for methods of eliciting information via interviews, and Books 3 and 4 for methods using audiovisual recording, focus groups, formalized elicitation techniques, and other data collection techniques

- writing down the *verbatim* responses of informants to interviews;
- taking dictation;
- recording stories, legends, spells, ditties, chants or songs; and
- keeping a running record of everything an individual says during a specific period of observation (Clifford 1990).

We add to this list recording respondents' commentaries when engaged in listing and sorting exercises, mapping the location of events and activities, completing sentences, responding to photographs and other visual stimulation, and answering survey questions. Transcription takes place throughout the fieldwork stages of a research process and often continues into the early stages of analysis away from the field. Focusing as it does on spoken language, transcription is particularly important for linguistic studies, when the objective of the research is collection of indigenous texts and stories or gaining an understanding of the meanings attributed to specific behaviors. Many studies rely largely on key informant and semistructured interviews, which are recorded and transcribed (and sometimes translated) in their entirety for analysis. Considerable thought must be given to how the transcriptions are formatted and organized to facilitate efficient coding and analysis of these data either by hand or by using a computer data management/analysis program. This is especially important when conducting research that includes group data collection, computerization, coding, and analysis.

Nonverbal behavior, however, also can be a focus of transcription. For example, school personnel often "script" the behavior of teachers whom they want to evaluate; this involves keeping a detailed written record of what the teacher says and does during a given period of monitoring. Similar scripting often is done in detailed monitoring of human behavior in situations where videotaping is not possible or is inappropriate, such as in classrooms or clinic settings.

The first stage of transcription, then, involves writing down verbatim, taking series of photographs, audio- or videotaping, or "copying," in Clifford's terms, what an informant says he or she knows of a tradition, practice, event, custom, ritual, object, myth, or song. If tape recordings or photographs are used, these then must be transcribed into texts. Or, in the case of "scripting," transcription creates a detailed written record of what a single person is observed to say and do in a given situation. Below are several examples of transcripts. The Arts Focus database included a set of over one hundred audiotapes of interviews which the researchers had conducted with students, teachers, and administrators in the program. These audiotapes had to be transcribed mechanically; one of these is excerpted below.

EXAMPLE 2.6

TRANSCRIPT FROM AN INTERVIEW BY DEBORAH HOLLOWAY WITH JT, A SIXTH-GRADE MALE ARTS FOCUS STUDENT, AGE ABOUT ELEVEN

DH: Hi. As I told you, my name is Deb, and we are working on an evaluation of the Arts Focus program. I know I've seen you in class this year, JT; I'm really happy that you agreed to talk with us because I think it's really important that we find out what students think about the program. So first I want to ask you a few background questions. Why did you choose to be in the literary arts program?

JT: I don't know. Well, I really thought I was good at, well, writing, and I thought it was fun, so my plan was that I'd do the literary arts because I'd really enjoy that. Then I wanted to go to visual arts [next year] because I really like drawing, you know, things like that.

DH: So when you say you really like literary arts, what is it about literary arts?

JT: Well, it's the freedom we have. I don't know, it's so concentrated and it's like, you are just surrounded by writers and books . . .

DH: Before you came to the program, did you write a lot?

JT: Yes. Not as much creatively, but you know, in science. I don't know, it was more the case of a journal than actually writing. I decided that I enjoyed writing and also I enjoy being creative.

DH: So you just did it!

JT: Yeah.

DH: Have you taken classes in any other arts areas, other than writing?

JT: Well, when I was little, I took art classes, I think I took something in the art museum.

DH: So you did visual-oriented art?

JT: Yeah.

DH: OK.

JT: See, I'm not into, well, I think I'd be good at drama, and I think it's fun to act out, and we kind of, I think it's easier not to be yourself, actually. Because a whole bunch of people would know that you are not purposely being an idiot. Yes, but, like singing, no, that's not for me. The drawing, yes. I probably draw every other day or something.

DH: You do? Right now?

JT: Yes. Or maybe more, unless I have too much homework. Or at least I pay attention more on my homework . . .

DH: Than you did before?

JT: Yeah.

DH: Let me ask you a few questions about your literary arts class. Can you tell me what you do in your literary arts class?

JT: There's this five minutes . . . sort of like where I don't get focused, then I'll make sure nobody's looking and I'll run to the other side of the room [Note: the class meets in the school's very large library] where we have a little place. I just write until we [the teacher and he] have our meeting, or whatever. There's not many distractions, but I'm an easily distracted person, so I have to find a good spot.

Another form of transcription also was used in the Arts Focus study. Because audiotaping was considered to be too intrusive, the researchers took down *verbatim* records of the conversations in faculty, parent, and administrative meetings. These were maintained in several dozen stenographer's notebooks.[2] In most cases they were nearly as complete as audiotaped transcriptions, and they served the same purposes.

EXAMPLE 2.7

TRANSCRIPT FOR APRIL 2, 1997, 3:05 P.M. LARGE GROUP STAFF MEETING FOR ARTS FOCUS

The meeting is in the school library conference room. Present are LeCompte and Holloway (the two researchers), the four Arts Focus teachers, two parents, and Rita, a consultant from the local arts alliance, who came to help the teachers identify possible sources of grant funding for the program. Some problems quickly surface with the effectiveness of the current fund-raiser. (That individual, Sue, not present, is not a staff member at the school, but she wrote the initial grant for the program, and her salary is paid from it. She is supposed to provide liaison with other arts organizations in the community.)

The teachers are talking among themselves with some dismay about how, although Sue is claiming responsibility for all grant writing, she is causing delays and problems because she won't consult with the teachers about funding proposals she's writing, and they don't know what obligations Sue's proposals might create for them if the proposals are funded. Maurita says, "She doesn't know what the red flags are, like that art exhibit at the university which she wanted us to attend with the kids, and there were big paintings of nudes in it. Can you imagine what the kids would have done if we'd just walked in there? We can handle that—we can preview the show and plan how to prepare the kids for it—but if we don't know what we are getting into, we'll have the whole community mad at us."

Pat (the art teacher) says, "Sue is just going off on her own, writing grants and working through Jeannette Farmer (the curriculum director with the school district). Jeannette and Fran (the Centerline principal) are in contact weekly with email, and they pass materials on to Sue, but nobody is talking to us, and we are the ones who will have to implement whatever they get money for. And it might not fit in with our program."

Rita: "What I hear from Sue is, she tells me that the teachers aren't coming to see her. And I'm giving Fran professional advice about what makes grant proposals stronger—I've been telling her that you won't get funded if there isn't collaboration between the teachers and all of the people involved."

Pat: "We did make a wish list of all the programs we wanted to try, and John [the music teacher] was going to type it up and give it to Fran so she would know what we were interested in getting funds for." [It is clear from Rita's response that she never saw the list and that Fran hadn't received it from John, either.]

Rita: "It'd really be good if you teachers could get your curriculum planned for the next year so we'd know how to plan for extra programs. And there are a lot of opportunities." She describes the local community art show, the arts festival at the local museum and library, and also the school's own arts festival. "I have the procedures for applying for funds from the school district. Fran says there is no way to get around the school district procedures, since there are particular officials who have to sign off on all grants. This means that Sue is working on grants [she names two] right now, and she isn't collaborating with you . . . that's not the wisest course for you . . ."

Pat: [sounding frustrated] "See, basically, this [she points at a grant proposal which Sue put in the Arts Focus teachers' mailboxes this morning] is out there, and we just didn't participate in it. Even though I totally agree with the concept [upon which the proposal is based], I just wish that we could get help from Sue for working with arts organizations other than the [local] symphony. It just seems to me that Sue is using this program to pay her salary and make opportunities for the [local] musicians."

Rita: "This is a problem. To have a successful grant, it [the proposal] needs clarity, it needs to speak directly to the questions asked. It has to be sexy, vivid, have color, catch attention. These [Sue's] proposals don't have it. I would guess that Sue isn't getting all her in-kind contributions recorded correctly, either, because she doesn't know enough about the school and what you teachers do. You'll also need letters for support for the [local arts alliance] council grant."

Pat: "Do you know about the Young Audiences program?"

Rita: "It's from the state council for the arts; you have to have part of the money to hire an artist, and then they pay some of the rest of the artists' fee."

They all talk about several other grant programs, what they each might do to write their own grant proposals. They ask Rita how they could start receiving the information and newsletters on grant opportunities that have previously been going to Sue, who doesn't pass them all on to the teachers. They then discuss all the logistics needed to bring an artist to the school under the Young Audiences program—facilities, time, administrative issues.

Deb (the research assistant) gives a report on the work of the videographer whom the research team wants to hire to film the final production of *Romeo and Juliet*; the school can't find a professional videographer they can afford, but they really want to document the performance for the historical record. The husband of one of Deb's friends (who is also LeCompte' student) is a videographer, and he's volunteered to do the work. "He usually charges one hundred dollars an hour, but he'll make a deal for us; he really likes kids' theater. He'll do the whole job for five hundred to seven hundred dollars, including the editing, and he'll also document the arts festival."

Maurita says, "Let's do it."

Rita says that they could get some publicity with the video on the public access television channel; "You could train your students to film your productions and then get them on TV." There is general agreement that this would be a good idea. It is 4:00 p.m., and I have to leave the meeting.

To record nuances of their instructional style and teaching content, the Arts Focus researchers also focused on individual teachers, scripting their behavior during instruction. The excerpt necessarily includes contextual information as well, documenting the setting and what students were doing in it so as to help the script make sense. This excerpt also illustrates the recording challenges posed by a lively setting filled with people.

 **EXAMPLE 2.8**

TRANSCRIPT FROM LECOMPTE'S FIELD NOTES, OCTOBER 4, 1996; 1:10 P.M., THIRD BLOCK, THEATER ARTS CLASS, SIXTH- AND SEVENTH-GRADERS (AGES ELEVEN–FOURTEEN)

Theater arts meets in the auditorium; it's their regular classroom. The students have been planning for their annual Halloween Night theatrical production; they will perform Ray Bradbury's *The Halloween Tree*, a fantasy thriller. I sit in the front row of the auditorium seats; the teacher is at her desk in the stage-left corner below the stage. Maurita, the teacher, told me earlier that she liked the play but also chose it because there were lots of parts in it that she could assign to girls; she says that girls can play male roles in some plays, which was good, since most theater programs have too many girls, and most plays don't have very many roles for girls. The buzzer sounds. Two boys *leap* into the still-empty auditorium, announcing in loud theatrical voices: "I am HERE!!" They then leap onto the stage. Four boys are now onstage, talking in loud voices and making theatrical gestures. They have been reading Shakespeare's *Romeo and Juliet*, and they are practicing the lines. Maurita Douglas, the teacher, moves to sit on a stool on the floor just below the stage at stage center. The students enter and sit down in a tight semicircle around her. Most of the twenty-five students are girls—I only count five boys. There is a deaf girl with a sign language interpreter in the class; the interpreter sits just behind the teacher, signing what Maurita says to the deaf girl. Maurita begins to list the decisions they have to make today to get ready for their performance. She says: "This is a production day; we aren't going to do much stage stuff today. And it isn't a democracy. We have to get organized. Now, I am going to need lots of volunteers—I need someone to take notes here. I am going to use my assistant director [AD] here for notes, that's what we use assistant directors for." The AD jumps up to the stage and starts writing down the high points of the discussion on a blackboard. They first discuss just how many performances they should have. The AD does ballet moves on the stage behind Maurita (whose back is to her). Most of the students want to have only two performances so that they can get bigger audiences; Maurita argues for more, so that more children will have a chance to participate and they will have a longer performance experience. They hold a vote, which is 8–13 in favor of having four performances.

Maurita: "Now, let's decide on the dates. We can't have just one performance on the second week; we'll all forget our lines. And we can't have one on Tuesday, which is a school holiday." The students all start talking at once with suggestions. Maurita listens.

Maurita: "OK, we're going to vote in one minute." The AD writes the possible dates on the blackboard; they decide to have two performances on the Thursday and Friday before Halloween [which always is the 31st of October], one on the night before Halloween, and one early in the evening on Halloween Night.

Maurita then changes the topic. "Now we have to talk about the stage combat. The two expert instructors are coming to tomorrow's class. You are going to practice falls, drops, body slams. You'll need something to use for a quarterstaff [a medieval weapon]. You can use an old broom handle, so bring one in, but remember to sand it with sandpaper so that there won't be any splinters in them—or you'll have splinters in your hands. Come dressed for gymnastics—old clothes—tennis shoes or gym shoes. Bring water. You'll get hot. And go to the bathroom before class. The two instructors aren't going to want people wandering out to go to the bathroom." Another change in topic.

"Now, let's talk about the rehearsal schedule for the play. I know this all is boring, but we have to do this or it'll be utter chaos." Various students tell her about schedule conflicts they have: soccer practice, ballet lessons, babysitting, a doctor's appointment. These kids have really busy schedules with many after-school commitments. It is hard to schedule rehearsals in which all the lead actors are present. She takes notes, asking each which role they have in the play and appointing a substitute. All of the girls are still sitting in the circle around Maurita, except for Danielle, the AD, still on the stage. Four of the five boys have moved to the center of the auditorium to join Mike, an eighth-grader who is directing all the sound and light work for the play, and who just came in to inspect the light booth. Two girls get up and climb onto the stage and begin mimicking the ballet moves that Danielle continues to make.

Maurita: "OK, now. We have to break up into groups to talk about sound effects. You are going to have to create the sound effects that will make this play live. Get out your scripts, and move into your groups." Somewhat slowly, the students move to five places in the room. Maurita tells them to read each page of the first act and think about all the sounds that might go with what's happening in the play. "It's fall, it's sort of cold; the wind is blowing and the leaves are falling. It's almost night. When you go up to the old house, what does it smell like? Imagine what you might hear. You're walking down the street with your friends. Just brainstorm together." Maurita resumes her chair in front. The kids begin to brainstorm, and it gets pretty loud. Maurita does some paperwork at her desk—far stage left—and then moves around the room, listening to the discussions. The students continue their discussion until the buzzer sounds for the end of class at 2:40 p.m.

This excerpt tried to include both teacher and student activities—a somewhat daunting process in a very large room with twenty-eight people—many of whom were engaging in different and sometimes unrelated activities. Somewhat different is an excerpt below of a teacher's instructional behavior from the Learning to Work study. This excerpt also has been coded for later analysis. LeCompte was interested in how teachers expressed norms and rules about working and keeping busy (W conceptual codes), use of time (T conceptual codes), achievement (A conceptual codes), and following rules (R conceptual codes). These conceptual codes at the structural level were further elaborated by the use of numbers (for patterns) and letters (for units or items). WlB, for example, represented a teacher statement about "work" (W) that involved the teacher reminding students what they *should* be doing (l) and related to current assignments (B). T2A was a reference to the time schedule (T), beginning with a "heads up" or alerting comment signaling an activity was about to begin, and a directive, indicated by a number, regarding what the students had to do next, for example, "get started," "take out pencils," "pay attention," "work a problem." LeCompte also recorded the exact time when activities changed so that their duration could be estimated.

EXAMPLE 2.9　　　　

TRANSCRIPT FROM THE LEARNING TO WORK STUDY FIELD NOTES

Valley School: September 15, 1977

Pat, the teacher, is sitting on a student's desk at the front of the room. The students' desks are haphazardly scattered throughout the room; four girls have pushed theirs together in a row diagonally across the room; some are clustered in twos and others are by themselves. There is no teacher desk immediately visible; it is obscured in the corner behind boxes of materials and a motorcycle engine. I am seated at the back of the room, in a corner diagonally across from the teacher (Table 2.1).

Definition: Selection involves the choice to include or omit recording of particular aspects of a scene, phenomenon or person

It is important to remember that both written and audio- or video-recorded transcription inevitably involves the researcher's conscious or unconscious **selection** and **translation** and hence, like any recording, cannot be a total or complete depiction. Selection is the process by which researchers record only part of what occurs as they chose among or omit details or portions of events that they record. Translation occurs when researchers tell and explain the story in their own words and according to their theoretical concepts. In the Arts Focus program, researchers tended to select for recording those events, stories, and materials that seemed to be most salient to their research questions or the ideas about learning and gender that interested them

TABLE 2.1 Field Note Excerpt from Learning to Work Study

9:06 Discussion	T2A	(T2A) OK, now, let's start. (Todd comes up and gives her a nickel.) OK, now, here's our new word for the day. What is it? (She writes it on the board.) Bazaar. (She writes "bizarre" and "bazaar" on the board, explains the differences. Goes through sentences using *bizarre* to illustrate bizarre things [italics added].)
9:10 Explication	T2A	(T2A) OK, I would like you to pay attention. We've had some problems with money. What is a dollar sign? (Children shout the answer. She explains how to read numbers as money.) Now I want you to pretend you just bought a house. Now, you gotta be careful because houses cost lots of money. (Writes $28560000 on the board. Larry volunteers the decimal placement.) Darn! I could not fool you! Let's see if I can fool this young man. (Does another. He gets it right.) Who wants a more expensive house? Bernie? (Does another, which Bernie gets right.) Let's see. I have not heard from some of these girls. Anna, that's what I spent at the grocery store. (Does another.)
9:15–9:26	R1A	Decimal points are very important when we are writing numbers. (She demonstrates how to add with decimals by using money numbers. She adds them incorrectly so that the children can correct them, calling out corrections from the classroom.) One way to help yourself, people, is to make sure all your dots line up. (R1A) All right, boys and girls, when you get our answers, be sure to put decimal points in.
Getting Organized	T2A	(T2A) OK, everybody, a pencil and a paper. We're going to do some problems. (Comes over to me and tells me it is not what she had planned to do, but that it was a good introduction to decimals and they needed the practice in this.)
9:26–9:30	A6 T3C T2A W1B	(A6) Remember two things. It's very important if you want a hundred: Dollar signs and decimal points. (T3C) I'll give you 15 minutes to do these (T2A). OK, are you ready to start? (W1B) When we finish this, work on contracts—your math contracts. If you do not have one, we'll have a conference and make one up for you. OK, here we go.

and to omit mention of others. LeCompte's "Learning to Work" scripts of teacher behavior (see Example 2.9) placed special emphasis on noninstructional speech and behavior, since her interest was in the so-called hidden curriculum (Friedenberg 1970; Jackson 1968) of classroom structure and organization, rather than on what was learned in formal content instruction. By recording the types of activities and how long they occurred, however, LeCompte was able to create a description of instructional priorities and the distribution of activities, material that turned out to

Definition: Translation is the process by which ethnographers describe in their own words and concepts the ideas, behaviors, and words of the people observed in the study

Key point

be very useful in her final write-up. Thus, *even when the researcher is taking verbatim notes or is using a recording device, items from informants' speech and behavior still are selected for recording by the researcher, and then recorded with the researcher's purpose in mind and an eye toward their utility in constructing an overall argument for the study. It is important to devise strategies that collect as much information as possible, even while recognizing the biases of selection and translation.* Ethnographers' observations and subsequent descriptions and transcriptions are filtered through their personal, professional, cultural, and theoretical lenses as well, and therefore serve whatever agendas the researchers might have.

SUMMARY

In this chapter we emphasize the recursive and sometimes even unconscious analysis that ethnographers do in the field because these early analytic processes often are not recognized as such by researchers who customarily believe that "real" analysis only occurs once the researcher leaves the field. While we disagree with Miles and Huberman (1984), who argue that researchers should always code their field notes the same night as they are recorded,[3] we do believe that some form of holistic or implicit coding and categorizing goes on throughout the fieldwork stages of research and sets the stage for rigorous analysis when fieldwork is over. If researchers follow the steps described in Book 2, beginning with conceptual taxonomies that guide the investigation and continuing through operational definitions of the concepts, a broad coding system will be partially developed even prior to the study, refined during the first stages of the study, and continually refined thereafter. This process provides a framework used throughout this book and is explained in detail in Books 1, 2, and 3 of the *Ethnographer's Toolkit*. These strategies help to clarify how early stages of data analysis—which we discuss in chapters 3 through 6 of this book—are linked to later stages of data analysis and interpretation. We now make a slight detour to describe how researchers set up data management procedures and prepare their data for analysis.

NOTES

1. Sanjek (1990) cites some cases where experienced researchers have had to rely almost exclusively on head notes because all their other data were destroyed. We believe that these are exceptional cases and should not be taken as guides for novice researchers.

2. LeCompte's preference for recording field observations are sturdily bound spiral stenographer's pads that have a stiff cardboard back. They contain many pages and are ideal for situations lacking a table or desk upon which to write. An indicator of the indestructible nature of these steno pads was the survival of one—completely filled and therefore invaluable—after LeCompte inadvertently left it on the top of her car and drove off. By the time she noticed its absence, it had lain in the middle of a busy street for thirty minutes and was run over by innumerable cars and trucks. Although its binding was crushed and two pages were rendered illegible by dirt, the rest remained intact.

3. Miles and Huberman assume that researchers already have done a considerable amount of fieldwork and have developed protocols or categories of behavior, speech, and events that they want to look for in the field—before they even arrive. Most ethnography today begins with a guiding theoretical framework that lends itself at least to broad-based categorization, of the kind we describe in Vadeboncoeur's work, later in this book. In these cases, the coding system used constantly evolves, based on interaction of the researcher with the field setting and the data collected to date.

3 ⬛⬤⬛⬤⬛

Steps in Organizing and Cataloging Data

Steps in Tidying Up

Reasons for Tidying Up

Summary

TIDYING UP, CATALOGING, AND CREATING DATA INVENTORIES

Once the data collection process is completed, in-the-field analysis ceases and the researcher withdraws from the field site or from data collection activities. At this point, the "out-of-the-field" stage of analysis begins. In the best case, this analysis begins with a serious housekeeping activity that must be completed as soon as possible after fieldwork really ends, and with luck, before the ethnographer is too far away from the field site. Various methodologists have called this process "data cleaning," "data management," and "cataloging"; we have described it in some detail as "tidying up" in chapter 10 of Book 3. We note that in some cases, the "tidying up phase" actually must begin to happen even at the beginning of the data collection process. This is especially true for group projects, in which team members must have common formats for writing up their notes and interviews and common organizing schemes for other forms of data that are brought in from the field, such as photographs, secondary or Internet references, relevant library references, and artifacts. Agreed-upon means of storing these data and making them accessible to all team members for analysis must be created prior to the project actually beginning. We describe these procedures in Book 3, chapter 3. The suggestions we make in this chapter for tidying up thus apply to

Cross Reference:
See Book 3, chapter 10 for discussion of team projects

considerations taken both before data collection begins and after the point where data collection ends. In this chapter, we assert that "tidying up" is no mere paper-shuffling exercise; it is a systematic form of data organization and initial analysis. Below we review what tidying up involves and the contributions it makes in the initial stages of data analysis.

STEPS IN ORGANIZING AND CATALOGING DATA

As we noted in Book 3, the first thing ethnographers must do, either before the project begins if it is a group project, or as they are leaving the field (or immediately after departing from it) if it is an individual project, is to plan for how to organize and catalog their entire mountain of information. This means creating a system with the team if the project is a group project or, as an individual researcher, going through boxes, piles of paper, bags of artifacts, tapes and photographs, and stacks of notebooks as well as computerized field notes and interviews. The objective is twofold: first, the ethnographer must create order out of the materials, and second, he or she must check to make sure that all research questions have been answered. Step one involves creating systematic inventories and indices; step two requires establishing a data inventory system similar to the data tracking matrices discussed in Book 1, chapter 6. The two steps necessarily occur in tandem, though for purposes of explanation, we treat them separately here. The data inventory checklist illustrated in Table 3.1 can be used to map the research questions against data collected. As the sorting and systematizing process described below proceeds, the questions in the inventory are answered.

Table 3.1 displays the dynamic nature of ethnographic research, in which questions are modified, added to, and sometimes abandoned as the collection of additional data mandates; data or informants anticipated to be available become unavailable or are inappropriate and substitutes must be found, and timelines alter as field situations change. Such conditions do not obtain in more structured experimental or controlled research, but they are hallmarks of basic, applied, and action ethnography. It is helpful indeed to make sure that such alterations in the original

TABLE 3.1 Data Inventory Matrix

Research Questions	Conceptual Rationale	Data Type	Data Source	Gatekeepers	Data Format	Timelines
What did I want to know?	Why did I need to know this (e.g., what theories or concepts make this an important question to answer? What theories and concepts will help explain the results?)?	What types of data were collected to answer each research question (e.g., interviews, field notes, audiotapes, documents from meetings, photographs)?	Where, or from whom, did I obtain these data (e.g., school archives, science teachers, known Ecstasy users, Native American elders)?	Whom did I contact for access to these data?	What form are the data in (e.g., transcribed audiotapes, field notes of observations, a collection of letters and emails from administrators, journals kept by teachers, maps of the community and environment)?	When were these data acquired and by whom (dates, name of researcher)?
		Planned	Planned	Planned	Planned	Planned
		Actually Collected	Actually Collected	Actually Collected	Actually Collected	Actually Collected

(continued)

TABLE 3.1 (continued)

Research Questions	Conceptual Rationale	Data Type	Data Source	Gatekeepers	Data Format	Timelines
Original Question 1	Concepts Informing Question (author and date of concepts)					
Original Question 2	Concepts Informing Question (author and date of concepts)					
Subquestion 2A	Concepts Informing Question (author and date of concepts)					
Subquestion 2B	Concepts Informing Question (author and date of concepts)					
New Question 3 (Explanation)	Concepts Informing Question (author and date of concepts)					
Modified Question 2 (Explanation)	Concepts Informing Question (author and date of concepts)					
Extenuating Circumstances and Explanations	Extenuating Circumstances and Explanations	Extenuating Circumstances and Explanations	Extenuating Circumstances and Explanations	Extenuating Circumstances and Explanations	Extenuating Circumstances and Explanations	Extenuating Circumstances and Explanations

designs or plans are made clear to readers so that distinctions can be made between what was planned, what really happened, and how events that actually transpired affected the study's results. While a matrix such as Table 3.1 does not have to be followed in excruciating detail, it does provide a checklist by which researchers can document and explain changes in research questions and foci, problems in obtaining data, delays and omissions in collecting data, and the specific forms in which data are held.

Tracking and filing systems can be set up electronically. Especially in team ethnography projects, it is very important to track the status of work assigned or self-assigned to each member of the ethnographic team as well as the classes of data. Further, as specific types of data enter the database, the use of an analytic matrix becomes useful in tracking whether, for example, key informant interviews or semistructured interviews are providing the expected or desired data. Entering data in a data recording matrix is useful both as a form of quality control and as a way of revealing specific patterns, such as demographic or other information on sampling protocols as respondents accrue or the presence or absence of indicators of key domains related to the research questions in the study. As we note in Book 3, chapter 3, and later in this book, spreadsheet programs such as Excel are very useful in managing these data tracking and quality controls. Further, these forms of management are useful for research conducted by both individual researchers and research teams. They facilitate organizing an analysis scheme, as does the crucial material in column two, which provides the specific concepts that will inform how the data will be chunked and categorized.

STEPS IN TIDYING UP

We now review the steps in tidying up.

Make Copies of All Important Materials

First and foremost, to the extent possible, make copies of all text materials, including transcripts, field notes, surveys, interviews, questionnaires, documents, and written artifacts (Patton 1990). Some researchers prefer to make both electronic and hard copies of electronic data and to keep both. It is difficult to overemphasize the importance of making copies. Example 3.1 has a happy ending, but not all such stories do.

EXAMPLE 3.1 ⬥•⬤•⬥

AND THEN A MIRACLE HAPPENED. . . .

Stephen Crosley had completed his doctoral dissertation fieldwork in Africa. He returned to his home in New Jersey in the spring, and while he was completing the cleanup and organizational activities described above, he accepted a job at a university in the northwestern United States, thousands of miles from where he had attended school. He packed up his Volkswagen van in the early summer with all of his belongings, including every scrap of data he had collected for his dissertation and the night before he was to leave went to a farewell party with friends. During the party, his van was stolen. Months went by and it had not been recovered. The dissertation data were lost. Crosley had to begin his new job with no degree and no research project with which to earn one. A year later, on a visit back home, he once again drove down the New Jersey Turnpike, noticing the many junkyards full of wrecked cars that lined the freeway. Suddenly, he spied a familiar looking, though battered, Volkswagen van. A quick investigation confirmed that it was indeed his van, stripped mechanically and empty of valuables, but with the boxes of data still intact. Nobody had thought them worth taking. If Crosley had actually kept a copy of all his data separately, his year of despair could have been avoided.

Store Copies and Originals Separately

Storing copies and originals in separate and safe places assures against theft, loss, fire, and researcher absentmind-edness. We cannot emphasize enough the need for careful storage of both original and copies of data. Researchers should make sure that all data are kept in locked file cabinets or in password-protected computers and computer files with project-controlled access. Fireproof storage also is a good idea. In group projects, all team members should turn in copies of their finalized materials for the project. Storage of project data should be managed by the study coordinator or data manager, whose job it is to keep track of all the data as they are copied into the master file. Group projects require a common storage site for the project; individual researchers must have access to all of the data so that they can copy it into their own working files (which also must be password protected) after they coordinate their activities with the study investigator and field coordinator.

Put All Field Notes in Some Sort of Order

There are many ways to put field notes in order. Most people organize their notes into several kinds of files. Keeping multiple kinds of files facilitates retrieval, but it also requires that the researcher have some idea of how he or she wants to chunk up the data. Below we list illustrative types of files; it goes without saying that copies must be made of all files.

TYPES OF FILES

- *Chronological files*, with all materials generated on any given day kept together.
- *Genre files*, which maintain specific kinds of data—logs, diaries, artifacts, story transcripts, descriptive notes, journals, meeting minutes—separately.
- *Cast-of-character files*, which maintain separate files for everything said, done, or relevant to each significant person, group of persons, or program in a study.
- *Geographic files*, which maintain separate files in accordance with the location where events occurred or people interacted. For example, a study of a school could separate data into geographic files containing material relevant to the principal's office, the teachers' lounge, individual classrooms, the auditorium, the gym, the bathrooms (boys,' girls,' male teachers,' female teachers'), the playground, and "off-limits" areas.
- *Event or activity files*, which maintain separate files for key events and activities or categories of events and activities.

- *Topical files*, which maintain data by categories of interest to the researcher—disease, type of meeting, specific class, theme, type of behavior.
- *Quantitative data files* of survey, network, elicitation, and other numeric data.

EXAMPLE 3.2

CREATING A FILING SYSTEM FOR A GROUP ETHNOGRAPHY PROJECT IN STAGES

A team ethnographic study of Ecstasy drug use among young adults in central Connecticut produced many different types of data, including key informant interviews, focus group interviews, in-depth interviews, field notes, recruitment notes, photographs, information downloaded from the Internet, and digital recordings. The study coordinator at the Institute for Community Research created a system for filing these materials that evolved along with the multiphased study. During the first phase of the study, file subdirectories were created to hold focus group sound and text transcriptions of digital recordings, field notes, field photographs, initial analyses and preliminary reports, and data tracking matrices. The second stage of the study required file subdirectories for pilot and final in-depth interviews, recruitment field notes and recruitment materials, and data tracking and master analysis/matrices. The third, or analysis, stage of the study called for yet more file subdirectories, including originals of transcribed interviews, an Atlas TI computer analysis software file subdirectory, an SPSS subdirectory, and subdirectories for analytic matrices. The fourth, or dissemination, phase of the study called for subdirectories related to the preparation and recording of dissemination workshops, papers for presentation, and peer-reviewed journal articles in draft and final manuscript stages.

Other details on data tracking and analytic matrices are located in this book, chapter 7. Any of these files may be duplicated for filing with other relevant files. Surveys on particular topics, for example, can be filed in both data-type files and topic files. It is easy to see that the kinds of files maintained for a project depend on the research questions asked and the purposes of the research; they also depend on the particular preferences and management style of the researcher or the research team. Since funded researchers increasingly are being asked to share their data, even de-identified qualitative data, other researchers who were uninvolved in the initial study may use the data in the future. Thus, it is very important to give careful consideration to the organization of these files and to document them in detail. An index accomplishes this purpose.

Create a Catalog or Index of All Documents and Artifacts

An index makes it possible for research data to be located and retrieved as necessary. The catalog should be kept in a separate place from the actual data. The index also could include information about who handled the materials and when, as illustrated in Table 3.2.

Create a Management System for Interviews, Surveys, and Questionnaires

The steps in creating a data management system include labeling all audio- and videotapes and numbering each interview, survey, or questionnaire. In a team project, these data are usually identified with a unique identifier in advance, and personal identity markers are removed from the instruments or interviews. Researchers also should create a log or notebook for audio- and videotapes and another log or notebook for interviews, surveys, and questionnaires. Each instrument or tape should be logged in on a form by its unique identifying number, followed by columns indicating its status, as indicated in Table 3.2.

Often digital data are transcribed by hired transcribers or transcription services. It is very important to maintain good records of the status of these recordings for both financial/billing and data quality control and management.

Some data may not be coded, and some kinds of surveys and questionnaires may not need to be transcribed. However, it is important to keep track of the dates when

TABLE 3.2 Instrument Log

Survey Number (or Tape Number)	Date Transcribed	Name of Transcriber	Date Coded	Name of Coder	Date Entered into Database
0001	1-15-98	LeCompte	1-25-98	Holloway	1-30-98
0002	1-16-98	LeCompte	1-27-98	Maybin	1-30-98

notes, instruments, or digital recordings were handled and who did what to them, regardless of how the data were manipulated or cataloged. The same kind of checkout and handling system should be created for artifacts and documents. These systems prevent materials from being lost and facilitate monitoring transcribers, coders, and other research personnel for accuracy and care.

Store All Materials in a Safe Space

Once logs, catalogs, and indices of data are created and data are stored in digital format, the instruments, recordings, photographs, documents, and artifacts themselves can be stored in files and boxes in a secure waterproof and fireproof place for safekeeping. These boxes should be labeled clearly and may be archived if not needed immediately.

Make a List of All the Box Labels

Listing all the box labels creates a complete "table of contents" of the boxes and their contents. The following example illustrates what can happen to data in a team project if they are not carefully monitored.

EXAMPLE 3.3   ◀▬•▬◀•▬▶

THE CASE OF THE DISAPPEARED ETHNOGRAPHIC NOTES

In a mixed-methods study of youth and drug use at the Institute for Community Research (ICR) involving observations, in-depth interviews, and a panel study (same data collected from the same people at two time points), the study team pooled ethnographers across two organizations. One of the ethnographers had conducted extensive fieldwork and had stored much of her data on her computer at the partner organization. When the time came for her to leave the project, she copied the data to a password-protected CD, erased her own project files at her organization, and handed one copy to the principal investigator and a second to the project coordinator at ICR. The coordinator copied the data from the CD into his own private subdirectory and password-protected it, but he did not place it in the ICR project "shared drive"; and he kept the CD in his own desk. His private subdirectory was transferred to a backup system, which was stored and archived by the ICR technical staff, but the subdirectory was not transferred into the project directory on the "shared drive." When the technical director left the project, the CD was stored with a collection of other backup CDs in a box in the computer/server room. No one knew where the data were stored. When the time came to analyze this collection of ethnographic data, the data were not locatable in the project shared drive. It was only because the team ethnographer had made a second copy for the principal investigator, who kept it as a backup with the password to the files, that these valuable data were recovered.

REASONS FOR TIDYING UP

As we explained in Book 3, chapter 3, researchers can lose track of all the data needed in the overall welter of things that they actually have amassed. Tidying up, then, serves a number of purposes. First, it creates a data inventory to check to make sure all research questions are answered, and if not, why not. It also facilitates checking to make sure all needed data have been collected as well as creates a rationale for why certain materials were not collected. Finally, it ensures that the data are properly protected and confidentiality is maintained.

   **EXAMPLE 3.4**

**EXPLAINING WHY SOME DESIRED DATA WERE NOT COLLECTED
AND WHY OTHERS, NOT ANTICIPATED, WERE**

May Lee, a science education graduate student, had planned to do a study of children's beliefs about science in an after-school science enrichment class for her spring research methods class. In the fall semester before her methods class began, she had observed the program to get an idea of how it operated; at that time the enrollment was over twenty children, which she felt was sufficient for her interview-based project of children and their parents. However, when she began her actual study in the spring, only five children were enrolled, and of those, one boy was too young for the program. He had been allowed to enroll because his older sister was enrolled. And since two of the enrollees were siblings, only four sets of parents were available, and even they were too busy to be interviewed when they came to pick up their children—as Lee had originally planned. Lee had to change her focus from interviewing children to a close observation of what the children did and how they seemed to construct ideas about science. Her data tracking matrix explained the change in data collection, as it did her change in data about parents. When she discussed the dearth of parent respondents with the program staff, the director told her that until the previous year, the program had administered an opinion survey to every parent, but no one had analyzed the data for lack of time. Learning that these surveys had covered many of the questions in which she was interested, Lee volunteered to analyze the data for them if she could use the results for her project. This fortuitous change also was documented in her data tracking matrix (Lee 2009).

May Lee's data inventory checklist included an explanation of the "extenuating circumstances" that mandated a change in her research design and data collection: low enrollment in the classes, few parents and their unwillingness to be interviewed, and the lucky discovery of hundreds of unanalyzed parent surveys that answered some of her research questions. It also explained how the data actually collected differed from what was initially planned.

Tidying up also permits researchers to confirm the relevance and validity of categories and codes initially developed as well as to develop new insights as a consequence of reviewing all the information they have collected. For example, in her "Learning to Work" study, LeCompte had originally thought that teachers would emphasize to children the intrinsic value of learning by highlighting how grades represented the acquisition of new knowledge. It was only during the process of organizing her data, after she had reviewed all of her teacher interviews and classroom field notes, that LeCompte discovered that this behavior occurred only once in six months of observation (LeCompte 1978). Similarly, in an HIV-related substudy of low-income women in India who were interviewed about the effects of alcohol consumption of their husbands on their lives, researchers Berg and Schensul expected to find many cases of sexual violence. Instead they found other types of abuse and violence, but few actual reports of forced sex (Berg et al. 2010). In the absence of forced sex, they had to reformulate their views about the role of alcohol in the transmission of HIV from husband to wife in this vulnerable population of women.

SUMMARY

In this chapter, we have explained how housekeeping actually is a preliminary and necessary form of data analysis. We have outlined plans and options for carrying out these tasks expeditiously and using them to create a sound set of data management procedures. In chapter 4, we return to a discussion of the recursive cognitive processes that researchers use to crunch their data.

4 ━◆━◆━◆━

RECURSIVITY, INDUCTION, AND DEDUCTION: MOVING BETWEEN LEVELS OF ABSTRACTION

RECURSIVITY REVIEWED

Analysis of ethnographic data is characterized by the cyclical and interactive process of data collection, analysis, and interpretation used by ethnographers and qualitative researchers. Throughout this book we have used the term "recursive" to describe this process. It includes the following steps:

THE RECURSIVE PROCESS

- Formulate initial questions and create formative theoretical models that reflect the research questions.
- Collect data to answer those questions and explore, deepen, and amplify the domains in the model.
- Determine on an ongoing basis what the data mean.
- Match the data against the original questions and models.

- Based on the data collected, retain, elaborate, modify, or discard the original questions and models.
- Reformulate original questions and raise new ones, deepening and revising the model in accord with the new information and questions.
- Continue data collection.

 Definition: Recursive analysis involves a cyclical process of raising questions, collecting data to answer them, conducting preliminary data analysis, and then reformulating old or generating new questions to pursue, based on the previous analysis

The **recursive process** outlined begins when researchers enter the field with general questions designed to roughly map out the environment, the numbers and kinds of people engaged in the environment, what they are doing, and why. The researchers then collect data that answer those questions. Next, researchers perform a preliminary analysis of these data. They then match the analyzed data against the original questions and the study model to determine whether or not the questions and the model (a) continue to be appropriate to the site, (b) must be modified, or (c) should be discarded because they have been negated or contradicted by the evidence gathered. This process also generates new questions and variable domains not anticipated in earlier stages. Finally, the researchers reformulate the original questions where necessary and add new ones. The process then cycles again, with data collection to continue answering the original questions as well as answering new and modified ones. While the steps just listed imply that the process is quite systematic, with one cycle ending before another cycle begins, recursivity actually is a dynamic process that occurs throughout a study as researchers constantly match information previously collected with new information and the research questions and then modify and adapt subsequent questions as the study progresses.

Examples 4.1, 4.2, and 4.3 show how researchers had to alter original research questions in the light of feedback from the field.

EXAMPLE 4.1

WHEN THERE IS NO INDIGENOUS MATH IN THE MATH CLASS: MODIFYING QUESTIONS AND DATA COLLECTION STRATEGIES WHEN WHAT THE RESEARCHER EXPECTS TO FIND DOES NOT APPEAR

For his dissertation, David Sanders, a Native American from the Lakota tribe and a doctoral student in mathematics education, planned to study how Lakota language and culture were reflected in the math classes of the elementary school he himself had attended in the Oglala community that was his home town. He planned to supplement what he found in the classroom with information about mathematical knowledge from Lakota elders. Unfortunately, the math teacher in the school was a white person with little knowledge of traditional Lakota culture, and while the elders did remember that mathematics-oriented games had been played by Lakota in the past, they themselves didn't know how to play them. They also could not remember much other information relevant to how the Lakota used mathematics traditionally. In a nearby community, however, an archive of research existed, compiled by the first anthropologists to study the community. These archives contained a great deal of information about Lakota games, star knowledge, migration patterns, and other mathematically relevant materials. Sanders then altered his research question. The study became not so much about what Lakota math *was* used in the classroom, but what kind of Lakota mathematical practices *could be retrieved* and revitalized from the archives for use in contemporary classrooms (Sanders 2011).

Like David Sanders, Jennifer Vadeboncoeur also did not find in her field site the behavior she had expected to be exhibited after students finished participating in their teacher education program.

EXAMPLE 4.2

WHEN A CRITICAL THEORETICAL TRAINING PROGRAM DOES NOT PRODUCE CRITICAL THINKERS: MODIFYING QUESTIONS AND DATA COLLECTION STRATEGIES WHEN WHAT THE RESEARCHER EXPECTS TO FIND DOES NOT APPEAR

Jennifer Vadeboncoeur began her study of an eighteen-month undergraduate teacher licensure program with the assumption that the coursework and class discussions, which were heavily influenced by the liberatory rhetoric of Paulo Freire and other critical theorists, would lead student participants to become more emancipated in their thinking and less narrow-minded in their approach to minority and low-income students. She felt that students gradually would shift their orientations from very self-centered (most of the students) to a few who might be called emergent critical thinkers (those able to consider individual, group, and structural influences on behavior and thought) who exhibited what Freire calls transformational thinking. Vadeboncoeur first documented what students said in small group discussions about classroom scenarios similar to what they would find in their practica and student teaching. She also examined what they wrote in their daily journals, looking for examples of the list of statements and behaviors she had used to operationalize orientations in each stage of the critical consciousness continuum (see Figure 5.1 in this book). To her surprise, she found no behavior or journal entries that exhibited what she thought critical thinking should look like, even at the end of the first semester. If anything, the students became less, rather than more, emancipatory in their thinking. Students were concerned only with surviving the first days in a classroom; most of the audio-recorded discussions were filled with complaints that teacher education students weren't learning enough about classroom management techniques, as well as lots of chatter about boyfriends and parties. The overall philosophy of the program eluded most of the students, at least until the very last days in their coursework. These data required that Vadeboncoeur modify her project from one in which she looked deductively for a match with her initial assumptions to one in which she explored inductively what the students actually *were* saying and to what material in the curriculum and pedagogy of the program the students actually attended (Vadeboncoeur 1998).

EXAMPLE 4.3　　⬤•⬤•⬤

CHOOSING A NEW CONCEPTUAL MODEL WHEN THE ORIGINAL ONE DOES NOT EXPLAIN THE DATA

Candice Miller's dissertation explored which factors facilitated graduation from PhD programs and which impeded them. A review of the literature, her exposure to the Council of Graduate Schools' (CGS) PhD Completion Project (http://www.phdcompletion.org), and her prior work as campus coordinator for the "Making the Implicit Explicit" study of doctoral study programs sponsored by the Alfred P. Sloan Foundation (Lovitts 2007) led her initially to choose the CGS model used in that study to inform her study of PhD programs in two academic departments (Miller 2009; Golde et al. 2006). It examined student characteristics as predictors of success as well as the presence or absence of certain aspects of graduate programs, including mentoring, transparent rules and regulations, and availability of information about program procedures. While these issues were important, they did not seem to explain all the variance in student success, especially given that the students themselves were a relatively homogenous group and the two programs did not differ radically. Miller also was constantly struck by what she felt was the discontinuous nature of learning in PhD programs. Once students had completed coursework and comprehensive examinations, they were thrown into a completely new set of performance expectations and standards. No prior educational experiences really prepared PhD candidates for the kind of thinking they would have to do to complete their PhD. What, then, explained the fact that one program graduated nearly all its PhD candidates and the other did not? Miller began to search for a model of teaching and learning that would better explain what students really needed to, or did, experience for doctoral success. She found it in the sociocultural learning theories of Lev Vygotsky (1978) and Barbara Rogoff (1990, 2003) and the apprenticeship experiences mandated in this approach. Miller's dissertation ultimately created a new model that described a continuum of formal and informal processes of learning that, if present, led to student success, and if absent or only partially present, left students struggling, often to drop out and fail (Miller 2009).

◆━◆━◆━◆

INDUCTION, DEDUCTION, AND LEVELS OF ABSTRACTION

Some readers will recall the general format of Table 4.1 from similar tables in earlier books in the *Toolkit* and from the first chapter in this book. We have used this format throughout the *Toolkit* to explain the processes ethnographers use in thinking about the models and processes that shape their work. Tables 4.1, 4.2, and 4.3 show graphically just how the inductive and deductive strategies for coding, developing taxonomies, and identifying structures and patterns within a cultural scene are interrelated processes. Tables 4.1 and 4.2 are used here to display the levels of the inductive and deductive processes that Vadeboncoeur used recursively to develop an understanding of what actually was happening in the teacher training program she studied. In so doing, she had to move horizontally between levels of abstraction from field-based actual behavior to "clumped" or "chunked" data describing larger units of information assembled in the field, and vertically between the simplest local explanations for phenomena through substantive explanations of similar phenomena in other settings, to overall theories of human behavior in general. Table 4.3 displays how students explained what one had to develop in order to become a "good teacher"; these local to more general explanations gradually emerged as a reflection of the students' preoccupation with survival during their first year of actual teaching. Survival concerns also clustered at the left of the table, indicating that students thought that being a good teacher simply was a matter of an individual's personal characteristics, experiences, and luck.

Vadeboncoeur had begun with a macro theoretical model for her study. She first identified the general theories about the causes of inequality in human social and economic life that she wanted to use to inform her study. She then isolated from them specific domains attendant to levels of consciousness linked to how people explained the origins of and responsibility for inequality *for themselves and others*. She operationalized these theoretical levels based on *a priori* assumptions about how they would look in practice. This process was, of course, informed by other research that had attempted to look at similar phenomena in different settings. She then went looking for evidence of those operationalized "variables" in the conversations, interviews, diaries, and behavior of her participants. In a sense, she was trying to impose a framework, organizing her work deductively, or from the top down, on her field site.

Table 4.1 shows how she originally thought teacher education students would explain why their own students failed to succeed. It displays the vertical or theoretical continuum from *local explanations*, which we call *locally situated theories*, about why people do or believe particular things, through substantive or middle-range theories that explain similar behavior across similar sites, to macro theory, which attempts to create theories of human behavior and belief in general. In this case, the continuum ranges from theories that show little social consciousness and blame failure on individual student characteristics to theories of transitive consciousness (Freire 1970) that show a sophisticated understanding of structural impediments to academic success. The successive domains factors, subfactors, and variables indicate how Vadeboncoeur thought these levels would appear in her data.

However, she found little in the students' talk that matched with her *a priori* categories. Instead of talking about theory or even about the possible explanations for student

TABLE 4.1 Vadeboncoeur Dissertation: The Theoretical/Conceptual Levels of Research: The Relationship between Freirian Levels of Consciousness and Students' Explanations for Student Academic Failure

Causes of Low Student Achievement	Semitransitive Consciousness	Semitransitive Consciousness	Transitive Consciousness 1	Transitive Consciousness 2
Domains	Personal characteristics	Life experiences	Discrimination	Socioeconomic status
Factors	Intelligence Motivation Personality	Parental background Education Peer group	Sexual orientation Race Gender Language Religion	Family income Parents' educational level Parents' occupation Place of residence Visible possessions
Subfactors: Intelligence, Motivation, Personality	"Worked very hard" (motivation) "Nice friendly person" (personality) "Was a good student" (intelligence) "Teachers didn't like him" "Lazy"	"Friends all went to college" "Parents were good role models" "Family was stable; both parents present" "Travel opportunities"	"Muslim students were ridiculed" "Having a Mexican accent is bad" "Only black kids get athletic scholarships"	"Can afford to live where there are good schools" "Well-educated parents can help their kids with homework" "Kids do well when their parents can buy them the latest books and electronics"
Variables	"Did not turn work in on time" (motivation) "Was absent all the time" (motivation) "Talked back to the teacher" (personality) "Fell asleep in class" (indicative of low motivation perhaps—and an indicator of not working hard)	"She and her best friend planned to be college roommates" "Parents helped with college applications" "Was accepted into best school in his area" "She studied Spanish in Mexico and got a good summer job with her language fluency"	"Why are all the computer tutors Koreans? Who can understand them?" "My math teacher says 'everyone knows that girls can't do math'" "Swastikas were painted on the dorm doors of Jewish students"	"She's wearing designer jeans and drives a Hummer" "Her father's an orthopedic surgeon" "They live in the projects behind the railroad tracks"

Local ← Theoretical/Conceptual → Paradigm

success, Vadeboncoeur's students were much more interested in talking about their own daily activities and their personal problems than in understanding some of the philosophical reasons behind their own and their students' behavior. What actually occurred looked more like the material displayed in Table 4.2. Perhaps if Vadeboncoeur had done some initial exploration before creating her model, there would have been a better match between theory and actuality.

Table 4.2 shows what her participants actually said about what they did and their explanations of behavior and concerns. A table such as this showed Vadeboncoeur that the students in fact did not talk in their work groups about the emancipatory theory that informed their teacher training program. The primary school-related topics involved what they needed to do and how far they had to go before they embodied their ideal of the "good teacher." Thus, there was a mismatch between her original theory and what the field data "told" her. Vadeboncoeur's predicament is typical of what can happen to a novice researcher who develops a the-

TABLE 4.2 Vadeboncoeur Dissertation: The Operational/Empirical Levels of Research: Students' Conceptions of Classwork and Teaching

	Abstract	← *Empirical/Operational* →		*Concrete*
Student Concerns	*Structure (Domain)*	*Pattern (Factor)*	*Unit (Variable)*	*Item or Fact*
	Topics students discuss in group work	Academic talk	—Subject matter insecurity —Management insecurity —Classroom dynamics	—Why won't the EL students speak English? —Don't feel ready to teach math —Can't control students —Stayed up all night doing homework —Student teaching: white kids picked on Mexican students today
		Nonacademic talk	—Social life —School workload —Money problems —Health	—Had fight with boyfriend —Working two jobs —Missed classes with the flu —Can't afford to repair car

ory prior to doing sufficient preliminary fieldwork. Her strategy seemed reasonable, given that the School of Education heavily promoted the notion that its program was strongly influenced by Freirian notions of teaching and learning. However, as Vadeboncoeur found, theory and action do not always co-occur. Even though many of the students' professors did, in fact, make Freirian teaching explicit, the prior experiences and current preoccupations of students overrode the curricular message. Vadeboncoeur had to abandon her previously deductive approach and generate alternative explanations for the failure of the program to imbue its students with a heavy Freireian message. Seeking inspiration in a body of research on similar programs, Vadeboncoeur discovered that the eighteen-month duration of the program probably was insufficient for the treatment to "take." Further, students were far more concerned with how to just survive in their first teaching assignments than in understanding the nuances of structural inequality theory. The questions with which they concerned themselves were not why their future *students* might or might not fail, but why and how *teachers*—such as they aspired to be—were effective or not. Table 4.3 shows how the students conceptualized what it was they thought they should become to emulate good teachers.

The students' fixation on daily classroom practice caused most of them to remain at the intransitive or semi-transitive level of consciousness, in which they evaluated most phenomena in terms of their own experience and needs. Thus the main theoretical concepts in her original model were useful after all.

MOVING BETWEEN LEVELS OF ABSTRACTION: FROM CONCRETE TO ABSTRACT AND BACK

In Table 4.4, we present yet another way of looking at the operational dimension. The right-hand column of the top two rows of Table 4.4 displays facts that a researcher could assemble about specific plants: they have a pattern in common—woody stems and softer leaves—but their structure is different. Some lose leaves in winter, and some do not. Further, there are different units, distinguished by their shape: trees are tall with single leading stems or trunks; bushes are shorter and have multiple leading stems and a rounded

TABLE 4.3　Vadeboncoeur Dissertation: What Makes a Good Teacher

	What Makes a Good Teacher			
Domain	"Good teachers"			
Factor		—Institutional criteria for good teaching —Student explanations regarding good teaching		
Subfactor (student explanations)			—Strong in subject matter —Treats all students fairly —Cares about students —Accessible to students	
Variable (strong in subject matter)				—Went to a top graduate school —Has an MA degree —Does hands-on experiments —Always explains material well —Comes to class prepared

Local ← Theoretical/Conceptual → Paradigm

shape. Bushes and trees have thick, strong supportive stems and are freestanding, while vines have long, trailing, relatively weak stems and need something to climb on for support. The bottom of Table 4.4 returns to Candice Miller's dissertation and similarly disaggregates her data into patterns, units, and items or facts in the second two rows.

GENERATING EXPLANATIONS: FROM LOCAL TO SUBSTANTIVE THEORIES AND BACK

Table 4.4 is descriptive, but it does not tell us *why* the structures that appear in the data do so at any level, whether

TABLE 4.4 Deconstructing Various Structures into Patterns or Factors, Units or Variables, and Items or Facts

Structure or domain	Pattern or factor	Units or variables	Items or facts
Plants with woody stems	Single trunks, soft leaves, loses leaves in winter	Deciduous trees Vines Bushes	*Deciduous trees:* elms, oaks, maples, redbud *Vines:* Bittersweet, poison ivy, clematis *Bushes:* Quince, spirea, forsythia, dogwood
	Single trunks, needlelike leaves, does not lose leaves in winter	Types of needles: Needles borne in clusters Needles borne in pairs	*Clusters:* Larch, fir *Pairs:* Ponderosa pine, pinion pine
Doctoral programs at universities	High completion rates; most students successfully earn a PhD and graduate	Level of funding	Full funding; A four-year scholarship; extra after the four years if needed
		Frequency of workshops and events	Workshops and social events throughout the program Regular cohort meetings; student/faculty social hours and beer busts
		Career counseling	Strong career counseling A staff member who was responsible for updating websites and providing career help
		Mentorship	Mentor matching at beginning of program
	Low completion rates; fewer than half of students admitted complete a PhD and graduate	Level of funding	Insufficient funding for five-year program Some students received full funding, others didn't
		Workshops and social events	Social events end after first year; students complained that it was hard to meet colleagues
		Career counseling	Career counseling limited to professor interests
		Mentorship	Students find own mentors in course of program Students didn't understand how to get an advisor

locally explanatory or at the level of substantive theory. Table 4.5 is an attempt, using Miller's dissertation, to depict and integrate both the descriptive and the explanatory arenas. In this case, the figure displays how explanations move from local explanations given by students, to categorization of these explanations, to translation by the researcher of those categories into terminology and language used by sociocultural learning theorists, and finally, to an overarching conceptual domain. In this case, the vertical dimension displays how particular aspects of a program contribute to learning in the *zone of proximal development* (Vygotsky 1978), a concept that provided a model for Miller's characterization of successful PhD-level learning and development. Miller actually developed Table 4.5 because her data, which ended up illuminating institutional impediments to doctoral success, challenged prior work that had attributed success almost exclusively to students' personal characteristics.

Miller noticed that the items on the lower right recurred repeatedly in the interviews and observations she conducted among PhD students in the two programs she studied. She aggregated these into patterns that helped to explain why the completion rates of one program were higher than the other. However, Miller had structured her initial interviews to focus on mentoring, a specific subfactor that her prior research indicated was important in assuring that students would graduate. Her approach, therefore, was both inductive (from right to left and bottom to top in Table 4.5) and deductive (from left to right and top to bottom in Table 4.5). Some of the things she looked for had been established as conceptual categories prior to data collection; other things emerged in the process of analysis. This example clearly illustrates the benefits of prior experience in the field and/or discussions with diverse people familiar with the study question and the field situation before creating a formative model.

TABLE 4.5 Miller Dissertation: The Theoretical/Conceptual and Empirical/Operational Levels of Research: Explaining Student Success in PhD Programs

	Abstract ← Empirical/Operational → Concrete			
Domain (structure): Zone of proximal development (Vygotsky)	Training and experience are provided for all skills needed for the professoriate			
Factor (patterns): Apprenticeship under experts and more capable peers Community of learners Just manageable challenges Authentic practice experiences Mentoring		Teaching, writing, research, fieldwork practice. Group social activities		
Subfactor: Personal experiences Professional opportunities Sufficient funds Appropriate coursework Advice and support Mentoring			Doing research and publishing articles with professors. Five years of funding; Research assistantships; Early assignment to good advisors.	Students organized research methods class to supplement regular program.
Subfactor: Personal characteristics				I'm smart, persistent; I worked hard; I made friends and formed a good study group
Variable: Student "Folk Theories" of Success (Ogbu)				I didn't get sick. In the right place at the right time. I was lucky.

SUMMARY

In this chapter, we have explained how different levels of abstraction are used and manipulated in achieving research results. The horizontal dimension creates descriptive taxonomies that shift from concrete to abstract. The vertical dimension links these descriptive taxonomies to explanations at each level. Both move between more and less abstract or between more or less closely linked to empirical evidence. Local explanations given by participants are most closely related to substantive meanings assigned to the least abstract items, events, and units in the given setting. As the level of abstraction increases, the level of explanation becomes more and more global or general and in a sense becomes more applicable to events and phenomena in larger arenas. Similarly, the least abstract categories become subsumed in higher levels of a taxonomy. Explanations of why these groupings exist also are created at each level. In the chapters that follow, we discuss the tools needed to carry out these processes.

concrete ——⟶ abstract

5 ❖❖❖

WAYS TO BEGIN ANALYSIS

A COMMON STEREOTYPE

A stereotype commonly applied to ethnography is that ethnographers never enter the field with the kind of formative model described in Book 2 and in previous chapters throughout the *Toolkit*. Ethnography is thought to be virtually atheoretical, proceeding without any prior presumptions guiding it; that is, faced with a problem or phenomenon that is poorly understood or documented, if at all, ethnographers are thought to enter the field with a completely empty brain and then to collect and pore over all manner of qualitative data, reading through interviews, field notes, and transcripts until themes and patterns begin to "emerge" from the materials and explanations for those themes somehow magically materialize from the ether. Of course, virtually no researcher approaches the field with *no* preconceptions; most realize that at the very least, their own training and interests create so-called tacit or personal theories about how the world works (LeCompte and Pre-issle 1993) and as such influence what researchers notice in the field, see in the data, and determine how they proceed. Beyond tacit theory, though, most researchers do build their initial forays into the field studies around some guiding concepts and theories that provide a starting point for investigation. Without such a starting point, even knowing what data to collect, much less trying to analyze it, is virtually impossible. In this chapter, we describe how the guiding theories, hunches, and informing concepts that

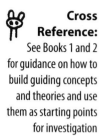

Cross Reference:
See Books 1 and 2 for guidance on how to build guiding concepts and theories and use them as starting points for investigation

ethnographers carry with them as part of their intellectual experience, plus the data from the field and strategies for aggregating and disaggregating them, combine to inform the analysis of the database.

INITIATING AN ANALYSIS

Once tidying up has been completed, the masses of accumulated data must be organized and reduced so that the ideas, meanings, explanatory theories, and themes emerge and the units, variables, patterns or factors, and structures or domains within it become visible. Allowing what is of interest in a study to emerge from the data requires both consideration of *all* the data collected and **triangulation** of data or evidence from a variety of sources to achieve credible findings. However, before triangulation is possible, researchers must subject their data to a process of reviewing and then chunking, crunching, and coding of data. Chunking, crunching, and coding of data each are used to analyze different kinds of data. Which process the researcher chooses to initiate analysis depends on the form of the data and the purpose of the study. Types of data and their relationship to analysis needs include:

Definition: Triangulation is the use of data from two or more different sources or several different kinds of data to corroborate what an informant has said or what an ethnographer has concluded

- Data that are completely qualitative, such as field notes or unstructured interviews. These must be treated initially as big clumps or pieces, usually of text, that evoke or represent a particular concept or phenomenon of interest in the study. This is called *chunking.*
- Data that are essentially qualitative but that already have been chunked. These data can be transformed into more quantitative data by a process called *"crunching."* Crunching creates clear taxonomies of distinct items or units of data. Crunching actually can transform qualitative data into data that can be counted or enumerated. Crunching also can allow for exploration of the relationship between qualitatively defined variables or factors (groups of variables).
- Data in qualitative text materials that already are in quantitative form or that have been transformed

into quantitative data. These data can be coded into discrete items and units using a coding system developed from a formative—and usually revised—theoretical framework, or inductively, or both. The units thus coded can be organized into taxonomies and structures and relationships among them identified and explored.

- Data that already are precoded and simply need to be crunched, scaled, or tallied up and manipulated to show relationships among variables, factors, and domains. These data are those usually found in systematic structured surveys or survey-like formats.

Taken together, these processes often are called the process of "coding" data. However, in the *Toolkit*, we differentiate between "general coding" and "specific coding."

GENERAL CODING AND SPECIFIC CODING

Coding involves organizing data into categories related to the conceptual framework and/or the questions guiding the research in order to provide evidence supporting analysis and interpretation. General coding and specific coding are two different processes; they tend to take place at different stages of the research process and with different kinds of data. While all "coding" does involve organizing data into categories related to the framework or model and questions guiding the research, lumping all of these complex processes together significantly oversimplifies what really happens. Initial stages of organizing data involve finding underlying themes and structures in the data; later stages involve finding discrete components with the themes and structures once they are identified. Too often, novice researchers assume that the process of "coding" simply involves using a preexisting system that represents concepts, categories, and themes from a theoretical framework by numerical or alphabetic codes. They believe that coding only means assigning these codes to sentences or paragraphs of text or to segments or units in the database. Such a deductive process is, of course, rarely used by itself by ethnographers, even though they do use it at times in studies that call for

Definition: Coding involves organizing data into categories related to the framework and/or the questions guiding the research so that they provide evidence supporting analysis and interpretation

Cross Reference: See Book 3, chapter 9 for more information on how to construct ethnographically based surveys and other structured observational materials; how these data are analyzed is addressed in chapter 9 of this book

 Definition: A model is a diagram showing the initial hypothesized relationships between concepts and phenomena thought to be important in the study. These concepts and relationships reflect the research questions

Cross Reference: See Book 2, chapters 4–6 and Book 3, chapter 1 for a discussion of how to construct models

certain types of "mixed-methods" approaches involving the simultaneous collection of survey and qualitative data on the same domains, factors, and variables. Ethnographers, by contrast, create their qualitative coding systems recursively in the course of preliminary fieldwork; they are successively modified until no new changes emerge. Only when they arrive at the point of creating a survey based on their qualitative data do they precode all of the variables by assigning values to them.

BEGINNING WITH FORMATIVE THEORIES

Most ethnography begins with research questions and an explicit, or at least an implicit, formative or guiding **model**. The term "model" refers to a diagram that shows the initial supposed relationships between important domains in the study that reflect the study questions. Most qualitative and ethnographic research involves creating an initial formative theoretical framework or model that ethnographers use to structure initial inquiry in the field and whose "goodness of fit" as an explanatory framework then is assessed against what actually exists in the study site. The examples previously provided in chapter 4 and in Book 2, chapters 4–7, illustrate how such initial models guided first forays into the field and subsequently were revised.

To begin analysis, rather large categories or conceptual "bins" deriving from the formative model or theoretical framework are created, into which to chunk various elements of the database. The process of clarifying and identifying components within each of these bins leads to a revised and more specific set of items and units and a rough outline of their relationships to one another. This is the process described in chapter 4 and followed by Vadeboncoeur and Miller in their initial pass through the data. These researchers began by following a formative model based on prior research and created in advance of the study. They first "chunked" data (including nontextual data) into large conceptual categories congruent with the theoretical framework informing the study. The larger chunks were then examined in ways that followed logical and semantic rules and were congruent with the theoretical framework informing the study. After aggregating and disaggregating bits of data, Miller and Vadeboncoeur found they had to modify their original set of categories. Eventually, they were able to formalize a more or less stable system of categories that they could use on the entire database without having to add or delete codes. It is this process that often is used to quantify qualitative data so that it supports the results and conclusions reached at the end of a study.

Similarly, in Schensul, Schensul, and Oodit's study of relationships in Mauritius (see Example 5.2), a preliminary or formative model included peer, family, and work "domains" as contributors to the development of intimate relationships and sexual risk. This model was based on initial discussions with a few critically placed, well-informed Mauritian researchers and service providers. However, the study team was not sure whether other domains might be missing or exactly what would/could be included under each of these domains. In the process of ethnographic research using local expert interviews, cultural consensus analysis, and in-depth interviews, this framework was modified and extensively expanded to the point where the analysis of the qualitative data was saturated (that is, no more new codes at the domain, factor, variable, or item levels emerged), and a survey based on the qualitative data could be developed.

THE RECURSIVE PROCESS AGAIN

We already have suggested that data analysis in ethnography uses deductive, recursive, and inductive processes. *Discussing only induction and deduction, as many research methodologists do, is an oversimplification because, in fact, ethnographers actually use both induction and deduction throughout their analysis, and they move back and forth between the two in a third strategy, which we have called* **recursivity.** Another way of explaining recursivity is that researchers explore their data both from "top down" (deductively, using predefined coding categories for analysis) and from "bottom up" (inductively, developing newly identified codes/analytic categories). This spiraling or *recursive* process allows researchers to respond to variation and contradiction in the field, altering their models

Key point

and explanatory theories so that they remain congruent with reality as it occurs at the study site.

Recursive analysis can be as simple as dividing data into piles according to their congruity with the principal concepts informing a program the ethnographer is studying—as in Vadeboncoeur's research, described in Example 5.1.

EXAMPLE 5.1

CODING AT A GENERAL LEVEL: USING A CONCEPTUAL MODEL TO ORGANIZE DATA ABOUT A TEACHER TRAINING PROGRAM

Vadeboncoeur (1998) studied the attempts by a U.S. university to restructure its teacher training program. In the early stages of her fieldwork, Vadeboncoeur came to understand that one of the principal themes of the three-semester program had to do with helping teachers-in-training to become critical thinkers who understood themselves, their own biases and background, and the impact of the social and political environment on their potential students and the schools in which they would teach. She visualized the program as emphasizing three interconnected circles (Figure 5.1), which she called "understanding the self," "understanding other people," and "understanding the environment."

These circles—which we call "bins"—constituted her conceptual framework. Taken together they provided a formative model for the study. Her database included field notes taken during observations of students in their classes and while they were student teaching, transcripts of interviews conducted with the students and their instructors, a survey she administered to students when they began the program, transcribed audiotapes of students' group work, and the journals that students kept throughout the program. To begin the organization of her data, she used her computer to mark the codes "S" (self), "OP" (other people), and "E" (environment) wherever she found references to *self*-reflection, comments on the impact of *other people*, and discussion of the influence of the *environment* in all of the interview transcripts, journals, and field notes of observations. This rough coding gave her a way to examine her data more closely and to separate material that was relevant to the overall themes of her dissertation from other material which—at least at first glance—she did not consider relevant. Once having completed this initial sorting, she went on to organize her data within each large category or domain in a more finely grained manner (Vadeboncoeur 1998).

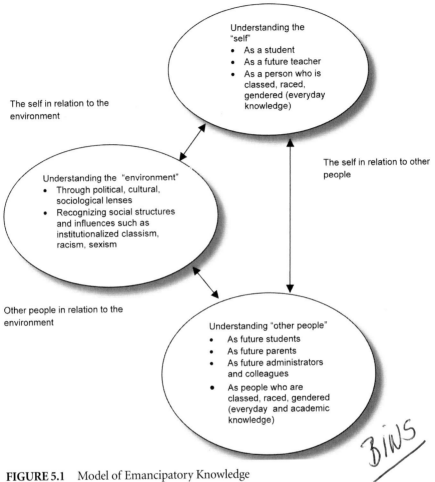

FIGURE 5.1 Model of Emancipatory Knowledge

General coding also can be as complex as starting with a set of categories based on an initial model and then developing a larger number of codes, as was the case in Schensul, Schensul, and Oodit's study of sexual risk in Mauritius (see Example 5.2).

EXAMPLE 5.2

CODING AT A GENERAL LEVEL: USING SEMISTRUCTURED INTERVIEWS WITH YOUNG UNMARRIED WOMEN FACTORY WORKERS FROM MAURITIUS

Researchers Schensul, Schensul, and Oodit guided a team of researchers and health educators to conduct exploratory and semistructured interviews with young women factory workers in Mauritius. Jean Schensul developed a coding system based on an initial or formative theoretical model guiding the study (Figure 5.2, Table 5.1). The model included three independent domains—family, peers, and work—and two dependent domains—sexual risk behavior and sexual knowledge, beliefs, and attitudes. These so-called bins were very broad and encompassing. Based on in-depth interviews with key informants, at first each domain was subdivided into between five and ten factors. A semistructured interview schedule was constructed in which one or more open-ended questions were asked for each factor. The initial coding scheme had two levels: domain and factor. When the interviews were reviewed for coding, items or concepts at the factor and subfactor

Cross Reference: See Book 3, chapter 8 on semistructured interviewing and observation

levels were developed and added to the coding scheme. The formative ethnographic theory and the fully evolved coding taxonomy are as follows in Figure 5.2 and Table 5.1.

The coding system in Table 5.1 is the final coding system that was used to code and manage all text data in the Mauritius Young Women, Work, and AIDS study. The coding system includes items at the domain, factor, and subfactor level. The

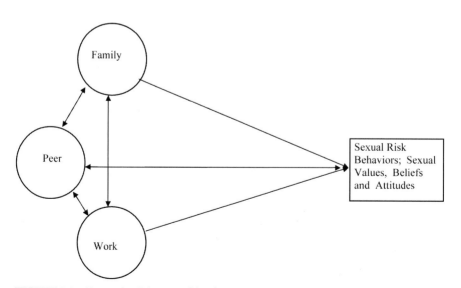

FIGURE 5.2   Formative Ethnographic Theory: Young Women, Work, and AIDS Risk

TABLE 5.1 Coding Tree Diagram: Young Women, Work, and AIDS Study, Mauritius

Factor	Subfactor	Variable (examples)
FAMILY (INDEPENDENT DOMAIN)		
FSTRUCTURE	**Family Structure**	
	MAROLE	**Mother's role**
	FMCHCARE	**Mother's caring for children 16 and under**
	FWKHIST	**Father's work history**
	FAROLE	**Father's role**
	FSIZE	**Family size**
	FSIBS	**Number of children**
	FBIRTHOR	**Birth order of young woman**
FMHEALTH	**Health of family members**	
	FHLTHMO	Mother's health status
	FHLTHFA	Father's health status
	FOTHER	**Health of other family members**
FWORK	**Family members' work**	
	FSIBSWK	**Siblings' work**
	FVIEWWK	**Family views of work**
FMAT	**Family's attitudes toward peers and social life**	
	FMATPR	**Families' attitudes toward respondents' peers**
FMSOC	**Family socialization practices with respondent**	
	FAMTALK	Family members discuss issues with respondent
	FMACTIV	Family activities with young woman
FMPROB	**Family problems**	
FWHYWORK	**Reasons for going to work**	
	FSELFINC	**Work for personal income**
	FFAMINC	**Work for household income**

(continued)

TABLE 5.1 *(continued)*

Factor	Subfactor	Variable (examples)
WORK (INDEPENDENT DOMAIN)		
WKENVIR	**Work Environment**	
	WKRESP	**Work status of respondent**
	WKPROBS	Problems at work
	WKSOC	Social practices at work
WKTYPE	**Type of work of respondent**	
	WKADMIN	**Supervision/administraton**
	WKLINEMC	Line mechanical work
	WKELECT	Work on computerized machines
WKSALARY	**Salary**	
WKCHARR	**Characteristics of respondent related to work**	
	WKSAT	**Satisfaction with work**
	WKED	**Education of respondent**
	WKAGE	**Age at entry into work**
WKSAT	**Work satisfaction**	
WKREL	**Relationships with co-workers**	
	WKTRUST	**Trust of co-workers**
	WKMEN	**Meeting/knowing men at work**
PEERS (INDEPENDENT DOMAIN)		
PEERS	**Peer environment and activities**	
PSIZE	**Size of peer network**	
	PSIZEM	**Size of male peer network**
	PSIZEF	**Size of female peer network**
PACTIVS	**Activities with friends**	
PROMANCE	**Boy- or girlfriend or fiancé**	
	PRBEHAV	Restrictions/violence in a romantic relationship
	PRCOMMUN	**Communication in romantic relationship**

CONDOMS (DEPENDENT DOMAIN)		
CONHEAR	Hear of condoms	
CONKNOW	Knowledge of condoms	
CONATT	Attitudes toward condoms	
CONUSE	Use condoms	
SEX BEHAVIORS (DEPENDENT DOMAIN)		
SEXACTS	Specific sex behaviors	
SEXVAL	Values about sexual behavior	
SEXVALPRE	Values about premarital sex	
AIDS (DEPENDENT DOMAIN)		
AIDSHEAR	Hear of AIDS	
AIDSATT	Attitudes toward AIDS	
AIDSKNOW	Knowledge about AIDS	
RISKS		
RVIRGIN	Virginity	
	RVCONCRN	Concern about loss of virginity
	RVKNOW	Knowledge of virginity
	RVRISK	Perception of exposure to risk
RPREG	Pregnancy	
	RPCONCRN	Concern about getting pregnant
	RPKNOW	Knowledge of pregnancy
	RPANAT	Knowledge of reproductive anatomy
	RPNOPREG	Knowledge of avoidance of pregnancy
	RPRISK	Perception of exposure to risk
RAIDSTDS	AIDS/STDS	
	RACONCRN	Concern about STDs (including AIDS)
	RAKNOW	Knowledge of STDs
	RASTDSPRV	Knowledge of STD prevention
	RARISK	Perception of exposure to risk

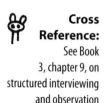

Cross Reference: See Book 3, chapter 9, on structured interviewing and observation

boldfaced items emerged from *key informant interviews* and were added to the formative theoretical model portrayed in Table 5.1. This revised and enhanced model then guided the development and administration of a semistructured interview schedule. Unboldfaced factors and subfactors and variables in Table 5.1 were added to the conceptual model as a *result of semistructured interviews*. Together, they guided the development of a structured survey instrument described in Book 3, chapter 9, on survey research.

HOW RESULTS EMERGE FROM DATA

Many key variables are not known in the early stages of a study. Neither are the items that are indicators of the variables clearly spelled out. Knowledge of these is required for development of survey questions; they must be derived from descriptions of observations and photographs, field notes and commentaries, quotations, transcripts, books and articles, elicitation data, documents, and excerpts from interviews. As the noted analysts Matthew Miles and A. H. Huberman (1984, 54) have said, words are fatter than numbers; they have multiple and sometimes ambiguous meanings, and they have little meaning without context, whether that context is as simple as the words immediately preceding and following a word or phrase of interest or as complex as the complete event in which it was uttered. The problem faced by ethnographers is that they must somehow organize and classify segments of texts (or collections of words) in a systematic way and, in some instances, translate them into numbers for quantitative analysis.

Here, we are concerned with the way that results "emerge" from qualitative data. While many ethnographic accounts seem to suggest that emergence is a rather mystical process, such a view diminishes the complex cognitive activities required to facilitate that process. Emergence occurs because the researcher is engaged in a systematic cognitive process that clumps individual items at the concrete level together into more abstract statements about the general characteristics of those items *as a group* and in relation to an emerging implicit or explicit conceptual "model" and/or explanatory framework. Researchers must identify locally relevant explanations of phenomena and then look for connections between the local explanations and factors that are more generally relevant to settings beyond the specific study site to build such a framework. This is a process of continual comparison that involves clustering concepts, behaviors, or other dimensions of the data that are alike, and differentiating them from others that are different on some dimension, and then organizing them into increasingly abstract ideas. In this chapter, we discuss what we would call the most qualitative of approaches and then move successively in chapters 6, 8, 9, and 10 to more and more specific treatments of data. The processes follow the figures presented in chapter 4, in which the horizontal dimension displays phenomena from the most concrete to the most abstract levels and the vertical dimension presents explanations for those phenomena from the most locally meaningful to the most globally applicable.

EMERGENCE AND COGNITIVE PROCESSING: HOW DOES IT BEGIN?

We believe that the process of emergence begins systematically, if intuitively, with a loose kind of counting process. As researchers go over field notes, they observe that certain phrases, events, activities, behaviors, ideas, or other phenomena occur repeatedly in the data. However, these observations do not occur just by chance; of key importance is which things ethnographers *notice* in the data and why they do so. Basically, ethnographers are sensitized to *noticing* specific ideas within the data both because of the conceptual frameworks or models within which they work, and because of their guiding research questions. What they are engaged in when they are noticing things are specific cognitive processes.

COGNITIVE PROCESSES INVOLVED IN "EMERGENCE"

- Noticing or perceiving
- Describing
- Defining
- Listing
- Classifying
- Comparing
- Contrasting
- Aggregating
- Ordering
- Establishing linkages and relationships
- Speculating

These processes require researchers to notice, define, and describe, count, compare and contrast, and match up "things" in the data that go together. The processes are iterative and operate at different levels of abstraction. When addressing the "things" that emerge from the data, researchers array them from the very concrete to the more aggregated and abstracted; when addressing reasons for or explanations of the things observed, researchers array them from those given for the most local and individual events or phenomena to those generalized to phenomena even quite far from the specific site or linked to theories explaining human behavior more generally. This complex twofold process occurs simultaneously. Fortunately, there are a number of strategies for picking apart both the phenomenal and the theoretical aspects of a database. We begin with how to isolate and identify phenomena—the "things." We then discuss how to identify the explanations—the "reasons why."

AGGREGATING AND DISAGGREGATING PHENOMENA: FINDING THE PIECES AND EXPLAINING WHY AND HOW THEY GO TOGETHER

Working inductively, we have borrowed from James Spradley's approach to data by beginning to find pieces (things) within a database and classifying them empirically into "items," "patterns," and "constituents" or "structures." We call these "the pieces" and think of them as arrayed on a continuum from least to most concrete. We also could classify them into items, variables, factors, and domains, another way of combining the rationales for categorizing "things" from smaller or more concrete categories to larger and more abstract groupings and concepts. That we use multiple names for phenomena at the same level of abstraction derives from the fact that different analysts have used different terminologies for these levels. Table 5.4 at the end of this chapter equates this language across some of the better-known analysts.

THE PIECES

- *Items* or *facts* consist of discrete and concrete activities, objects, persons, or other lower-level classifications fit together under a single definition. That is, items and units are alike on the basis of some criteria that cause them to be clustered or classified into a single category.
- *Units* or *variables* consist of clusters of items. The multiple ways these items differ, despite sharing common criteria within a cluster, constitute *variation* in the variable.
- *Patterns* or *factors* consist of groupings or collections of these categories.
- *Structures* or *domains* consist of larger groups of patterns that are linked together in ways that form the foundation for an overall cultural portrayal or theory that explains a cultural phenomenon.

Another way of describing the pieces is the following:

- *Variables* are the range of possibilities within a category of units or items.
- *Subfactors* are groupings of variables that make sense to the researcher as they emerge from the local situation.
- *Factors* are groupings of subfactors or variables that can be created by using middle-range or substantive

theories to explain larger aggregates of concrete data such as patterns and structures.

- *Domains* are groupings of factors (larger cultural units or phenomena) that can be explained by referring to how people, including the researchers, "make sense" of and organize their world.

Researchers can choose to use either of these rubrics for building the patterns and structures that are the basis for interpretation. In addition, as the pieces begin to emerge in larger and more abstract groupings, so too do the *reasons* why these pieces achieve a specific organization. We call these "the explanations" and array them from the most emic and local rationales given for phenomena to more etic reasons, those that are couched in social theories or applicable to human groups more generally. The reader will notice that the box above reflects the organization of the tables presented in chapter 4. Both actual pieces and patterns and the reasons and explanations for their appearance actually "emerge" somewhat simultaneously in the process of analysis. Below, we discuss them, beginning with the lowest level of abstraction.

DEFINING THE ITEM AND VARIABLE LEVEL OF ANALYSIS

Items are the components of *units* and *variables*. The lowest level of analysis involves identifying and marking items, units, and variables in data sources. Item- and variable-level analysis is utilized at any and all points in the analytical process. Item-level analysis can even be reintroduced after the study is over if researchers are revisiting the ethnographic database with new questions and domains of interest. A number of theorists have systematized procedures for facilitating this level of analysis. We discuss a number of these approaches, including those of Spradley (1979), Glaser and Strauss (1967), Znaniecki (1930), Lofland (1971), Lofland and Lofland (1984), and Mishler (1986).

Finding Things: Playing with Pieces

Item- and variable-level analysis begins as researchers laboriously look over, read repeatedly, tidy up (Romagnano 1991), and organize their data and then relate it to their formative models. The earliest formulations of items and variables may appear in formal formative models or research questions, but it is more likely that early formative models will include initial domains and possibly factors, leaving variables, units, and items to emerge from the actual data. As researchers pore over their data, they inevitably begin to notice events, behaviors, statements, or activities that stand out, either because they occur often or co-occur, because they are crucial to other items, because they are rare and influential, because they are totally absent despite the researcher's expectations, and because they are related to the study's formative model and/or research questions. The identification of items helps researchers make sense of what otherwise would be an undifferentiated morass of information. Isolating these specific items or elements and determining how they are related to each other and the research questions is the first step in the analytic process. In the latter part of this chapter, we provide a number of strategies to facilitate this process.

Finding Explanations: Playing with Ideas

Locating things that are significant within a database requires knowing why and for whom these things are worth noticing. The same process used to find the bits and pieces of culture in a site also facilitates the simultaneous generation of substantive theories of behavior and belief. What we have called general processes of chunking data and playing with ideas also make it possible to locate explanations for why data are patterned as they are at different levels of abstraction. These explanations range from those closest to the informant's own local understandings to those that apply more generally to groups of informants within a site, and finally to theoretical explanations that apply to phenomena beyond the immediate study. Developing explanations also involves a series of steps to create, re-create, and refine conceptual models. As researchers initiate research, they:

- notice the phenomena around them;
- differentiate these phenomena from each other by comparing and contrasting them with each other,

past experiences, sets of values, or their own or others' conceptual frameworks or theories;

- select those explanations that they feel are most important for further examination;
- organize them into explanatory hierarchies of abstraction—domains, factors, subfactors, variables;
- identify which variables, factors, and, eventually, domains are associated with one another;
- develop explanations for these associations;
- organize them into verifiable patterns and structures by describing, interpreting, and explaining the relationships among them

 Definition: Theorizing is the "cognitive process of discovering abstract categories and the relationships among them; it is used to develop or confirm explanations for how and why things happen as they do" (LeCompte and Preissle 1993, 239)

Cross Reference: See Book 2, chapters 1–5

This is achieved by a process of **theorizing**, or for thinking about how items, patterns, and structures, as well as variables, factors, and domains are related and the reasons for their occurrence. (ibid.). Theorizing is a way of playing with ideas; another way of describing it is as the "cognitive process of discovering abstract categories and the relationships among them" (ibid.). Theorizing, then, is used to develop or confirm explanations for how and why things happen as they do. In Book 2, Schensul, Schensul, and LeCompte describe how theorizing is used for *building formative theory* to guide the initial stages of research. We believe that theorizing—at any stage—resembles the kind of thinking that people do in everyday life—except that theorizing is done in a more systematic manner. Both everyday thinking and theorizing involve playing with ideas, but theorizing in research also involves the laborious and time-consuming tasks of pulling apart field note narratives, interviews, and documents; identifying relevant information from them; matching that information with relevant information from other sources of data such as maps, surveys, and questionnaires; and then trying to figure out why they fit together as they do. Theorizing expands and further develops the explanatory dimension of a study by refining formative theoretical models; it is the process by which new items, patterns, and structures are identified and their corresponding explanatory variables, factors, and domains can be explored. Item-level analysis, then, is a foundation for all subsequent analysis of both phenomena and the reasons for their existence but, as we said earlier, as well as in Books 1 and 2, theorizing is a fundamental process in ethnography and can take place at any level, and throughout the course of a study.

SOME ANALYTIC STRATEGIES

Using Spradley's "Domain Analysis"

One of the most useful strategies for playing with ideas was developed by James Spradley. His approach was particularly useful for identifying and differentiating classes of items in a culture. He began by using what are called descriptive questions that induce people to describe the components of the world they live in. Weller and Romney (1988) refer to this and other elicitation tools, including listings, taxonomies, sentence completions, and triad sorts, as "systematic data collection." The components identified through such systematic data collection consist of "things"—components of larger units of cultural knowledge, which Spradley called "domains." These things are identified during interviews or elicitation strategies used with research participants. When they list the "things" or items in their world, researchers can then group those things into taxonomies. The taxonomies are created within domains (or large units of cultural knowledge). The listings themselves do not create the domain; they are the result of asking questions (the process of eliciting) to identify the elements or things in a domain; the taxonomies researchers create from them in turn identify the different levels of abstraction within a domain.

Cross Reference: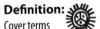
See also Book 4, chapter 3, "Elicitation Techniques for Cultural Domain Analysis"

Spradley focused on the concrete, defining domains as classes of objects, things, ideas, or events in the real world, or at least in the world as people understand it and perceive it to be. Each domain in a study is given a distinct name, or "cover term." **Cover terms** simply are the most inclusive or general terms that can be applied to the array of things included in a given domain. Cover terms or domains are like overviews that can be deconstructed to their constituent components or elements. Any given domain consists of **included terms**, or the names for those things subsumed

Definition:
Cover terms are the most inclusive or general terms that can be applied to the array of things included in a given domain

TABLE 5.2   Cover Terms and Included Items for Domains

Cover Term	"Trees"	"Musicians"	"Ways to annoy professors"
Included Items	Oaks, palms, banyans, elms, bamboos, larches, redwoods, pines, etc.	Pianist, guitarist, harpist, violinist, singer, sousaphonist	Turn papers in late, chat in class, forget your book, arrive late to class, plagiarize

 Definition: Included terms are the names for things subsumed within a domain

 Cross Reference: See Book 1, chapters 2 and 3, and Book 2, chapters 4, 5, and 6 for a discussion of theorizing, building formative theory, and operationalizing

by the domain. Elements in a domain are arranged in taxonomies, or hierarchies of terms. Table 5.2 includes the domains or cover terms "trees," "musicians," and "ways to annoy a professor"; it also includes some of the associated included terms (which could be factors, variables, or items) for each cover term. This same kind of figure can be used for guiding the early stages of the research; unpacking the cover terms or domains is what we have referred to as "vertical modeling" in chapters 2 and 3 of Book 1 of the *Toolkit* and in chapters 4–7 of Book 2.

Table 5.2 also can be said to display "domain taxonomies"—tree diagrams that illustrate the components of each cultural domain. Initially, the category "musician" could include the terms "singer," "professional," "amateur," "orchestra player," or "band member." While all of these terms could apply to people who are musicians, only the term "singer" is at the same level of abstraction as "musician" presented in Table 5.2 because all of the latter terms refer to the specific instrument that the musician plays—and a singer's instrument is his or her voice. Thus the researcher who obtains a listing for "musician" that includes "singer" may decide to redefine the term singer as another domain and unpack it in terms of its components—what people sing, how they sing, where they sing, the life of a singer, and so on. One of the most important things the domain analyst does, then, is to establish the *boundaries* of the domain by using rules that permit the ethnographer to make distinctions between what is and is not included in the domain.

 Definition: Semantic relationships are sentences describing how two or more objects or phenomena are related to each other

Spradley's rules for identifying boundaries involve looking for the way that the items are connected by **semantic relationships** that Spradley feels are culturally universal. Semantic relationships are stated in the form of sentences,

TABLE 5.3 Types of Semantic Relationships

Form	Relationship
x is a kind of y	Strict inclusion
x is a place in y; x is a part of y	Spatial
x is a result of y; x is a cause of y	Cause-effect
x is a reason for doing y	Rationale
x is a place for doing y	Location for action
x is used for y	Function
x is a way to do y	Means-end
x is a step or stage in y	Sequence
x is a characteristic of y	Attribution
x can be found in y	Location

Source: Adapted from Spradley 1979.

as indicated in Table 5.3. The relationships expressed are not all hierarchical, but all Xs are related to Y in some way.

Domains are categories or arrays of distinct things that ethnographers—or informants—treat as related to one another in some way and existing at more or less the same level of abstraction. Spradley's and Schensul, Schensul, and LeCompte's domains generally include subdomains. For example, *musical instruments* is a domain that includes violins; *violins* is a subdomain that includes modern and baroque violins; *modern violins* might be a domain that includes violins made after 1900 and violins made at any time since the 1600s that have been modernized. **Taxonomies** such as the ones in Table 5.2 visually represent the hierarchical ordering of items as well as the linkages and relationships among various items in a domain. They not only help to classify information, but they are a critical first step in identifying structures in the cultural life of whatever group an ethnographer studies. Ethnographers can code their data by domain, by subdomain, by factor, or by variable, depending on the level in the domain taxonomy at which the data should be placed and how detailed the coding system is. They also can code by item, pattern, and structure.

Names and Symbols: Connotative and Denotative Meaning. All domain names, cover terms, and included terms are symbols; they have no real meaning other than that

Cross Reference: See chapter 3 in Book 4 for a discussion of hierarchical relationships in domains

Definition: Taxonomies help to classify information by visually representing both hierarchical orders of items and patterns and the linkages and relationships among items, factors, and patterns in a domain

which people give to them. Within each domain are other verbal symbols that refer to subsets of the larger domain. Symbols can have a wide variety of connotative meanings independent of their denotative or referential meaning. For example, the word symbol "mouse" refers to or denotes a small rodent. However, the same word symbol can also refer to part of the auxiliary equipment necessary for operating a personal computer or the discolored tissue around the eye that results when a person runs into a door or is punched in the face. Thus a "mouse" can be a rodent or a small plastic piece of electronic equipment or a black eye. Its connotative meaning, however, can be quite different; to many people, the word symbol "mouse" also *connotes* filth or a threat. A single verbal symbol thus can be included in multiple taxonomies or "sets" depending on its meaning. A good researcher will explore the conceptual hierarchies that include all of the meanings associated with a verbal symbol. A large rodent *is* a rat, but "rat" also refers in English to someone who double-crosses or deceives others. "To rat" also is a verb meaning the procedure used by hairdressers to tangle women's hair into a mass that creates the illusion of much more hair than women actually have. For many young teenagers, "college" connotes more than its denotative meaning of "an institution of higher learning." College, or going to college, also can symbolically represent independence, since going to college also can refer to leaving one's parents' home and becoming an adult. It also can connote a split from family, which may or may not be desirable, or an insurmountable obstacle that one can never overcome. Ethnographers need to engage in sufficient fieldwork to ensure that they understand all the various connotative and denotative meanings possessed by the symbols their research participants use, prior to organizing them into domains.

The ethnographer must elicit the relevant symbols in the world of his or her informants and then, during the analysis phase of the research project, organize them taxonomically. Determining the relationships and equivalent levels of abstraction may not always be easy or straightforward; symbols may have the same referent but different connotative meanings. For example, the word symbols "juvenile," "young person," and "adolescent" can have the same denotative meaning, but for many people the terms "juvenile" and "adolescent" can have negative connotations. "Juvenile" can be associated with delinquent behavior, and "adolescent" with naive or foolhardy actions. Similarly, while the cover term "plants" could apply to such things as seaweed, oaks, forests, palm trees, cacti, crabgrass, roses, grains, living organisms, tea, and rice, it is clear that the above list of "plants" consists of many varied things at several levels of abstraction, none of which are very much like each other except at the most general level. As we said earlier, in order to sort out and make decisions about these classifications based on connotation or meaning, one has to know a great deal about a cultural setting and to read the collected text data closely.

Using Glaser and Strauss's Constant Comparison and Analytic Induction

One of the most well-known strategies for identifying items was initially spelled out by Barney Glaser and Anselm Strauss in a study of death and dying in a hospital. Glaser and Strauss wanted to know at what point a person was, in the minds of those who had known him or her, truly deceased, and whether these different definitions had any impact on the behavior of the deceased person's health-care workers and family. They called their strategy *constant comparison*; they used it to look for similarities and differences in behaviors, settings, actors, and other dimensions of cultural life and then made inferences about the meaning and origins of these differences (1967). Using a formative model, the researchers began by studying changes in the way doctors, nurses, and other health-care personnel talked about patients who were terminally ill as those patients moved through stages from being very ill, to death, and finally to removal from the hospital for burial. They noticed, for example, that patients who had died within the past few hours were still described in the present tense, as if they were still living. The researchers kept careful records of the names or identifiers that different kinds of health-care workers applied to patients at varying stages of their illness,

reasoning that aides and nurses would have different jobs—
and therefore different relationships to patients—which
might affect how they defined—and therefore described—
the dying person. They constantly compared the language
used by one set of workers with that of the others and the
language used to describe patients in one stage of illness
with that used to describe patients in other stages. In the
process of comparison, they looked for similarities and differences in behaviors, settings, actors, and other dimensions
of cultural life and made inferences about why these differences existed and what factors could predict them. The
thinking process in constant comparison is very similar to
that required in quantitative data analysis when researchers explore differences in, for example, educational performance or compliance with medical treatment by gender,
ethnicity, age, socioeconomic status, or other factors.

The process of constant comparison permitted Glaser
and Strauss to elaborate on their initial model by developing a set of consistent identifiers that both marked
the stages of life from serious illness to death and also
denoted the "social worth" of individuals in each stage.
Social worth was a new and mediating variable introduced
to the model and was measured by the quality and kind of
treatment and the level of respect implied in the names
applied to those various stages of life. Glaser and Strauss
also recorded the way that these identifiers denoted a form
of progressive distancing used by medical personnel to
protect them from too much intimacy with patients who
they knew would soon die.

The organization of Glaser and Strauss's analysis is
similar to, and not incompatible with, Spradley's domain
analysis. Glaser and Strauss recorded the stream of behavior or language and then separated it into discrete concepts
using constant comparison. The items were then "chunked"
into categories. Subsequent steps link the categories into
concepts or theoretical constructs, which, in turn, permit
selection or development of theories that the researcher
can use to explain what was observed in the field. Table 5.4
displays a comparison of the stages in the principal forms
of analysis reviewed in this book, showing their similarities
and differences.

TABLE 5.4 Comparison of Inductive Analytic Strategies

LeCompte	Schensul and Schensul	Mishler	Spradley	Glaser and Strauss	Lofland
1. Item-level analysis Identifies items or units; creates taxonomies (classifies and orders items or units)	**1. Variable definition** Identifies items and hierarchically organizes them into variables	**1. Constructs a chronological narrative** Identifies all narrative clauses or units that can not be moved elsewhere without changing their meaning **2. Categorizes the narrative clauses as** a. Abstract or summary b. Orientations to place, time, person c. Complicating actions or what happened d. Results or resolutions e. Coda or returns to present f. Evaluation or how the speaker felt	**1. Descriptive analysis** Identifies items and units from behavioral or data stream and names them **2. Groups items into categories and taxonomies**	**1. Separates discrete items from behavior stream** **2. Chunks units or items into categories**	**1. Identifies acts** **2. Identifies activities and settings in which specific activities are located**

(continued)

TABLE 5.4 (*continued*)

LeCompte	Schensul and Schensul	Mishler	Spradley	Glaser and Strauss	Lofland and Lofland
2. Pattern level of analysis Establishes linkages among taxonomies or classifications	**2a. Factor definition** Organizes groups of variables or taxonomies into domains **2b. Subfactor definition** Organizes groups of variables into larger taxonomic units that can then be grouped into domains	**3. Identifies the moves** (interactions that alter or threaten to alter the position or interactants) **4a. Analyzes the text** (the content domain, telling what the function of each category is) **4b. Finds the coherence relations** (the ideational domain or meaning of the story), whether local coherence, global coherence, or thematic coherence	**3. Develops and identifies linkages among categories and taxonomies**	**3. Aggregates categories into structures or factors**	**3. Identifies patterns of participation**

Structural or constitutive level of analysis	Definition of domains and relationships among domains	Develops themes	Develops theoretical constructs	Links empirical categories, structures, or factors with theoretical constructs	Links patterns together to identify relationships and structures
3. Structural or constitutive level of analysis Organizes relationships among patterns into structures or constituents	**3. Definition of domains and relationships among domains** Organizes factors and subfactors into larger sociocultural or ecological units	**5. Develops themes** (recurrent assumptions, beliefs, goals, values, worldview cognitive maps)	**4. Develops theoretical constructs**	**4. Links empirical categories, structures, or factors with theoretical constructs**	**4. Links patterns together to identify relationships and structures**
4. Interpretation **Assigns meaning** to structures in relation to existing or new theoretical frameworks and paradigms	**4. Interpretation** **Describes the meaning** of relationships among domains, given related factors (blocks of variables), and between individual variables in relation to existing or new theoretical frameworks and paradigms	**6. Interpretation** **Interprets meaning** of themes	**5. Interpretation** **Identifies meaning** of theoretical constructs	**5. Interpretation** **Develops or selects theories** to assist in explanation of theoretical constructs	**5. Interpretation** **Elicits meanings** used by participants and assigns them to relationships and structures

Using Analytic Induction

One specialized form of comparison used in all forms of analysis is analytic induction. It was developed in the work of Florian Znaniecki, a Polish sociologist who based his book about the experiences of Polish immigrants to the United States on an analysis of letters that immigrants wrote to family members remaining in Poland (1930). The principal feature of **analytic induction** is its focus on searching for "negative" or disconfirming cases or what sociologists call "counterfactuals." Researchers find it easier to look for items that are similar to what they have just identified as being of interest in a study; similarity, after all, tends to confirm a researcher's insights. However, Znaniecki cautioned that good science requires a principled skepticism regarding the goodness of research results. Researchers must not ignore negative or disproving cases—those that are dissimilar to the majority of cases or items found so far in a study. In some ways, negative cases serve to protect researchers from excessive enthusiasm about the credibility of their initial findings. They also help researchers to refine the definitions of their items, pay attention to variance within a population, and record nuances and dimensions of meaning and perception that would be ignored were a systematic search for such differences not done.

Systematic analytic induction not only helps the researcher identify omissions of items, ideas, events, behaviors, explanations, and the like that investigators thought might or should be present, but also sensitizes them to those absences that researchers do not anticipate. For example, in the early stages of the AIDS epidemic in the United States, the absence of cases of women infected with HIV/AIDS led researchers to define the disease as one affecting homosexual men only. As a consequence, when some women did begin to exhibit AIDS symptoms, their illness was misdiagnosed. In other countries, however, HIV/AIDS was known to afflict both men and women. Had researchers looked beyond the U.S. data, or had they looked closely at the improbability that an infectious disease would afflict only one sex, they might have earlier and more clearly identified the nature of the disease and women as a population vulnerable to infection.

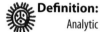 **Definition:** Analytic induction refers to the identification of negative or disconfirming cases or counterfactual evidence

 Cross Reference: See Book 3, chapter 11 for a discussion of spurious conclusions and their threat to validity

Using Lofland's Structure of Activities

John Lofland's (1971) and Lyn and John Lofland's (1984) analysis focuses more narrowly on the structure of human interaction and moves from a rather microscopic examination of the constituents and details of human interaction to a more macroscopic perspective on how those constituents are aggregated into the behavior and beliefs of larger groups. Rather than beginning with a process of item identification, as is the case with both Spradley and Glaser and Strauss, Lofland's and Lofland's strategy begins with a hierarchically organized set of categories which could be called domains, as they do constitute organized bodies of cultural knowledge. These are:

- Acts and actors
- Activities
- Settings
- Ways of participating
- Relationships
- Meanings

This is roughly parallel to the categories that Pelto and Pelto (1978) advocated for observing, documenting, and categorizing field situations. Although researchers could begin with any of the first four categories (acts, actors, activities, and settings), the Loflands' approach involves first identifying all the individual actors in a particular setting as well as the acts in which they are engaged. The researcher might do this for several settings encompassed by the research site; in the Learning to Work study, for example, LeCompte observed students and teachers (actors) in classrooms, on the playground, in the library, and at lunch in the cafeteria (settings). She then worked to identify the different acts and activities in which the actors engaged in each of these settings. The Loflands define "acts" as small-scale interactions, engaged in by individuals and conducing to one specific goal. Individual acts can be combined into activities. For example, you, the reader of this book, are currently engaged in the act of reading. When you stop reading, you will do so to engage in other acts, such as hearing the telephone ring, rising from your chair, walking across the room to the telephone, picking up the phone receiver, and uttering a greeting. Taken together, the last four acts constitute part of an "activity" called "answering the telephone," in which you (an actor) are engaged with a friend, family member, colleague, or some other actor.

Actors participate in settings in different ways; some actors may prefer to read a book with a television or radio turned on for background noise; others need silence. Some may prefer to slouch in a comfortable chair; others need an upright chair and writing desk for taking notes. The participative style may also depend on the relationship that the actor has with the particular book and the reasons why it is being read. A book read for schoolwork will be more likely to require the chair and desk. This is because the relationship the actor has with the book is different from the relationship the actor has with a friend who recommended it or the teacher who required it, and the set of meanings attached to that relationship dictate different ways of interacting and participating. Lofland suggests that an outline of the structure of activity be developed first, followed by a systematic search for the meanings that people attach to their activities, relationships, and ways of participating. Listings, events and activity sequences, and other strategies outlined in books 3 and 4 are helpful in eliciting such meanings.

Using Mishler's Linguistic Analysis to Identify Items in Stories

Elliot Mishler (1986), a sociolinguist, focuses on the analysis of texts, in particular, texts created from interviews or stories told by informants. Mishler recognizes that the stories people tell during an interview often do not "make sense" without some kind of rewriting by the researcher. They may lack any kind of chronological or logical order; they may jump around, addressing various topics in a nearly random manner; and they may stretch over several different interviews conducted at different times. It is the researcher's job to reorganize the information so that it can serve as evidence in support of whatever propositions the researcher is exploring in an investigation. Mishler suggests first restructuring the interview into a narrative form, one that resembles the "story" form of Western literature. This means orienting the reader to the time and place of the story, identifying the persons involved (or characters) in the story, describing what happened (the drama or plot), identifying the resolution of the plot (or how it all turned out), and finally, giving an evaluation or indication of how the storyteller felt about the events covered in the story itself.

Once these procedures are followed, Mishler argues that the researcher can identify the critical elements in the story, telling which ones predicted change in the events or behavior of individual characters; categorize the content of the story and indicate the function each category performs; and discuss the meanings in the story and then connect those meanings to more global assumptions or worldviews held by individuals or within the culture under study.

SUMMARY

In chapter 5, we have discussed how researchers begin to create taxonomies and categories of items they have identified in their data and to refine, modify, and develop explanatory frameworks for those data. Table 5.4 arrays the analytic schemes of six strategies (LeCompte, Schensul and Schensul, Spradley, Glaser and Strauss, Lofland and Lofland, and Mishler) and roughly equates the stages of each with stages in all of the others. The first and second columns represent a synthesis of the scheme utilized by LeCompte and Schensul to organize this book.

It is important for researchers to realize that the schemes presented in Table 5.4 are compatible and can be used together in a study. They simply represent different ways of cutting up, dissecting, and rendering manageable the complex "stream of behavior" that ethnographers try to understand. We suggest that readers may want to refer to the original source books in which these strategies are described for more details about their use. We also point out that none of the researchers mentioned in this chapter began their work without a framework that guided their discovery of items, units, variables, factors, patterns, and structures. That framework stemmed from their research questions and the research literature, which guided the construction of a rudimentary or formative model that could be diagramed quite readily. The degree of induction varies, depending on how elaborated that conceptual model or blueprint is, but most studies proceed in stages in which the original model is continuously modified as new information is obtained. Finally, when there is no new information, all data have been classified, and relevant associations made, the conceptual model or jigsaw puzzle is complete and the data are ready to be published.

In the next chapter, we define what specific codes are and explain how to create and use them. We discuss how researchers develop and use schemes that are congruent with their own research questions. We also present an extended example that illustrates how a researcher not only developed a coding system for a large team project but used computer software to assist in the process of managing the data. Then, in chapter 7, we discuss code books (records of codes and their definitions) for qualitative and quantitative data and procedures for coding verification and team coding. In chapter 8, we discuss how computers can be used in analysis of qualitative data; in chapter 9, we present different approaches to quantification of qualitative data. In chapter 10, we discuss how coded data are assembled to create cultural patterns and structures. In the final chapters, we describe how data are displayed and interpreted.

6 ━━◆━●━◆━●━◆━━

SPECIFIC CODING AND INITIAL QUANTIFICATION

BEGINNING WITH GENERAL LEVELS AND MOVING TO MORE SPECIFIC LEVELS OF AGGREGATION AND DISAGGREGATION

The previous chapter outlined how to do a rough pass through a database. In it, we first discussed how general codes are identified and applied to various forms of data. General coding is sufficient to identify concepts, components, themes, and initial sets of meanings in the database; it also provides a sense of the range of behavior and belief in the study population. However, it is by no means the end of the analytic process. Qualitative and ethnographic research not only seek to identify the qualities of things and determine whether these qualities are present; they also need to determine which qualities are absent when they were expected to be present, which are present only in a specific degree, and which are present only in specific instances or under specific conditions. In order to answer these questions, some sort of quantification is required, at least sufficient to determine which is "more" or "less" of an entity or what the relative sizes or frequencies of items in each category are. Whether it yields actual frequency counts or is limited to more subjective depiction of relative weights or quantities, such a process helps to establish the variance within the cultural scene under study. This process is critical to outlining the complete cultural portrait, which is the ultimate goal of an ethnographer's work. In this chapter, we discuss "specific coding," which involves marking discrete

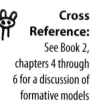

entities and meanings in the data and then assembling them into patterns. These patterns are then assembled into a more complete portrait of the cultural scene under investigation.

In the *Ethnographer's Toolkit*, we distinguish for explanatory purposes between the terms "*general coding*," which is based on major domains or bins in an initial formative model, and "*specific coding*," which involves more detailed coding based on major domains and subdomains, factors, and even variables that emerge during a pilot phase and are then incorporated into revisions of the initial formative model. Vadeboncoeur's initial organization of data is based on general coding, while Schensul and others' (1994, 1995), LeCompte and Holloway's (1997, 1998), and LeCompte's (1978) work begins with general and proceeds to specific coding.

Coding involves identifying and marking not only concrete things but also ideas and meanings. Consider these statements: "I started college *because I wanted to become a diplomat.*" "We don't move furniture or make any changes to daily routines for forty days after someone dies *because we do not want the soul of the dead person to become confused or get lost.* If they do, they might never be at peace, and *that could cause us trouble.*" "I started doing volunteer work in high school *because I thought it would make my resume look better when I started applying to colleges.*" "The statewide 'uniform' of people from the state of Oregon is a waterproof parka *because it rains nearly every day for nine months each year.*" The italicized parts present the logic or rationale explaining why something happened or why people behaved as they did. These could be coded as reasons for actions. In the next few pages, we present three examples of studies that began with general coding and then moved to more specific forms of categorizing and organizing the data.

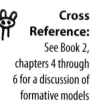

Cross Reference: See Book 2, chapters 4 through 6 for a discussion of formative models

EXAMPLE 6.1

GENERAL CODING DURING FIELDWORK, FOLLOWED BY SPECIFIC CODING WITH THE HELP OF ASSISTANTS

Angela Smith, a doctoral student at the University of Colorado, noticed that her fellow students seemed to make wide use of humor to defuse the stress of graduate school. For a course project, she explored the kinds and frequency of humor use among her colleagues. She began by asking her fellow students to write down all the kinds of humor that graduate students used, from writing satirical pieces and performing skits that lampooned faculty and staff to teasing, practical jokes and using irony and puns in their classes. She assembled a list of all the various uses of humor generated by these brainstorming sessions and created a grid on which she could make check marks each time that she observed a "humor event" occur. She herself concentrated on coding "humor events" in the hallways, coffee lounge, dean's office, meetings of the graduate student association, and her own classes throughout the semester. Because she could not be present in each class, she also gave her grid to a representative group of other students, who recorded data for her in their own classes.

➤➤➤

This example illustrates how preliminary data collection can lead to a coding scheme that can be tested and shared with other coders, who use the coding scheme as a guide in collecting data for study purposes.

Example 6.2 shows how Margaret LeCompte moved recursively—both inductively and deductively—to develop a coding system for the Learning to Work study that fit both her theoretical framework and the phenomena occurring in the classroom. Her initial general codes, Work, Time, Responsibility, and Achievement, formed the basis for the initial general coding; she then modified and elaborated on this system after her fieldwork was completed.

➤➤➤ **EXAMPLE 6.2**

CREATING CODES INDUCTIVELY IN A PILOT STUDY, THEN USING THEM RECURSIVELY: THE LEARNING TO WORK STUDY

LeCompte's dissertation research was influenced by the work of John Dewey and other reformers' belief that schools facilitated the formation of a democratic society and attitudes about freedom, individualism, and creativity. Dewey in particular had suggested that the social organization and management structure of elementary classrooms helped children acquire attitudes appropriate for their future roles as citizens and workers; if the school were democratic, children would learn to be participants in a democratic society. LeCompte planned to investigate to what extent schools really did emphasize democratic values. She included these general categories in her initial conceptual framework as well as concepts addressing children's understanding of the world of work (1974, 1978). Initially, she conducted a pilot study in the town where she lived, quite distant from her field site. She spent days observing two fourth-grade classrooms, writing down everything the teacher said and did. LeCompte read her "scripts" of teacher behavior over and over, trying to identify inductively the specific behavior patterns and deportment that the teachers most often tried to instill in their students. Though LeCompte had wanted to study how schools inculcate democracy, what she found was that teachers mostly focused on teaching children to conform to authority, be on time, stay in their seats, work hard, keep working, and be quiet. LeCompte also had expected to find that teachers stressed the intrinsic value of learning, creativity, and autonomous decision making at least some of the time. However, what LeCompte's pilot study showed was that elementary school teachers really emphasized a set of categories that she termed:

- Responsibility/Accountability ("R" codes)
- Timeliness ("T" codes)
- Achievement ("A" codes)
- Keeping Order and Staying on Task ("W" codes)

Still hoping to retain her original focus on democratic learning but also mindful of what the pilot study was telling her, LeCompte altered her conceptual framework to include not only the original ideas of autonomy and democratic participation but also a focus on good study habits as embodied in the list above. She also added some new coding categories, such as "Opportunities for Students to Choose Their Own Assignments" and "Valuing Learning for Its Own Sake," which she thought *should* be visible in teacher behavior and which were in her theoretical model, even if they weren't found in her pilot study.

LeCompte's final coding system consisted of the headings of an outline she created using the initials of the main coding categories or study domains for the domains (R, T, A, and W) as the initial letter of the code, and the number and letter corresponding to the specific behavior within the list in each category. Thus, "1" codes under "T" referred to nonverbal reminders of items on the schedule and signals invoking the schedule or preparing students for a change in activities. "2" codes in the "T" domain were "tellings" or verbal utterances by the teacher that referred to the schedule, deadlines, and appropriate activities to engage in at specific times. Since it evolved from an outline, this coding system was not really a full and ranked taxonomy because LeCompte did not know which of the activities or utterances would achieve prominence during the fieldwork. However, it did respond to the challenge raised by her advisory committee to create a system clear enough to convince them that she (and other researchers) would recognize an instance of a category if it appeared. The codes, therefore, had to be operationally defined and clear. Table 6.1 shows how some of the codes were operationalized behaviorally.

TABLE 6.1 Developing Operational Categories for the Learning to Work Study during a Pilot Study, Then Modifying It after Initial Fieldwork Was Completed

Code	Operational Examples
CATEGORY/DOMAIN: TIME	
T1A	Visual schedules displayed; notes or reminders for kids' appointments written on the board; reminders of special classes or assignment deadlines written on the board; putting up clock faces as reminders of when to do things
T1B	Cutting off an activity before it's done because of the schedule; talking about "things being messed up" because of the schedule; complaining about things that disrupt the smooth flow of schedule
TIC	Preparatory rituals signaling a new activity; rituals whose purpose is getting ready to do something else
T2A	Statements signaling the end of one activity and beginning of another ("Now put your books away and take out your spellers."); statements telling students when something will be done or what will happen next ("It's time for recess and after that we'll do a story.")
T2B	Statements that tell students to hurry up or rush and that aren't related to specific tasks
T2C	Nonjudgmental statements about being late ("We're late getting started today, so let's get out our math books.")
T2D	Telling a child that an activity is inappropriate for this specific time ("Put the clay away; this is study time," or "You can't talk now; this is quiet time.")
T2E	Statements reminding students of emphasized deadlines, when things are due or expected to be finished; queries about a task's status ("Are you done? If you are, you can go outside.")
T3A	Punishments or reprimands for being late, handing work in late, or coming in late
T3B	Withholding time for fun as a punishment; taking away recess if a child misbehaves or doesn't do a task; not letting them leave at the end of the day until they are quiet, even if the bell has rung
T3C	Speaking of time as a commodity ("Spend five minutes on this," "I'll give you ten minutes to relax," "Time goes quickly if you use it wisely.")
CATEGORY/DOMAIN: WORK/STAYING ON TASK	
W1B	Dispatching orders, short commands telling individual students or small groups what to do. No explanations accompany these orders. ("John, finish page 3.")
W2A	Get-moving, get-to-work comments designed to get a child working immediately or working harder or faster. They are aimed at accomplishment of a specific activity or task. ("Mary, have you nothing to do? Your math is waiting. Come on; you have four problems to do.")
W2B	Moral lectures distinguishing between work and play and on the necessity of work in school. Not used as a reprimand, though it may follow one.
W2C	Descriptive comments that indicate the teacher has observed a student working; meant to encourage others to do so, too. ("Boys and girls, George is doing his spelling.")
W3A	Reprimands: detention for not working; losing recess for not working
W3B	Isolation for not working
W3C	Reprimand to individual or group for not working or for playing

Once it had been approved by her dissertation committee, LeCompte put the coding system away and began her four-classroom study, scripting everything that the teacher said and did in handwritten field notes and trying to do so without any preconceptions as to what the teachers would or should say. She did so in accordance with positivistic requirements for "objectivity" imposed by her advisory committee; therefore, in the first pass through the data, she did not refer to the coding categories at all while collecting data. Instead, she tried to record everything that teachers said and did that might express a teacher's value system regarding what was important to do in school. With the wisdom of hindsight, of course, it is apparent that LeCompte had to be viewing the classrooms through some sort of lens developed during her graduate studies. However, she had been urged to set all her preconceptions and theoretical hunches aside, which she did, to the best of her ability. Only when she had finished collecting data did she resurrect the coding system, applying it deductively to her new data set in a first pass through the data. After coding the entire data set once, she found that she was unable to classify all the behaviors of her four teachers using the coding system she had developed and modified during the pilot study. However, she had kept track of the "nonconforming" teacher utterances, so the next step was to categorize them. She then revised the coding system once more, adding more categories and subcategories and many individual behaviors. In a final step, she then reapplied the revised system to the data set, generating the results she published for her study. Example 2.9 in chapter 2 of this book shows what her coded field notes looked like.

EXAMPLE 6.3

CODING DATA BASED BOTH ON A FORMATIVE MODEL AND EMERGING, MORE SPECIFIC, CODES: WOMEN AND WHITE DISCHARGE IN INDIA

A team of researchers led by Stephen Schensul and Ravi Verma conducted a study of men's sexual risk behavior in Mumbai, in which sexual health problems were a marker of exposure to sexual risk. Conflict in marriage was one of the factors leading to sexual risk behavior for these men. Because rates of infection were increasing among women in rural areas, they wondered whether women in their rural-origin sample might show risk markers that would indicate exposure to sexual risk through their husbands (or even via their own behavior). Initial interviews with women identified white discharge (*safed pani*) as an indicator of tension in a woman's life. They obtained a supplemental grant to study white discharge among women in the same community. They began with a formative model in which *tension* (viewed as a result of the burden of responsibilities women bore), *conflict* between the marital couple, and *insufficient financial resources* were posited as the main domains associated with white discharge in the pilot interviews. Because they also were the main domains that were known through the men's study to contribute to sexual risk behavior among men, Schensul and Verma thus thought that white discharge might be considered as a possible marker of men's sexual risk taking.

The study team then conducted forty-one interviews with married women, exploring their current life situation including their family responsibilities, household stresses, and relationships with their husbands as well as their stories about white discharge. These constituted the main study domains. From a review of the first ten or so interviews, coders on the project produced a list of thirty codes related to the main domains, which were applied and then modified in accordance with the remainder of the interviews. The final coding scheme, which several study team coders applied to the data, included the codes that best helped to refine the theoretical model linking components of women's life situation to the presence or absence of white discharge and to answer new questions about medical help-seeking behavior and home treatment of white discharge. The final code list is presented in Table 6.2.

These codes were organized into operationalized taxonomies with conceptual (explanatory) underpinnings. An example of an operationalized taxonomy is reproductive health (*safed pani*, vaginal symptoms, *kamjori*, HIV/STI, and history of pregnancy). An example of another operationalized taxonomy is marital relationship (marital communication, evaluation of husband, marital problems, marital violence, support from husband, marital process). A third taxonomy is emotions (emotional health, emotional violence, jealousy), and a fourth is sexuality/sexual health (sexual satisfaction, sexual risk, marital sex, male sexual risk, female sexual risk, health consequences). These were

TABLE 6.2   Codes Used for the White Discharge Study

alcohol	marital process
autonomy/empowerment	marital relationship
children	marital sex
communication-marital	other addictions
daily routine	physical health
economic condition	physical violence
emotional health	religious issues
emotional violence	reproductive health
environmental description	reproductive history
evaluation of husband	safed pani/white discharge
family relationships	sexual risk
female sexual risk	sexual satisfaction
gender ideals	sick role
health consequences	social relationships other than
HIV/STI	family
hygiene	socioeconomic conditions
intervention	support from husband
interview logistics	taboo
jealousy	tenshun/tension
kamjori/weakness	treatment seeking
leisure	vaginal symptoms
living/sleeping arrangements	violence
male sexual risk	what doctors say
marital problems	

linked in a model in which the predictor or independent variable domains were emotions, sexuality, and marital relationship and the dependent variable domain (the focus of the study) was reproductive health. The emergent theory suggested that these three predictor domains contributed separately and together to reproductive health problems. The original list of codes emerged from the formative model structuring the study and from interaction with the data. They were available to combine in a variety of different ways for descriptive and analytic/explanatory write-ups and for the development of both a social norms survey and an instrument measuring changes in intimate relationships and sexual health as a result of an individual- and couples-based *intervention*. The codes developed in Example 6.3, as well as the entire data set, are now available for use by other researchers who may employ all, or only some, of the codes or even devise their own coding system, depending on what their research questions are and what they have in mind in terms of data analysis (Kostick et al. 2010).

These examples demonstrate that coding can be quite holistic, as in the very first stages of Schensul and Verma's project, or in Vadeboncoeur's study, where the researcher really only "clumped" the data into three piles or conceptual domains. They also can be quite specific, as in LeCompte's (1978) Learning to Work study, in which data were divided into very small segments, usually no longer than a sentence or two, and then coded. Coding can be used after data are collected, as was the case in LeCompte's and Vadeboncoeur's studies, or during the observation phase, as Smith did, as an actual data collection strategy or as antecedent to a survey as in the Schensul and Verma study. Further, a coding scheme devised by one researcher or research team can be applied by more than one observer, as in the case of Smith's research, when she used fellow students to help her collect data. Finally, it is important to remember that codes, as we refer to them here, are not mutually exclusive. Many of the codes in the above list overlap or coincide. And in the analysis process, the intersection of codes (conceptual categories or "things") within data sets and in the same blocks of texts is an important feature to be explored in the data.

All of the above researchers used coding systems that they developed themselves. However, there are many other ways to arrive at coding systems. Frequently, researchers borrow a coding system developed by others in another similar field site and use it in their own study, or they use a system that they developed themselves and apply it to a different population or use it in a different site. They may also use a standardized coding scheme devised for archived qualitative data, such as the Human Relations Area Files.

EXAMPLE 6.4

USING THE HUMAN RELATIONS AREA FILES (HRAF)

The HRAF files were developed by anthropologist George Murdock to compile and code ethnographies written by anthropologists and other social scientists anywhere in the world (Murdock 1971) (Table 6.3). The coding system he developed enables ethnographers to use a collection of ethnographies that is stored at the Peabody Museum, Yale University. The purpose of the file is to make these ethnographies available for cross-site comparison or for the conduct of meta-analyses or quantitative analyses of qualitative ethnographic data.

TABLE 6.3 Examples of Generic Codes from the Eighty-Eight Major Coding Categories in the Human Relations Area Files Outline of Cultural Materials

20.	COMMUNICATION	
	201.	Gestures and Signs
	202.	Transmission of Messages
	203.	Dissemination of News and Information
	204.	Press
	205.	Postal System
	206.	Telephone and Telegraph
	207.	Radio and Television
	208.	Public Opinion
34.	STRUCTURES	
	341.	Architecture
	342.	Dwellings
	343.	Outbuildings
	344.	Public Structures
	345.	Recreational Structures
	346.	Religious and Educational Structures
	347.	Business Structures
	348.	Industrial Structures
	349.	Miscellaneous Structures
46.	LABOR	
	461.	Labor and Leisure
	462.	Division of Labor by Sex
	463.	Occupational Specialization
	464.	Labor Supply and Employment
	465.	Wages and Salaries
	466.	Labor Relations
	467.	Labor Organizations
	468.	Collective Bargaining
48.	MARRIAGE	
	581.	Basis of Marriage
	582.	Regulation of Marriage
	583.	Mode of Marriage
	584.	Arranging a Marriage
	585.	Nuptials
	586.	Termination of a Marriage
	587.	Secondary Marriages
	588.	Irregular Unions
	589.	Celibacy

Source: Data from Murdock 1971.

Murdock and his colleagues developed a generic coding system consisting of major domains and subdomains that represented every possible dimension of cultural, social, economic, and political life. Any ethnographic data can be coded using this system, and the coded chunks can be stored. Because the generic coding system is not theoretically based—that is, it is not embedded in a particular way of conceptualizing human behavior—its cultural classification system can be used by ethnographers working in a variety of different topic areas, whether or not with the HRAF archives, in their own research. The entire coding system is available to ethnographers, but, depending upon their topic, studies will utilize some codes more than others, and many codes will never be used. Ethnographer Bryan Page of the University of Miami Medical School, for example, used the HRAF files coding system to code in-depth interviews and observations with injection drug users in central Miami.

Although the HRAF categories are intended to be comprehensive and universally applicable, someone using the HRAF files in the twenty-first century clearly would have to add categories such as "Internet Communication" and "Cellular Devices" to the "Communication" category and might wish to do the same for "Marriage" to accommodate for the wide range of blended, extended, and same-sex marriages currently in existence.

In the examples above, we have used the term "code" without defining it very specifically. Below, we present an elaborated definition that encompasses both the very general "bins" used in the initial stages of organizing data and, as well, the more discrete and specifically operationalized items that are disaggregated from the larger conceptual "bins."

WHAT IS A CODE?

Codes are names or symbols used to stand for a group of similar items, ideas, or phenomena that the researcher has noticed in his or her data set. In order to determine whether or not items or other phenomena are present, present in some degree or intensity, or absent altogether, researchers have to code specific bits of data. *For qualitative research, the codes are "qualitative"; that is, they describe the qualities or characteristics of people, places, or events. For quantitative research, the codes are numerical, and each*

Key point

number represents a specific kind of item within a category (for example, codes of 1 = male, 2 = female, 3 = transgender for a category called "SEX"). Both qualitative and quantitative data can be tabulated or counted after coding for each coding category. The variance that occurs among the various categories then can be determined. Here we focus mainly on qualitative codes; we address quantitative variables in chapters 8 and 9 in book 3 and in chapters 8 and 9 of this book.

Codes usually are given short names that represent, in a somewhat abstracted fashion, the nature of the more concrete items to which they are applied. For example, in the Learning to Work study, LeCompte used the code "Time" whenever the teacher referred to the qualities or characteristics of time. These included references to deadlines, schedules, time limits, being on time, or the specific time of day. Similarly, Vadeboncoeur coded under the category "Self" all stories that students told about their personal experience, any instances where students judged the behavior of other people by their own personal value systems, or whenever they held up their own background as the standard by which other experiences should be evaluated. These references might be considered as factors within the domain "Self." In another example, Berg and colleagues (2010) used "marital abuse" to refer to any instances in which women described situations where they experienced verbal, emotional, financial, or physical attacks from spouses. Schensul and colleagues used the code "spousal relationship" to refer to many different dimensions of interaction/communication between husband and wife in a study of women and HIV risk in India (S. Schensul et al. 2010).

WHAT DO QUALITATIVE CODES LOOK LIKE?

In qualitative research a code usually is a person, an object, a kind of event, an idea, a theme, or any number of other things that have "qualities." Qualitative codes are used to identify and compare events, persons, and settings in terms of these qualities. Codes thus can identify similar "events," "types of persons," "kinds of settings," "activities," or "rituals." They also can be used to identify and even to express variance in the things coded, in that they denote differences in a quality, for example, the presence or absence (categorical variables yes or no, present or not) of a quality, or they represent variance in the degree (more of, less than) of the quality present. Qualitative codes have the following characteristics:

- They are operationalized; that is, they are carefully defined so that both the researcher and others can easily and consistently recognize in the data the phenomenon to which the code is being applied. **Operational codes** respond to statements such as " 'X'[name of code] looks like this!"

- They have names, often a single term (such as "sex," meaning anything related to sexual activity; or "alcohol," meaning anything related to the use or purchase of alcohol; or "sharing," meaning instances in which children share information, toys, or other things with each other) or a phrase that represents a concept, such as "showing respect for elders" (demonstrated by the presence of behaviors such as standing in the presence of elders, speaking politely to elders, offering assistance to elders, and doing what elders tell one to do) or "dropping out of school" (measured by factors such as the fact that a student has exceeded the permitted number of unexcused absences, is not currently attending school, and has no plans to return to school).

- Code names are close to the concept they describe. "Religion," for example, could be the code name for various faiths to which people adhere. They may be subdivided/subcoded into different types of religions, for example, Catholic, Muslim, and Baha'i, if this is useful to the study.

- Codes may exist at different levels of abstraction or explanation. The code "showing respect for elders" is an abstraction rather distant from the actual empirical actions it subsumes. The code "religion" is much more concrete, as it refers to membership in a specific religious grouping.

- Codes reflect "qualities." In most qualitative work, a code is most likely to be organized as present/absent

Definition: Operational codes mark items or units in the data that have observable boundaries and are defined such that others understand what they mean and can apply them to data with a high degree of congruency.

Definition: A scale is a measure of the degree of presence or absence of a concept or quality

Definition: Level of inference refers to the degree of interpretation or evaluation done by the coder. Low-inference coding stays very close to actual concrete description. High-inference coding involves interpretation; it requires that the coder make more difficult and complex judgments as to which code is more appropriate. High-inference codes are the building blocks of analysis, interpretation, and theory generation.

 Cross Reference: See Book 2, chapter 5 for a continuum reflecting levels of inference and abstraction

or by degree of presence (e.g., high, moderate, low). They can be a point on a **scale** with multiple points.

- Codes usually are not numbers.
- Individual code names are distinctly different from one another. Unlike quantitative codes, qualitative codes are not mutually exclusive—the same block of text can include a number of different codes that intersect.

In the initial stages of coding, codes must be kept at a low **level of inference**. A high-inference descriptor referring to "neighborhood quality" might be the following statement: "The run-down house was located in a bad neighborhood." However, such a description does not give a photographic impression of the house; what is run-down to one person might seem quite adequate to another, and different people have different ideas as to what a "bad neighborhood" looks like. Low-inference descriptors, by contrast, create a rich description unaffected by value judgments of coders. For example, the descriptors used to describe a house—which might all be subsumed under a high-level descriptor such as "house maintenance"—could include the category "Paint" (meaning "quality of the paint" as indicated by such elements as whether the paint condition is intact and bright or dirty, patched and peeling), "Roof" (meaning "condition of the roof" as indicated by fresh matching shingles, none missing or, by contrast, mismatched patches and holes in the roof), "Windows" (meaning "characteristics of windows" ranging from intact Thermopane glass with painted wood frames to windows with broken and missing glass), and "Screens" (meaning "presence and condition of screens as indicated by present and intact, present but torn, or shredded and missing). After all descriptive text in the database is sorted into the categories of Paint, Roof, Windows, and Screens, the researcher will actually have assembled a list describing the exact qualities of the house itself. Adhering to low-inference descriptors helps keep the coded items discrete from one another and avoids the unreliability involved when coders have to make too many value judgments about how to classify items. However, creating too many low-inference descriptors can generate far more codes than a researcher can handle with ease. This is why researchers usually begin their rough coding with big chunks at a higher level of inference and then create more discrete codes within each bin. One caveat is that coders employed to do high-inference coding must be well trained initially, or their work will be inconsistent and unreliable, simply because their judgments can vary in accordance with differences in their backgrounds and biases. It is important to note that these examples show a unique characteristic of qualitative codes—they are complex, often consisting of a "package" of subcategories that in a quantified system would be given distinct variable names.

Codes used later in the analytic process can be at a higher level of inference or abstraction. Using the example of the house above, a conceptual category could be "Deterioration." Rather than simply designate the categories of coding as "High," "Medium," and "Low," the codes within the category could be based on how coders interpret descriptions recorded in data, using those interpretations to code the condition of paint, windows, roof, and screens. *As noted, high-inference coding requires greater attention to training of coders to ensure that judgments are consistent across all coders.*

Key point

OTHER CHARACTERISTICS OF CODES

If possible, codes should be related to more or less obviously bounded, spontaneously reoccurring or repeated text chunks, qualitative units, or items. The coded blocks of text can be paragraphs, units of time (hours, minutes, days, weeks) specific utterances, observable behaviors, parts of narratives, and so on; however, they should *not* span pages and pages of notes. LeCompte, for example, defined her coding unit as a chunk of text data she called a "verbal episode"; she defined a verbal episode as all those words, sentences, or even paragraphs uttered by teachers or students between the beginning and end of a distinct topic. Most of the time the verbal episodes were limited to several

Cross Reference:
See Books 1 and 2 for a discussion of how to identify and define units of analysis

sentences or phrases, but some were quite lengthy, such as minilectures on some serious misbehavior on the part of the students or complicated sets of instructions for a coming activity. More complicated was a coding unit called an "utterance" that Michele Berke (2012) used, in a study of how deaf mothers read storybooks to their deaf preschoolers. Because the mothers used a variety of means to communicate the text, including American Sign Language, finger spelling, facial expressions, and gestures, what actually constituted an "utterance" was not so clear-cut as in LeCompte's use of a spoken "verbal episode."

Jean Schensul's study of alcohol use among men in Mumbai used yet another type of unit. Her coding unit was called the "critical event," which consisted of stories of men's sexual encounters with and without alcohol use (J. Schensul et al. 2010). These were first general-coded (as "critical event") and then subcoded with a combination of locational and behavioral variables important in the study. In this case, the team developed sixteen different subcodes involving use of alcohol, location, type of partner, and protected/unprotected sex within the general code "critical event." Subsequently, they were further coded for other aspects of the critical event—such as whether friends were present, type of alcohol used, pattern and duration of alcohol use, and so forth. In the analysis, these variables and their associations were considered in relation to type of critical event.

Codes should reduce data to a manageable form, not expand it. Therefore, they should subsume or place into larger groups many smaller items or groups of items, as was the case in Vadeboncoeur's and LeCompte's studies described earlier. Although researchers have different opinions regarding the number of codes to be developed, most studies, other than those that are extremely complex or longitudinal, will not generate more than twenty to thirty coding categories for the master list.

Codes can be manipulated, collapsed into larger categories, and subdivided. Researchers also can add or delete codes as they work through their data and find that evidence for coding categories originally anticipated do not exist or that new codes have to be created for unanticipated categories. However, the lack of evidence for a code may not mean it should be deleted; it may simply mean that something we have good reason to suspect should be present is absent. For example, LeCompte's finding that teachers did not emphasize the intrinsic value of learning at all contradicted her initial theoretically driven model; this was an important finding during the pilot phase, given the nature of her study.

Codes often are organized hierarchically and can be thought of as branching tree diagrams, with sub-subcodes collapsing into subcodes, which in term are subsumed into larger codes or taxonomies. In addition, Tables 5.1 and 5.2 in the previous chapter illustrate this type of organization.

Cross Reference: See how formative taxonomies and tree diagrams are constructed in Book 2

WHERE DO CODES COME FROM?

Codes can be derived directly from the study data in the process of collecting it. They also can be created prior to initiating a study, based on a formative theoretical model and the researchers' experience, and then revised in the light of experience in the field site. We already have indicated that researchers often borrow coding systems from other researchers or from studies they have already done themselves. They also frequently adapt an existing set of coding categories that they or someone else has developed.

EXAMPLE 6.5

ADAPTATION OF A PREVIOUSLY USED CODING SYSTEM

LeCompte adapted the coding categories for "Responsibility," "Accountability," "Time," "Task Orientation," "Opportunities for the Students to Direct Their Own Instruction," and "Taking Initiative" from the Learning to Work study (see Table 6.1) for use in her study of the Arts Focus program. Even though the former study was done with elementary schoolchildren in regular classes and Arts Focus was a middle-school arts program, the teachers still placed great emphasis on these specific norms, and the categories fit the Arts Focus data very well.

Similarly, the formative theoretical model and coding scheme used in Mauritius and illustrated in Figure 5.2 and Table 5.1 in the previous chapter were adapted for use in a study of a similar topic—AIDS risk among youth—with young workers in the industrial sector, college students, and out-of-school community youth in Sri Lanka's Central Province (Silva et al. 1997).

Coding categories can come from quite mundane sources. One of the most common sets of categories are the demographic categories used by the United States Bureau of the Census and other mass survey organizations to delineate the general characteristics of a population. These include categories such as age, sex, race or ethnicity, educational level, occupation, income, place of residence, religious preference, and political party preference. Often these categories constitute important *variables*, or categories whose component parts vary along a given dimension in the study and that are used for comparative purposes. For example, researchers frequently compare males and females, people with different party preferences or religion, or people with varying levels of education and income. It is this variance that often explains why people behave as they do. Thus, variables structure the hypotheses that researchers want to test or the research questions of interest in the study. For example, in the question "Does instruction in the arts have a greater impact on the identity formation of *boys* or *girls*?" sex or gender, with its coding categories of male and female, is a variable that can be expected to influence or to explain the differential outcomes of a program. Or, in the question "Do arts education programs enroll fewer *males*, *minority* students, and *poor* students than females, whites, and affluent students—even when the programs are located in public schools and require no special fees?" sex (coding categories of male, female), minority status (coding categories of African American, White, Hispanic or Latino/a, American Indian, Asian American), and income (coding categories of high, upper middle, middle, lower middle, and low) are variables that are well-known markers of variance in a population. Or, in the question "In which kinds of *communities* are *minority* school dropouts most likely to live: the inner city, city borders, the suburbs, or rural areas?" *type of community* is a variable with precoded categories embedded in the questions, and the variable of minority status can be coded according to categories recognized in the census, by the way that participants self-identify, or by other strategies. At least some of this kind of information customarily is included for future comparison and analysis with every set of in-depth interviews, surveys, testing instruments, questionnaires, or elicitation tools (such as pilesorts) so as to maintain information on the possible demographic variance within a population.

Rough deductive coding categories also can be derived from the conceptual and theoretical frames or research questions around which the researcher built the study, as was the case in Vadeboncoeur's study.

EXAMPLE 6.6

BUILDING A CODING SYSTEM DEDUCTIVELY FROM A CONCEPTUAL FRAMEWORK

Vadeboncoeur had hypothesized—and administrators of the teacher training program she studied had hoped—that over the three-semester sequence of professional seminar courses she studied for her dissertation, teacher training students would develop more and more sophisticated explanations for why public-school students succeeded or failed in their studies. Vadeboncoeur conceptualized developmental growth as a movement from a preoccupation with "self" toward more cognizance of the influence of "other people," and finally to a recognition of the impact that "the environment," or structural forces—such as social class, patterns of discrimination, economic disparities, and academic ability grouping in schools—could have on students' chances for success (see Example 5.1 in the previous chapter for a description of her original "general formative model"). She hypothesized that over the course of several semesters, she would be able to see evidence of this shift in her qualitative data.

To test her hypothesis, Vadeboncoeur sorted her coded data into three other "groups" according to the semester in which the specific pieces of data were collected. By examining the relative frequency during each semester of different types of statements made by students, she was able to get a rough idea of how and whether the students' descriptions changed over time. A content analysis of what the students said further enabled her to see in what direction the changes occurred and to what the changes might be attributed. She displayed her data in a table arranged as in Table 6.4.

TABLE 6.4 Changes in Student Attitudes over Time

	Student Name	Semester One	Semester Two	Semester Three
"Self"	Dale Sue Cary Ella	# of Examples from Data for Each Student	# of Examples from Data for Each Student	# of Examples from Data for Each Student
"Other People"	Dale Sue Cary Ella	# of Examples from Data for Each Student	# of Examples from Data for Each Student	# of Examples from Data for Each Student
"The Environment"	Dale Sue Cary Ella	# of Examples from Data for Each Student	# of Examples from Data for Each Student	# of Examples from Data for Each Student

These data were assembled in part from texts produced by the students—journals, papers, and transcripts of their discussion in small groups. The counts from the text data were fairly precise. Estimates of change in observable behavior were rougher since the researchers could not document everything that students did during their class activities and student teaching. Thus, observational data were able to provide only a gross estimate or guideline regarding any shifts. Vadeboncoeur searched through her data again to determine what might have caused shifts in consciousness, if any; evidence for shifts consisted of rationales given by students in their journals as they documented their thoughts and actions over time.

PRECODED DATA

 Definition: Precoded data have been categorized so that a given number or letter represents a single kind of information about a given person, group, setting, or other researcher-defined unit of analysis

Some of the easiest data to crunch are those that are **precoded**; that is they have been collected in a form that can be counted or enumerated. That is, the instrument generates answers to closed-ended questions. Demographic data using census categories have been precoded in this way; it also is the customary format for standardized structured surveys and questionnaires. As noted, these kinds of data are not used as often in qualitative and ethnographic research, except when the survey instruments have been developed and/or adapted in the specific research site and after considerable preliminary fieldwork.

Researchers who do have such data often like to begin their analysis with this material because the analysis is quite straightforward and the yields—in terms of results—are rather immediate. This can help make the ethnographer feel as though progress is being made even though field notes and other data have not yet been analyzed. Precoded data can include enumerated (or numerical) data, such as test scores, purchase records, attendance figures, and so on; so-called nominal data, which involves specific, named categories of things, such as sex (male, female), province or state of residence, political party affiliation (Christian Democrat, Socialist, Green, Labor), and to which church or religious organization respondents belong. Interviews and all standardized surveys and questionnaires contain responses that consist primarily of such material—that is, of answers to closed-ended questions. Many such instruments have built-in coding systems which, once applied, yield categories of things that can be counted, such as sex, age, preference for particular kinds of food or entertainment, places of residence, and estimated frequencies of specific types of behavior, such as drug use or number of moves a household has made.

Other forms of precoded data represent efforts to test theories. Intervention studies are often implemented using approaches that reflect specific theoretical assumptions or domains. In observing the implementation of the intervention, researchers will note and code for the presence, or degree of presence, of key variables. For example, an Institute of Community Research study testing the idea that youth action research programs can be used to curb substance abuse is driven by a social learning approach (Berg, Coman, and Schensul 2009; Berg and Schensul 2004). Facilitators leading the intervention are taught to implement the action research curriculum using four instructional techniques that are intended to produce specific responses in the young students: modeling, scaffolding, explication, and reflection. Observers learn the techniques with the facilitators; the observers are taught to record and code examples of the desired behaviors in teachers and students as they occur. The data collected test the hypothesis that these facilitation techniques produce the desired responses in youth, preparing them to reduce their substance use and increase their risk avoidance attitudes and behaviors. One problem with this form of recording data, however, is that unless researchers use video-recording to capture all instances of such phenomena, they cannot obtain a fully accurate account either of the number of times such events take place or the students' reactions to them. Only if video is used can the data can be quantified and analyzed through variable interaction. We discuss these forms of analysis in later chapters on management and analysis of quantitative data in which variables, rather than cases, are interrelated.

KINDS OF CODES OR CATEGORIES

Descriptive codes are those most commonly used in pre-coded instruments and in qualitative studies where data on previously identified variables are collected for comparison between and among cases. Such codes usually are categorical, that is, they are "yes/no" codes. They include such things as whether or not a person is enrolled in school, an injection drug user, the parent of a student enrolled in a particular educational program, a lover of classical music, a known sufferer from hypertension or diabetes, or whether or not someone has ever had cancer, a hysterectomy, or a tooth extraction. The answer to all of these questions usually is unambiguously yes or no; "yes" can be coded as a "one" and "no" as a "two" and all the yeses and nos can be counted to give the researcher some idea of the profile of participants. The importance in a qualitative study, however, is that these answers are used to make comparisons across "cases" in relation to other, qualitative characteristics that have been coded.

Other kinds of variables, such as the number of homes, cars, or telephones a person owns or the number of times people attend concerts, purchase prescription drugs, or take trips away from their home community can be recorded in actual numbers. In a qualitative study, such questions can be asked in the context of an in-depth interview and quantified later, or they can be asked on a separate survey instrument that can be amalgamated with the more qualitative data and used for comparative purposes. If numerical consistency is called for across observations or interviews, however, it is best to use a precoded supplemental instrument or checklist in addition to other more qualitative data collection to avoid the very real possibility that information will be left out and not available for coding and analysis later on.

Some kinds of descriptive data can be grouped so that each of the possible answers can be given a number, which serves as its code. Such information includes such things as political party (Republican, Democratic, Socialist, Socialist Worker, Green, Liberal) or religious affiliation (Protestantism, Catholicism, Judaism, Buddhism, Islam, Hinduism, Shintoism, etc.); occupation (professional, managerial, educational, clerical, service, technical, manual, agricultural, child care, home care, unemployed); educational level (elementary school, middle school or junior high, high school, postsecondary school); place of residence (inner city, periurban, suburban, semirural, and rural). Again, these data can be elicited in an in-depth interview or can be asked in a supplemental survey as background information. To be sure of collecting these data systematically and consistently from all respondents, we recommend using a survey instrument.

As we have noted in Books 1 and 3, it requires a considerable amount of preliminary fieldwork before study data are collected to create *valid* codes that are more detailed or conceptual than those defining the main domains in a study. This is because the options or codes that researchers use in their **instruments** or data collection tools have to include *all* the options or information that reasonable informants would think of in trying to answer the questions. And these options or response alternatives need to be clearly stated so that they will be equally well understood by respondents. Usually for an ethnographic/ qualitative study, we do not recommend trying to create or use valid codes in advance beyond the "domain," factor, or "chunk" level unless they have been used by others in the same or similar study sites or are used in national surveys, which ensure their validity and reliability.

Definition:
An instrument is a tool for collecting data, which can consist of open-ended or closed-ended questions or both

LIMITATIONS OF CODING

Codes do not tell us everything; for example, knowing how many years a person went to school wouldn't tell a researcher whether specific individuals repeated grades or attended part-time or the kinds of institutions they enrolled in. Similarly, researchers would not be able to tell from the codes above whether an individual attended or graduated from a two-year college, a four-year university, a postsecondary technical/vocational school, or a secretarial institute. Indeed, the educational codes above might not make sense to individuals who had received certificates from one- or two-year technical or clerical institutes and did not know how to classify them. Further fieldwork might be needed to make sure that the categories included all the possible responses. Questions about *willingness* to attend a seminar or participate in a program will not reveal to the researcher whether people actually *did* attend. Additional questions— and perhaps some observations at such programs or seminars—might be needed to determine fine points. However, precoding can be refined, and it certainly permits researchers to make rough descriptions of a population in a relatively short period of time by showing how many people fall into each category of a given code. In short, when well done, survey instruments with precoded answers permit us to learn very efficiently a considerable amount of information about a great many people. And a mixed-methods approach involving collection of quantified qualitative and quantitative data provides the best and most well-rounded portrayal of results in a complex study setting.

SUMMARY

Specific coding can begin with theories and hypotheses—as was the case in Vadeboncoeur's study, in which the theories that guided her research also were the basis of her initial coding or "clumping" categories: "Self," "Other," and the "Environment." By contrast, coding can be associated with little theory at all, as is the case for the precoded demographic data that researchers always collect as a way to identify characteristics of respondents. However, these same "theoryless" categories can come in quite handy when researchers need to explore the strength of a theory with regard to a particular group or set of individuals. In all of these cases, however, the codes are applied "on top of" the data, whether the application is done during the data collection phases of research or after the data are all collected. Applying codes to data and doing so consistently over time and with multiple coders requires a kind of reference to which researchers can refer to assure that definitions do not "creep" over time and use. We discuss how to create codebooks for qualitative data in chapter 7.

7

CODING AND CREATING
QUALITATIVE AND
QUANTITATIVE
CODEBOOKS

As stated in earlier chapters, coding is a way to classify and organize data systematically in accordance with a conceptual framework, regardless of whether that framework is a formative one initiating the study or one that emerges during the study. Codes are developed using an inductive/deductive or recursive process; they render data amenable to further steps in analysis. All data that ethnographers collect can be classified using conceptual organizing categories or codes. Researchers create lists or books of their codes to assure that the codes they ultimately use are stable over time. This is particularly crucial when multiple researchers are coding data in a team project, when the project involves more than one site, or in a longitudinal study when data are coded over different periods of time. Obviously, if different researchers interpret data differently, coding will be inconsistent. If care is not exercised, the meaning of a code also can "creep" and change over time and with use by different coders. "Codebooks" that not only list the names of codes but provide standardized operational definitions for each code provide a consistent set of conceptual and operational definitions to use across a large data set, with multiple coders, over multiple time periods, or when data sets consist of multiple kinds of data. The **codebook**, then, is a standard reference.

The development of a codebook is intrinsically related to a researcher's search for answers to research questions and the domains and factors and their relationships highlighted in the study model. However, the *process* as well as the *product* of coding depends on the type of data that are being collected; different kinds of data require different kinds of coding. In this chapter, we first discuss the preliminary processes used to develop the codes that constitute a codebook; we then provide examples of codebooks and how different analytic and pragmatic processes are used to develop them.

CREATING INITIAL CODES IN ETHNOGRAPHIC RESEARCH

Ethnography utilizes three main ways of creating codes and accompanying codebooks: codes used with qualitative data and derived from qualitative analysis, codes created by quantifying qualitative data, and codes deriving from pre-coded survey data. We describe each of these below.

Creating Codes Based on Qualitative Analysis That Identifies the Qualities of Variables

Much of what we have described already is concerned with the creation of qualitative codes. As we have said, qualitative codes may involve a single item, unit, subfactor, or factor or be complex enough to involve the interaction of several dimensions. They also may range from descriptive (less abstract) to analytical (more abstract). Lwendo Moonzwe's research (2011) illustrates how she interacted with in-depth interview data at multiple levels to arrive at a final coding scheme for an important subcomponent of her paper on the use of the recreational drug Ecstasy for self-medication and mood management.

EXAMPLE 7.1

DEVELOPING AND FINALIZING A CODEBOOK FOR STUDYING FACTORS RELATED TO SELF-MEDICATION WITH ECSTASY

Like other researchers whose work we described in earlier chapters, Moonzwe had a general sense of what she was looking for: she wanted to explore a theme, "self-medication," that had arisen early on in her study. She was looking for individuals who appeared to be using the scheduled (FDA controlled) drug Ecstasy to solve emotional problems. She wanted to test the idea that use of the drug was a response to difficult life circumstances. In her analysis of self-medication with Ecstasy, Moonzwe first read and reviewed 118 in-depth interviews and sorted them into those people who had ever experienced any kind of negative life circumstance (a master intuitive conceptual code or domain that included, at first pass, any kind of abuse, loss, imprisonment, significant failures, abandonments, etc.) and those who had not. She marked quotations in the interviews in which participants described examples of negative life situations, but on first pass, she merely "chunked" them rather than classifying them in more detail. Next she searched through the quotations and sorted them into groups by similarity, creating codes for four main subdomains (groupings or factors): "abuse," "loss," "life circumstances," and "conflict."

Her next step involved looking through each factor grouping to make sure that the quotations/examples fit the general concept she thought underlay the grouping, and then she searched for any variation that existed *within* the grouping (counterfactuals). She made sure that all the quotations were properly sorted by checking to see that all the quotations fit into one or another discrete group. She then established definitions for the codes at the factor level. "Abuse," for example, included descriptions of occasions when respondents had been hurt physically, verbally, or emotionally in any way by someone close to them. "Loss" included descriptions of situations involving the loss of a person close to the respondent. "Conflict" included any examples of fighting, arguing, irreconcilable disagreements, or continuous disagreements. Lwendo could then define negative life situations as consisting of the factors identified from the data, separately or together, and either over time or at the present time.

Next she examined each of the four groupings to identify and count different types of situations within the factor—for example, physical as opposed to verbal abuse, and physical and verbal abuse versus financial abuse. At this point, Lwendo had a choice. She could decide to code in further detail within a coding/conceptual taxonomy, which would have meant first going through the cases that displayed abuse and then subcoding for each different type of abuse; or she could simply have counted and provided examples of different types of abuse in the section of her paper that described abusive negative life experiences. Because there were only approximately forty cases of abuse in the data set she was using, she decided to count examples of types of abuse by hand and describe them with examples in the text rather than coding the data set. In constructing her simple codebook, Lwendo recorded the main domain, "negative life situations," and defined it as subsuming the five different classes of experiences. She then constructed definitions for the five factors.

Coding in this way can be done on hard copy by hand or by using text management software programs that block text with codes and export the blocked text so that it can be compared across instances and cases.

Lwendo's codebook included only a few codes at the domain and factor level. However, she also could have included codes for different types of abuse at the variable level. She would have done this had she believed that these were of theoretical rather than descriptive interest, if there had been more cases to count and enumerate, or if she were planning to develop a survey. Developing a survey from her data would have required her to become more explicit about the ways in which variables and items are defined and measured. This is because surveys, with their closed-ended questions, require advance identification and quantification of codes.

Describing and/or Quantifying Qualitative Codes in a Coding Matrix

As mentioned, qualitative codes can represent characteristics that are present or absent, or rated quantitatively as high, medium, low, or absent. This type of coding can emerge through a comparison of the cases (persons, sites, types of incidents) in a qualitative database. It is important to remember that coding can be effective and valid only if the variables to be enumerated are sufficiently described across cases. One way to ensure consistency is to follow the guidelines for semistructured data collection and prepare a checklist of topics to be covered. As the data are being observed or collected through interviews, the topics can be checked off as they are covered in the interview. Later, the researcher should review the notes or transcriptions to make sure that all the topics required are included in the data. It also can be useful to do an introduction to each recorded interview in which the topics covered are listed. This makes checking for completeness and coding easier and makes case comparative analysis more systematic. It is also very useful to use a word-processing matrix such as Excel to record and manage data, such as the one displayed in Table 7.1.

Cross Reference:
See Book 3, chapter 7

TABLE 7.1 Summary Matrix of Data and Variables

IDI No.	PD#	Pregnant Now	Age	Age at Marriage	Educ.	Occupation	Age Started	Product Name
IDI 001	1	yes	22 years	15 years	6th	Housewife	16 years	Paan (with tobacco)
IDI 02	2	yes	22 years	13 years	8th	Homemaker	6 years	Started paan no supari at 6 years
IDI 03	3	no	37 years	16 years	1st	Teacher in tailoring class	18 years	Tobacco (kalipatha)
IDI 04	5	no	32 years	20 years	Illiterate	Housewife	13 years	Mishri
IDI 05	6	yes	16 years	12 years	Illiterate	Housewife	16 years	Mishri

Variables in the matrix are those considered early in the study to be important to investigate in every single interview or observation. This is especially important in conducting semistructured open-ended interviews or collecting other types of data for systematic case comparison, especially when there is high potential for missing data during the interview or observation. The matrix records presence of important variables, and summarizes content. These data are useful for a number of comparative purposes. The matrix can serve a number of different purposes: it is a checklist for researchers to make sure all of the critical topics are covered in a "case" or interview. A matrix can summarize the qualitative information on some of the more important codes. When an interview is completed, data on the key variables should be inserted into the matrix. If data are missing, the researcher can then return to the respondent or try to fill in the data through observations or other means. Completion of the matrix for every single case observation or interview improves the quality of later data collection by serving as a self-monitoring and feedback system. It is also useful, as we will note later, in group or team research.

Quantitative coding of qualitative data requires clearly differentiating among alternative responses. For example, in the case of Lwendo's classifications, the experience of abuse for a respondent (for example, "Case Participant 1") listed in a matrix can be coded for abuse as "yes" (it occurred) or "no"(it never occurred). Further, the abuse might be disaggregated by type of abuse (e.g., "physical ____yes____no"; "financial ____ yes____no"; "verbal ____yes____no"). In a matrix or SPSS file, each type of abuse would constitute a separate variable, for example, physical abuse, financial abuse, verbal abuse, and each would have a yes/no answer. A clear operational definition of physical abuse would be found in the primary coding scheme/codebook, and it would be repeated in the matrix. That same variable "physical abuse" could be further coded in the matrix for severity (low, moderate, or high). Thus "Case Participant 1" might be coded as abuse-yes, abuse-physical, and physical abuse-low.

These matrices must be rechecked when the data collection process is complete. Once they are filled in, they provide an invaluable tool for summarizing the study, describing the cases, examining patterns, and selecting cases that represent specific patterns for illustration in the write-up. They also provide the basis for categorizing cases for further comparative analysis. We have found these checklist and summary matrices to be very useful tools for data management, data quality control, organization of the data for analysis, and rudimentary analytic comparisons. We will describe how we use them along with quantitative data analysis programs for analysis of qualitative data in chapter 8 of this book.

Coding Data Using Predefined Demographic Codes

The easiest data to crunch are those that have been collected in a form that can be counted or enumerated. As stated in chapter 6, some researchers like to begin their analysis with this material because the analysis is quite straightforward and the yields—in terms of results—are rather immediate. This can help the ethnographer feel as though progress is being made even though the field notes have not yet been analyzed.

Precoded data such as demographic information always should be collected along with other text data that is coded and analyzed inductively. Sometimes, when the questions to be asked and the response alternatives are already known, these data in a fundamentally qualitative study can be collected using an accompanying survey instrument. This is especially important when the same data are needed from each person and the answers are usually categorical or nominal scales. Such instruments often include "locational data" (community of residence, street address, neighborhood), demographic data (gender, age, ethnicity/social race, educational level and experience, marital status, relationship status), type of residential situation (rent, own, live in a shelter, live with family member), condition of housing (temporary, permanent, or semipermanent), type of employment and material style of life, family size, number of children, and recency of migration.

Cross Reference: See Book 3, chapter 9 for a discussion of different types of scales

Precoded Survey Data. Standardized surveys or structured questionnaires always consist of precoded data that are mutually exclusive options to closed-ended questions. Ethnographic research, which emphasizes the behaviors, perspectives, and lived experiences of the study participants, uses three sources of precoded data. The first consists of demographic variables, such as education, religious affiliation, migration history, income, gender, and marital status. These indicators and the language used to describe them all must be adapted to the setting. For example, the term "grade," used to denote school level in the United States, should be replaced by "standard" in South Asian countries because that is the term more commonly used in those countries. An indicator of an affluent material lifestyle in one location might be possession of a car; in another, where no one has cars, it might be a bicycle or a home built of permanent materials rather than sticks and canvas. Making an accurate assessment of income may be very difficult if people work intermittently or engage in bartering, or if income received is nonmonetary. Each demographic variable must be constructed carefully with help from colleagues in the research setting and weighed against similar questions used in other surveys conducted in the study setting or settings like it.

A second source for precoded data consists of questions and item responses derived from the study model and variables and items related to the study questions. Developing survey questions and scales requires identifying the relevant domains, factors, variables, and items from the qualitative database (or from elsewhere) and transforming them into survey components (major domains), questions, and item responses, each with proper alternative response categories. This is a time-consuming task, but it is worthwhile because it facilitates socially valid generalization to a larger and more representative sample than that used in initial observations and interviews with key informants.

Other types of quantified precoded data also can be collected for comparative analytic purposes. For example, Geoffrey Hunt, a qualitative sociologist, studies substance use among young women, gang members, and Asian youth of different backgrounds in San Francisco. His predominantly qualitative research is based on in-depth interviews of young adults in samples varying from one hundred to three hundred individuals. Along with interviews, he uses a "numerate data" form that includes the above types of demographic and background data along with quantified data on patterns of drug use (frequency of use, amount of use, type of substance, use in past thirty days, use ever, and location of use). These data are used to describe the general demographic characteristics of his sample and general patterns of substance use. They are also used as the basis for developing the frameworks for comparing subgroups with the qualitative sample based on gender, education, and substance use classifications (e.g., marijuana use only, alcohol use only, polysubstance user) (Hunt et al. 2002).

To ensure a complete data set, researchers must make sure that they collect responses from every respondent for each and every question in the survey or structured questionnaire. Survey instruments must be completed and checked for accuracy before they are entered into the study's survey database. Such checking resembles the use of a data matrix in qualitative comparative analysis that we have described above; it can create a data set that can be very useful in comparing cases across variables to construct patterns or configurations of variables.

CREATING QUALITATIVE CODEBOOKS

Once ethnographers have worked through one—or several—of the recursive/inductive procedures described in chapters 5 and 6, they will be ready to begin systematically reading through and coding data. There are a number of tasks which must be done to facilitate this process, the most important of which is to create a codebook. As mentioned earlier, codebooks can be qualitative, quantitative, or both.

Codebooks are created once a coding system has been **Key point**
devised and more or less finalized—and we must emphasize that in ethnography, when using qualitative *or* quantitative data sets, analytic tasks almost never are completely finished and etched in stone! New qualitative domains, factors, and variables can be defined at any time and added to the codebook and other record-keeping systems.

A Side Note on When to Code

Some methodologists argue that data should be coded as soon as they are collected; Miles and Huberman (1984) even say, "Don't go to bed until the day's fieldnotes are coded." However, that admonition can apply only to those situations in which the fieldworker has done considerable research prior to entering the field, already knows what things are important to notice and what those things look like in the field, is knowledgeable about where in the field these things are to be found, and has a protocol or list of codes already established to use on the field notes or observations. Angela Smith's research on humor (see Example 6.1) is such a study; while she coded directly from observation, she also could have written down her observations in the form of field notes first and then coded them. Doing so, incidentally, would have preserved more of the context in which humor events were used and could have permitted explorations of how, under what conditions, and with whom graduate students used humor, rather than simple frequency counts of types of humor use alone.

While we strongly recommend that ethnographers write up their field notes as soon as possible after interviews or observations and make initial notations about possible items, coding categories, emergent themes, and other in-the-field very preliminary analytic activities, we also suggest that ethnographers not engage in rigorous and specific coding unless and until they have done enough fieldwork to be able to develop codes that meet all of the requirements spelled out in the previous pages. Premature coding is like premature closure; it can prevent the investigator from being open to new ideas, alternative ways of thinking about a phenomenon, and divergent—and sometimes quite correct—explanations for events. It could be argued that Angela Smith prematurely closed off her coding procedures and thus limited what she might have learned about the use of humor not only in graduate school, but as a tension-reducing strategy in a number of stressful situations. We explained earlier that analysis is a kind of playing with ideas; part of the usefulness of the play is its creativity and

 Key point   flexibility. ***We suggest that individual ethnographers avoid finalizing their coding schemes until they have completed their field research.*** Ethnographers should not stop playing the game before it's over!

WHAT IS A CODEBOOK?

A **codebook** is a list of all the codes (or variables) used for the analysis of a particular collection of data, the names of the variables that the codes represent, and a description of the characteristics (behaviors, appearances, activities, items, and other content) that are to be coded for each variable.

Table 7.2 displays a typical codebook that was used in a study of American Indian students' feelings about their school and teachers. It includes both quantitative/numerate and qualitative codes. Creating a codebook such as the one for the Black Knight High School study requires researchers to:

- name each variable;
- describe each variable; and
- label each variable.

Definition: A codebook reflects what is in, or expected to be in, the data set. Basically, a codebook is a list of all the codes used for the analysis of a particular collection of data, the names of the variables that the codes represent, and a list of the kinds of items that are to be coded for each variable

Naming the Variables

A variable name is a mnemonic shorthand for the variable. Software requirements sometimes limit the number of letters in a variable to eight. For example, YEARGRAD = year student expects to graduate from high school; BORING = reasons why the student is bored in school; LIKETEAC = whether or not students like their teachers; NOTLIKE = reasons why students don't like teachers, and so on. *Because of time constraints, some researchers may be tempted to list variables by number rather than naming them. This is not advisable as it makes learning and remembering the variables much more difficult.*

Key point

Describing the Variables

Describing a variable requires knowing how the variable is to be represented. Qualitative codes are operationalized or represented in words—sometimes quite a lot of words—and qualifiers, and they often consist of several different kinds of activities or events, together or embedded one within the other. They are not mutually exclusive, and multiple codes can be used to code a single piece of text data. Qualitative codes can be quite complex.

TABLE 7.2 Codebook for Black Knight High School Student Survey: Examples of Variable Names, Labels, and Values

Column	Variable Name	Question#	Codes
1–3	ID#		enter number
4	GENDER	1	1 = male, 2 = female
5–6	GRADE	2	enter number
7–8	YEARGRAD	3	enter number
9–10	AGE	4	enter age
11	NUMBNG	5	enter number[a]
12	HELP	6	1 = yes; 2 = no; 0 = blank
13	LIKETEAC	7	1 = yes; 2 = no; 0 = blank
14–15	NOTLIKE	8	01 = talk too much 02 = disorganized 03 = unavailable 0 4 = don't listen, don't care 05 = poor appearance 06 = too easy, no challenge 07 = unfair 08 = other 09 = unfriendly, don't joke 10 = complain too much 11 = negative attitude toward students 12 = uninterpretable response 13 = too much work for time 14 = teachers are good 00 = blank, no answer
16–17	BORING	9	01 = talk too much 02 = teach something we already had 03 = teach a boring subject 04 = when they don't get kids involved in class 05 = when they do nothing 06 = when they talk about themselves 07 = don't put in effort to teach 08 = other 09 = too rigid, strict, no time to relax 10 = when they are absent 11 = when students misbehave 12 = uninterpretable 00 = blank, no answer

18–19	INTEREST	10	01 = involves kids in class 02 = lots of activities 03 = well-organized 04 = interesting subject; interesting activities 05 = helps students, is understanding 06 = allows games, play, make up time 07 = positive attitude 08 = other 09 = teacher likes students 10 = uninterpretable 00 = blank, no answer
20	PROBLEMS	11	1 = yes; 2 = no; 0 = blank
21	WHATPROB	12	1 = I don't have problems 2 = teachers lie 3 = they are naive, innocent 4 = insult students; are unpleasant, jerks 5 = they ignore students; don't care 6 = flirting; sexual advances with female students 7 = physical contact; hit, grabbed, shook a student 8 = other 9 = give you time out 0 = no answer, blank
22	THREAT	13	1 = yes; 2 = no; 0 = blank
23	PHYSTHRE	14	"
24	EMOTHRE	15	"
25	CLASSEAS	16	"
26–27	EASCLASS	17	01 = all 02 = reading 03 = English 04 = mathematics 05 = band 06 = U.S. studies 07 = Spanish 08 = other 09 = vocational education 10 = seminary 11 = state studies 12 = art 13 = P.E. 14 = none 15 = science

[a]"NG" in this coding scheme referred to "no grade," an evaluation given for failing performance rather than an "F."

Labeling the Variables

Labeling describes the variable and labels its values, or the attributes or items that characterize it. Most software packages for statistical analysis do not require the labeling of variables in order to perform analyses. However, it is always best to insert labels and values in the definition of the variable, since they are printed with the output. This makes reading the output much easier. Variable and value labels should be clear. Examples of nominal and categorical measures (or variables) are illustrated in Table 7.2. Other tables display scaled or Likert-type data or interval data.

Qualitative codebooks always include a complete list of:

- all the options available for each code; or
- a substantial number of examples illustrating the kinds of units—behaviors, actions, beliefs, ideas, persons, events, activities, and so on—that coders should be looking for when they are searching for items upon which to use each particular code; or
- a set of criteria spelling out what characteristics should be present in a unit before it is coded with that particular code.

As new variables are created and added to the database, they should be added to the codebook as well as defined in the software database.

For the Black Knight study, researchers first created variable/code names, which are displayed in Table 7.3 on the left, associated with the question eliciting the needed information on the right.

The researchers next listed the codes for each of the closed-ended (precoded) questions. They then did a content analysis of the answers to the open-ended questions to determine appropriate categories and associated codes for them and added them to the codebook, parts of which are displayed in Table 7.2. Coders coded information from the completed survey instruments onto coding sheets first, after which the lead researcher recoded a sample of the surveys to check on the accuracy of the coding. Once the accuracy

TABLE 7.3   Variable Names and Associated Questions for the
Black Knight High School Survey Codebook

Variable Name	Questions
LIKETEAC	Do you like your teachers?
NOTLIKE	What don't you like about your teachers?
BORING	What makes a teacher boring?
INTEREST	What makes a class interesting?
PROBLEMS	Have you had any problems with your teachers?
WHATPROB	What problems have you had with your teachers?
THREAT	Have you ever been threatened by a teacher?
PHYSTHRE	Have you ever been physically threatened by a teacher?
EMOTHRE	Have you ever been emotionally threatened by a teacher?
CLASSEAS	Do you think your classes are easy?
EASCLASS	Which of your classes is the easiest?

check was done, the data were entered into a computer for tallying and descriptive statistical analysis.

There are times when qualitative codes are quantified in terms of "degree of presence" of a specific phenomenon, but such categorizations are infrequent and usually done in terms of three or four "points" (e.g., a lot, some, not much, none). Several such codes are included in Table 7.2, such as when students were asked to assess interest or other factors on a three-point scale: "yes," "no," and "blank" (for no response or don't know). These classifications are made while coding and are defined based on what the data suggest rather than in advance of coding procedures.

Data sets can be defined in multiple ways. *All* of the data collected in a study, taken together, can be considered a data set. However, most ethnographic studies include multiple smaller data sets that must be "triangulated" or integrated to produce a holistic analysis related to the study question. To make sense of codes and codebooks, it is easier to talk about these smaller data sets as bodies of information consisting of data collected in the same way. They often represent different steps or phases in the evolution of the study. So, for example, Schensul and Schensul's qualitative study of Ecstasy use among young adults included the following different data sets:

- The Focus Group (FG) data set: a data set derived from focus groups and in-depth key informant interviews on beliefs and perceptions of Ecstasy use
- The Free List data set
- The Sort data set: a data set based on an open-ended pilesort and structured sorts on relationship to sexuality and assessment of risk
- The Semistructured Interview data set: interviews with participants on life use of drugs, relationships, and events when they used Ecstasy (or not) and had sex, and
- The Survey data set: an SPSS file of data collected from the qualitative sample and using a survey instrument that included variables related to locations of Ecstasy use and sexual innovation.

Each of these data sets was associated with a codebook that acted as a guide to the data for current and future use.

Codebooks can be created as "hard copy" (formatted electronically and then printed, preserved, and used for coding) or maintained in a text management/analysis program. A hard copy/electronic codebook would list all of the codes and describe them, including precoded questions. Almost all qualitative data sets include both qualitative and some numerical data, so qualitative codebooks usually reflect both. A text-management-based codebook (codes listed and described within the data set) might or might not code for precoded variables such as age or marital status, depending on the purposes of the researcher. However, text-management programs are best used when coding for more complex qualitative variables that are represented by blocks of text. When using such a program, we prefer to list precoded demographic variables within the data itself, in an introductory section, so that the cases or instances that constitute the database can easily be organized into groups or families for comparison based upon the variables of interest and enumerated in a separate matrix for description of the study sample. Below we show several examples of code-books that include both qualitative and numeric data.

In Table 6.2 in the previous chapter, we showed a list of qualitative codes used in an analysis of forty-one inter-views with married women in a low-income area of Mum-bai conducted to explore factors associated with white dis-charge (*safed pani*) in their lives. *Safed pani* is an "idiom of distress" among Indian women, reflecting stressful life situations, among them conflict-filled marital relation-ships, alcohol use of husbands, and husbands' sexual rela-tionships with partners outside the marriage. The research team evolved a list of codes in interaction with the data and finalized the code list presented in the table. Each of the codes was defined in sufficient detail to distinguish it from other codes but general enough to encompass a num-ber of different situations or behaviors. The final coding scheme included only those codes that were used five times or more. The others were subsumed under other codes or eliminated. The data set was used to develop an interven-tion strategy and is available with documentation for others to use for additional analyses. This data set does not include quantified demographic data such as age, age at marriage, education level, age of husband, length of time in Mumbai, whether marriage was arranged or not, and so on. These variables are included in the introduction of the interview notes and are summarized by hand when describing the sample. They are used to organize comparative analyses.

In the following example, we show how a codebook was constructed for a study in which the codes applied to the entire data set reflected use by several different research-ers for different paper topics. Each paper topic used a dif-ferent subcodebook.

━•━•━•━ **EXAMPLE 7.2**

A QUALITATIVE CODEBOOK FOR STUDIES OF MDMA, THE DRUG ECSTASY

The major focus of a previously described study of Ecstasy use and sexual activ-ity involved the identification of instances when Ecstasy contributed, either alone or with other factors, to any form of exposure to risk of infection through sexual engagement. The study team initially developed a general set of codes based on close reading of the first ten interviews and awareness of the primary theoretical lenses for the study: gender/power, sexuality, social influence, and socioecological factors. However, after careful re-review of the interviews, the team decided to focus on both the primary question and several other emergent questions about the way users managed the risks and benefits of Ecstasy use, the use of Ecstasy for coping with negative life situations, and the role of Ecstasy in intimate partner relationships. These became the focus for analysis and several paper topics.

Each team member chose a paper topic and coded all the data for that topic using a computer text management program. The coded data sets were merged so that future researchers would have access to all of the codes used for each paper as well as the most useful general codes. The topic codes are shown in Table 7.4.

◆▬◆▬◆▬◆

The analyses conducted used these codes for each of the topics addressed in three different scholarly papers. The codes helped to identify the primary domains in the model for each paper; topics included, for example, risks and benefits of Ecstasy use, different types of coping, and different circumstances involving Ecstasy, condoms, and types of partners. Demographic data are used to organize the qualitative codes for comparative analysis.

CREATING QUANTITATIVE CODEBOOKS

Codebooks for standardized survey data can be constructed in a variety of different ways, depending on the study, the purpose, and the variables. Generally they include the variable name, its description, and the items that make up the variable. Important elements in the description of a variable are whether it is:

- numeric;
- a date;
- a currency unit; or
- alphanumeric (letters/words).

The width of the numeric variable (the number of characters it requires) and whether it includes a decimal place also are important. These decisions are embodied in the codebook formats and instructions. The computer software chosen for analysis of quantitative data will determine these

TABLE 7.4   Codes for Three Papers Based on a Single Data Set

Codes for Examination of Risks and Benefits	
E Addiction_	Self-defined addiction to Ecstasy use
Perceived Benefit	Respondent's statements of benefits of Ecstasy use
Messages	Messages from media or peers about Ecstasy use
Peer use	Peers' use of Ecstasy
R/B balance	Examples of weighing risks and benefits
Risk	Respondent's statements about risks of Ecstasy use
Codes for Coping with Negative Life Situations	
Depression Diagnosed_ Medication	Respondent's statement of diagnosis of depression, past or present, and use of medication, past or present
Drug Other_ Coping	Examples of coping with negative life events with other drugs, not Ecstasy
E Use	Statements about Ecstasy use
E_Coping_Abuse	Statements about abuse, including use of E to cope
E_Coping_Current Life Situation	Statements about negative current life situation (housing, loss of job, economic stress, problems caring for children, family)
E_Coping_Loss of Loved one	Statements about losing loved ones (friends, parents, partners, etc.)
E_Coping_Other	Other types of coping
E_Coping_Partner Relationship	Statements about conflict or problems in intimate relationships
Negative Life Situation	Any negative life situation including those above
Reason for E Use	All stated reasons for E use
Sexual Abuse	Any descriptions of forced sex or early sex
Master Codes for Ecstasy and Sex Risk Analysis	
CE_Ecstasy_ Condom_BfGf	(Ecstasy use, condom use, with boyfriend or girlfriend)
CE_Ecstasy_ Condom_Hetfd	(Ecstasy use, condom use, with heterosexual friend)
CE_Ecstasy_ Condom_HuWi	(Ecstasy use, condom use, with husband or wife)
CE_Ecstasy_ Condom_Smsxfd	(Ecstasy use, condom use, with same-sex friend)
CE_Ecstasy_Het_ Other	(Ecstasy use, condom use, heterosexual other)

(continued)

TABLE 7.4 (*continued*)

CE_Ecstasy_No Condom_BfGf	
CE_Ecstasy_No Condom_Hetfd	
CE_Ecstasy_No Condom_HuWi	
CE_Ecstasy_No Condom_Other	
CE_Ecstasy_No Condom_Smsxfd	
CE_No Ecstasy_ Condom_Bfgf	
CE_No Ecstasy_ Condom_Hetfd	
CE_No Ecstasy_ Condom_HuWi	
CE_No Ecstasy_ Condom_Other	
CE_No Ecstasy_ Condom_Smsxfd	
CE_No Ecstasy_No Condom_BfGf	
CE_No Ecstasy_No Condom_Hetfd	
CE_No Ecstasy_No Condom_HuWi	
CE_No Ecstasy_No Condom_Other	
CE_No Ectsasy_No Condom_Smsxfd	

and other characteristics of the variable and provide space for entering them and part of the variable's definition. The same software will usually generate a printed version of the codebook based on the data entry system, once it is in place.

Survey data codebooks can also include "string variables," or descriptive statements from semi-open-ended questions that can be recoded later into numerate variables. One way to construct a survey codebook is to name the variables and place them beside the questions in the survey instrument. Scale statistics such as alpha coefficients and the items included in the scale also can be included. Using survey instruments as codebooks is a very easy way to provide a description of the survey variables included in a quantitative data set.

Another way to record variables in a survey is to use a variable table. Such a table can be constructed for *every* variable, including demographic variables, or it can be constructed for scales and composite variables only. Table 7.5 shows part of the scale table for a study of youth and hard drug use in Hartford. It is one of a series of materials that record variables, their characteristics, and their composition.

Another, more elaborate way of constructing a variable "codebook" is to create variable tables that include more than the statistical coefficients that show whether the items in the scale work together or not. These more elaborate tables are useful for team research because they also include the syntax (grammar) for constructing the variables. A complex variable table includes the variable name, any other forms of the variable (original, categorical, converted, etc.), the items included in the variable, whether it is a scale or an index or a single item, and how it is constructed in a quantitative analytic software package such as SPSS, Stata, or SAS. Table 7.6 provides an example of such a complex table.

Codebooks are guides to the ways in which researchers have organized, classified, and managed their data. They also are blueprints for understanding the researcher's conceptual pathways. They are thus important even if the researcher is counting tallies by hand. Too many researchers have piles of old data, all well coded but undecipherable because the researcher cannot remember what the codes stand for and has lost the all-important key: the *codebook*.

TEAM ETHNOGRAPHY AND CODING IN TEAMS: DEDUCTIVE, ABDUCTIVE OR RECURSIVE, AND INDUCTIVE CODING

Ethnographic research is still viewed by many as a solitary pursuit. The "lone wolf" ethnographer remains a stereotype, especially when students are required to "go to the field" to conduct and write up their own research. A number of

TABLE 7.5 Scale Table for a Study of Youth and Hard Drug Use ($N = 548$)

Scale (survey item numbers and SPSS variable name)	How Calculated	Alpha	Theoretical Range	Min	Max	Mean	SD	N (if different from 548)
Total Income a.6a–a.6g (**tincome1**)	Sum of individual incomes for all sources	.86	0 → ??	3.00	4000.00	277.78	375.70	482
Multiethnic Identity Measure (a.15a–a.15t) (**meim1**)	Mean of all nonmissing items	.81	1–4	1	3.85	2.92	.37	
Language Preference (a.17a–a.17e) (**lanpref1**)	Mean of all nonmissing items (higher score—more preference for English)	.77	1–5	1	5	3.72	.89	324
Optimism (b.1a–b.1h) (**optim1**)	Mean of all nonmissing items (higher score—higher optimism)	.88	1–4	1.33	4	2.99	.46	
Future Expectation (b.2a–b.2j) (**futor1**)	Mean of all nonmissing items (higher score—higher expectation for future success)	.78	1–4	1.80	4	3.42	.42	
Importance of Family and Friends (b.3a–b.3g) (**impfam1**)	Mean of all nonmissing items (higher score—higher importance)	.90	1–4	1	4	3.39	.52	
Family Loyalty (b.4a–b.4f) (**famloy1**)	Mean of all nonmissing items (higher score—more loyalty among family and friends)	.77	1–4	1	4	2.87	.70	
Connection to Hartford (b.5a–b.5m) (**cityinv1**)	Mean of all nonmissing items (higher score—involved in more civic activities)	.70	1–4	1	3.46	2.11	.47	
Connection to Neighborhood (b.6a–b.6l) (**comminv1**)	Mean of all nonmissing items (higher score—involved in more community activities)	.91	1–4	1	3.92	1.93	.44	
Money to Meet Needs Index (b.12a–b.12m) (**resourc1**)	Sum of all nonmissing items (higher score—had money to meet more basic needs)	.68	0–13	0	13	7.47	3.93	

Variable	Definition	α	Range	Min	Max	Mean	SD	N
Material Possessions Index (b.13a–b.13q) **(poss1)**	Sum of all nonmissing items (higher score—reported more material possessions)	.79	0–17	0	15	5.97	2.77	
Personal Attitudes toward Substance Use (c.1a–c.1i) **(myatt1)**	Mean of all nonmissing items (higher score—more favorable attitudes toward use)	.77	1–4	1	3.89	1.59	.43	
Friend's Use of Substances (c.2a–c.2i) **(fruse1)**	Mean of all nonmissing items (higher score—report more friends who use substances)	.82	1–4	1	4	1.93	.52	
Peer Pressure to Use Substances (c.3a–c.3i) **(pruse1)**	Mean of all nonmissing items (higher score—report more pressure by friends to use)	.75	1–4	1	4	1.40	.48	
Perceived Access to Substances (c.4a–c.4h) **(peracc1)**	Mean of all nonmissing items (higher score—report easier access to substances)	.90	1–4	1	4	2.82	.78	
Frequency of Party Going (d.1a–d.1e) **(club1)**	Mean of all nonmissing items (higher score—report going out more often)	.74	1–6	1	6	2.32	.99	547
Ecstasy Use by Friends (d.4a–d.4f) **(frxtc1)**	Mean of all nonmissing items (higher score—more friends involved with Ecstasy)	.90	1–5	1	4	1.53	.65	536
Dust Use by Friends (d5.a–d.5f) **(frdust1)**	Mean of all nonmissing items (higher score—more friends involved with dust)	.91	1–5	1	4	1.51	.64	536
Club-Going Behavior (d.6a–d.6l) **(clubgo1)**	Mean of all nonmissing items (higher score—more involvement the party "scene")	.88	1–5	1	3.83	2.02	.66	545
Number of Drugs Ever Used Index (e.1a–e.1j) **(drgever1)**	Sum of all drugs ever used on the matrix (higher score—more drugs ever used)	NA	1–11	0	10	3.00	2.11	

(continued)

TABLE 7.5 (continued)

Scale (survey item numbers and SPSS variable name)	How Calculated	Alpha	Theoretical Range	Min	Max	Mean	SD	N (if different from 548)
Number of Drugs Used Past 30 Days Index (e.2a–e.2k) (**drg30d1**)	Sum of all drugs used on the matrix in the past 30 days (higher score—more drugs used in the past 30 days)	NA	1–11	0	10	1.67	1.21	518
Number of Drugs Used to Have Better Sex Index (e.9a–e.9k) (**drgsex1**)	Sum of all drugs ever used for better sex (higher score—more drugs used for better sex)	NA	1–11	0	10	.66	1.14	518
Mean Number of Drugs Intentionally Mixed (e.15a)	Single-item response	NA	0 → ??	0	10	.98	1.47	547
Mean Number of Drugs Used at the Same Time (e.15d)	Single-item response	NA	0 → ??	0	13	1.47	1.62	543
Usefulness for Engaging in Risky Behaviors (f.1a–f.1o) (**userisk1**)	Mean of all nonmissing items (higher score—higher perceived usefulness of engaging in risky behaviors)	.77	1–4	1	3.33	1.48	.37	
Perceived Benefits of Drug Use (f.2a–f.2f) (**drgben1**)	Mean of all nonmissing items (higher score—higher perceived benefits to using drugs)	.87	1–4	1	4	2.27	.72	540
Locus of Control for Drug Use (f.3d, e ,g, h, i) (**loc1**)	Mean of all nonmissing items (higher score—higher 'chance' locus of control for drug use)	.77	1–4	1	3	1.69	.49	541
Self-efficacy for Resisting Temptation to Use Drugs (f.4a–f.4j) (**seftmp1**)	Mean of all nonmissing items (higher score—resistance self-efficacy)	.95	1–4	1	4	2.97	.76	541
Problems Associated with Alcohol Use (f.5a–k) (**probsub1**)	Sum of all nonmissing items (higher score—more problems associated with drug / alcohol use)	NA	0 → ??	0	950	58.30	134.16	545

Variable	Description	α	Range	Min	Max	M	SD	N
Problems Associated with Alcohol Use (dichotomized) (f.5a–k) **(dprsub1)**	Sum of all nonmissing dichotomized items (higher score—more problems associated with drug/alcohol use)	.75	0–11	0	11	2.96	2.5	545
Number of Drugs Ever Shared Index (g.2a–g.2h) **(share1)**	Sum of all drugs shared from the trade/sell/share matrix (higher number—more drugs shared)	NA	0–8	0	8	1.53	1.50	
Number of Drugs Ever Exchanged Index (g.3a–g.3h) **(trade1)**	Sum of all drugs traded from the trade/sell/share matrix (higher number—more drugs traded)	NA	0–8	0	7	.53	1.20	541
Number of Drugs Ever Sold Index (g.4a–g.4h) **(sell1)**	Sum of all drugs sold from the trade/sell/share matrix (higher number—more drugs traded)	NA	0–8	0	8	1.09	1.65	541
Involvement in Legal System Index (h.3c–h.3q) **(legal1)**	Sum of all nonmissing items (higher number—more times in jail or equivalent)	.85	0–15	0	15	3.15	3.26	547
Negative Interactions with Police (h.4a–h.4n) **(police1)**	Mean of all nonmissing items (higher score—more negative encounters with police)	.87	1–4	1	3.86	1.77	.49	547
Victim of Violent Activities Index (h.5a1–h.5a13) **(victim1)**	Sum of all nonmissing items (higher score—victim of more crimes)	.80	0–13	0	12	3.68	3.00	
Perpetrator of Violent Activities Index (h.5b1–h.5b13) **(perpet1)**	Sum of all nonmissing items (higher score—perpetrator of more crimes)	.84	0–12	0	12	3.16	3.06	
Observer of Violent Activities Index (h.5c1–h.5c13) **(observ1)**	Sum of all nonmissing items (higher score—observer of more crimes)	.89	0–11	0	11	8.30	3.21	
Depression (CES-D i.3a–i.3j) **(depress1)**	Sum of all nonmissing items (higher score—more symptoms of depression)	.77	1–30	9	27	17.28	4.12	
Somatic Symptoms Index (i.4a–i.4k) **(somat1)**	Sum of all nonmissing items (higher score—reported more somatic symptoms)	.84	1–33	11	33	17.03	4.38	

(continued)

TABLE 7.5 (continued)

Scale (survey item numbers and SPSS variable name)	How Calculated	Alpha	Theoretical Range	Min	Max	Mean	SD	N (if different from 548)
Mean Age of First Sexual Experience (**j.1**)	Single-item measure	NA	0 → ??	2	21	13.83	2.74	541
Mean Age of First Intercourse (**j.4**)	Single-item measure	NA	0 → ??	2	20	14.48	2.3	530
Protected Sex Ratio (Regular Sex) (j.8a, j.7a) (**vagpsr1**)	Single-item proportion—ratio of the number of protected encounters to number of total regular sex encounters	NA	0 → 1	0	1	.52	.45	496
Protected Sex Ratio (Oral Sex–Penis) (j.8b, j.7b) (**orppsr1**)	Single-item proportion—ratio of the number of protected encounters to number of total oral (penis) sex encounters	NA	0 → 1	0	1	.18	.36	363
Protected Sex Ratio (Oral Sex–Vagina) (j.8c, j.7c) (**orvpsr1**)	Single-item proportion—ratio of the number of protected encounters to number of total oral (vagina) sex encounters	NA	0 → 1	0	1	.08	.26	314
Protected Sex Ratio (Anal Sex) (j.8d, j.7d) (**anpsr1**)	Single-item proportion—ratio of the number of protected encounters to number of total anal sex encounters	NA	0 → 1	0	1	.44	.48	134
Protected Sex Ratio (All Sex) (j.8a–d, j.7a–d) (**allpsr1**)	Single-item proportion—ratio of the number of protected encounters to number of total all sex encounters (all types of sex encounters were summed)	NA	0 → 1	0	1	.40	.39	515
Sexual Experience (Ever) Index (j.9a–j.9p) (**sexexp1**)	Sum of all items (higher score—more sexual experiences reported)	.74	0 → 16	0	13	4.18	2.92	

Variable	Description	α	Range	Min	Max	Mean	SD	N
Sexual Experience (Last 30 days) Index (j.9a–j.9p) (**sex30d1**)	Sum of all dichotomized items (higher score—more sexual experiences in past 30 days reported)	NA	0 → 16	0	11	2.6	2.2	498
Use of Drugs to Improve Sex (j.10a–j.10f–j.10e excluded) (**sxdrg1**)	Mean of all nonmissing items (higher score—use drugs to improve performance more often)	.89	1–4	1	3.4	1.26	.47	545
Sex Life Satisfaction (j.11a,b,d) (**sxsat1**)	Mean of all nonmissing items (higher score—more satisfaction with sex life)	.77	1–4	1	4	3.14	.59	542
STD Symptoms Index (j.12a–j.12g) (**stdsym1**)	Sum of all nonmissing items (higher score—more reported STD-related symptoms)	NA	0–7	0	6	.61	1.05	545
Ever Heard of STD Index (j.14a–j.14k) (**stdhrd1**)	Sum of all nonmissing items (higher score—more STDs heard of)	NA	0–11	0	11	8.02	2.41	
Ever Tested for STD Index (j.15a–j.15k) (**stdtst1**)	Sum of all nonmissing items (higher score—more STDs tested for)	NA	0–11	0	11	4.6	4.02	535
STD Diagnosis Index (j.16a–j.16k) (**stddiag1**)	Sum of all nonmissing items (higher score—more times diagnosed with STD)	NA	0–11	0	5	.38	.79	454
Ever Treated for STD Index (j.17a–j.17k) (**stdtx1**)	Sum of all nonmissing items (higher score—more STDs treated for)	NA	0–11	0	5	.60	.92	284
Perceived Risk for STI/STD's (j.22a–j.22d) (**prisk1**)	Mean of all nonmissing items (higher score—more perceived risk for STIs)	.88	1–4	1	4	1.34	.64	545

TABLE 7.6 Complex Variable Table with Variable Names

Scale/Index Name	Description	Variables Included	Factors, Alpha	Variables Deleted	Final Decision	Variable Name
A	Work-related stress scale (p. 53, 5.12–5.18)	All except 5.13	1 0.6838	5.13	Treat as normal using raw score	scaleA
B	Childhood exposure to alcohol (p.54, 8.1–8.6):	8.1, 2, 3	1	8.4–8.6	Use as index	indexB
C	Social influence to drink (p.54, 8.7–8.10)	All	1	—	Use as index	indexC
D	Alcohol risk access self-efficacy scale (page 55, 9.1–9.4)	9.1–9.4	1	9.5	Use as index	indexD
E	General alcohol expectancies scale (page 55, 9.6–9.19)		2			
	Positive factors	9.6–9.12	Factor 1 0.7622	—	Use as normal, raw score	scaleEP
	Negative factors	9.13–9.19	Factor 2 0.6912	—	Use as normal, square transformation	scaleENz (original: scaleENz)
F	Alcohol and sexual expectancies scale (page 55, 9.20–9.32)	All	1 0.7664	—	Use as normal, raw score	scaleF

popular methodology texts, in fact, discuss only the conduct of ethnography by individuals. However, in reality, much ethnography is carried out in teams. Team ethnography requires a high degree of coordination that is often challenging for people who traditionally have been trained to "do their own work." The best way for ethnographers to work in teams is to become involved in all aspects of the research project from early conceptualization to data collection and analysis. Co-construction of the study model—which can be done (and redone) after a study is funded—is a critical step in making sure that all team members understand the study questions and have worked out the primary questions and the main domains of investigation. There will always be variation in the way individual ethnographers interact in a field setting. Regular discussions, debriefings, trainings, and coordinated efforts at building coding systems and conceptual frameworks in the early stages of analysis are helpful in ensuring the success of team ethnographic ventures (Guest and MacQueen 2008).

Ethnographers working in teams find it useful to begin thinking about a coding system from the outset. And there is no substitute for having team members sit down around a table and work through data together. The first—very preliminary—coding scheme may be the interviewer/observer checklist, which is created to ensure that team members focus on the same informational domains when observing and interviewing. A collection of ten to fifteen observations or interviews is sufficient to initiate the early stages of analysis. This involves reading the materials together, raising questions, speculating/hypothesizing, and identifying primary domains as well as other "interesting" observations in addition to those already flagged as guiding the study. This work can be done with hard copy. One useful technique is to print hard copies of all interviews or observations with line numbering designations. Team members can then use the line numbering to mark blocks of text and to assign preliminary codes. Color coding by theme and by interviewer is also useful. It is easy to skim through hard copy to find text examples that illustrate a topic or code. These excerpts can then be examined, discussed, and compared across researchers to determine whether there is consistency of understanding, classification, and interpretation. ***This step, involving shared understanding of the meaning of the code and how to apply it, is critical to preparation for team coding.***

Key point

One advantage of a computerized text management/ analysis program is that such tasks can be carried out on the same interviews in different program files. The files can be merged to illustrate consistency of classification. For example, a data set can be shared among five people. Each person may be assigned to identify important "quotes" or blocks of text, without coding them. The data sets can be amalgamated, and the collection of quotations can be viewed. When the results are copied and then viewed by all using an LCD projector, the team can discuss the blocked quotations, decide what codes could be applied to them, and begin to devise a coding scheme together. Once the coding scheme has been decided upon, each team member can code two or three interviews or observations in their own file. The files can be amalgamated and the degree of overlap across interviewers assessed to determine interrater reliability. **Interrater reliability** is a measure of consistency across coders in the degree to which they agree on what they code, their choice of code, and how much of the text they select for each code. Of course, interrater reliability can be assessed by comparing hand-coded text as well. The coefficient of reliability or agreement (for example, Cohen's kappa) should be above .90. Interrater reliability is not the only way to ensure accuracy and consistency of coding. Coders who devise the coding scheme together can critique each other's coding practices and arrive at consensus. A study coordinator can review coded texts to assess degree of comparability and flag areas that require closer agreement. This is an effective practice that offers the possibility of feedback and correction throughout the coding process. These processes vary, depending on whether the coding process is deductive, in that the coding scheme has been constructed in advance for application to a database, or abductive, such that the coding scheme emerges in analysis.

Definition: Interrater reliability is a measure of consistency across coders in the degree to which they agree on what they code, their choice of code, and how much of the text they select for each code

Deductive Coding

In the case of deductive coding, where codes are established in advance and coders are hired to apply them, the preparation of coders is straightforward. The researcher provides

- the coding scheme with predetermined categories and definitions,
- examples of earlier applications of the scheme,
- practice in applying the codes to subsets of the new data set or similar data sets, and
- feedback on the accuracy of application.

The sequence of instruction, demonstration, practice, and feedback must continue until coders have reached an appropriate level of precision in terms of accuracy, consistency of application, and agreement with other coders on the use of the scheme.

Cross Reference:
See Book 3, chapter 11, the material below in this chapter, and chapter 8 in this book for information on how to establish intercoder consistency

Abductive or Recursive Coding

Training coders in an *abductive* or *recursive* approach requires that the coders be participants in the research process. First, the coders, who often are members of the study team, review or receive information about the existing scheme, the assumptions underlying the scheme, and the focus of the current work. Then the team works together to apply and modify the existing scheme in the following steps:

- All coders together review data (transcripts, tapes, etc.) and discuss assignment of preexisting codes and inductive generation of new codes. In this phase, the focus of discussion is on the meaning of codes (existing and newly generated), distinctions among codes, boundaries of categories (i.e., what meaning is central to the category, what is peripheral, what is outside of the category—what fits, what does not), and starting to develop exemplars of the category for future reference. This phase continues until there is sufficient clarity to permit coders to work independently.

- The coders work individually with sample data sets and reconvene to compare and discuss coding. In this stage, all coders work with the same data set. The researcher and coders then meet and compare the application of categories across coders, identify points of agreement, and discuss discrepancies in coding. The focus, again, is on clarification of meaning and identification of category boundaries and exemplars. New codes can be added, categories collapsed or expanded, subcategories created, and so on. The purpose is to develop a coding scheme that fits the questions, population, and context of the specific study. In addition, the coding team is developing consistent application and interpretation of the coding scheme, progressing toward intercoder agreement. This process is guided initially by the primary investigator, but all team members participate.

- With practice, the coders become fully fluent in coding and agree consistently. The coding team meets periodically to monitor consistency of application of the abductively derived scheme, and the lead investigator monitors the coding. The team resolves discrepancies together and/or discusses further modifications of the scheme.

Inductive Coding

Developing an *inductive coding* scheme requires that coders be full participants or coresearchers. The process of preparing the coding process and developing the scheme for inductive coding is similar to that for abductive coding but begins with only a rudimentary coding scheme and a study model. In order for coders to participate as collaborators in generating and applying an inductive coding scheme, they first must become familiar with the underpinnings of the work, particularly the purpose of the research, the researcher's theoretical-empirical base and related work, the target culture, its context, and the population/sample. In the ideal situation, coders would have been involved from the beginning in study conceptualization, initiation, and data collection. Steps in inductive coding include the following:

- The coders familiarize themselves with the data by reviewing data sources and related documents.
- The coders generate categories for organizing the data. For example, the research-coding team members individually review data, suggest organizing schemes, and then meet to compare and discuss schemes.
- Through a process of consensus building, the research-coding team generates a scheme to be applied to the data sets. The process of application and refinement is similar to that for abductive coding. The research-coding team members independently code selected data sets, meet to discuss and clarify the meaning and boundaries of codes, and modify the scheme as needed.
- The coders reach a level of expertise that permits independence, seeking consultation with the research team leader and each other as needed.
- The team leader (or principal investigator) continues to monitor the process for consistency among coders and across the data sets.

The preparation of coders varies as a function of one's approach to selecting and developing a coding scheme. At one extreme (deductive coding), coders use a preexisting scheme. It is the research team leader's responsibility to make sure that coders learn to apply the scheme in a consistent and accurate manner. At the other extreme (inductive coding), coders are full participants in the inductive development of a coding scheme and are coresearchers. The abductive approach reflects a blending of these two extremes. How the selection or development of a coding scheme and the preparation of coders is approached depends on the approach to inquiry. In our experience, coders who are members of the research team and who have a deep understanding of the research focus and process and feel ownership of the research process generate more trustworthy (reliable and valid) data.

USING A COMPUTER TO CODE DATA

Computers have made the lives of ethnographers immeasurably easier and often cheaper. Ethnographers who use computers for their data entry and manipulations—and most ethnographers now use computers for virtually all but the most simple of studies—should decide on the software they will use and learn its characteristics and requirements first, *before* they create the kinds of codebooks discussed in this chapter. This is because different software packages require different setups and different kinds of input. Regardless of the software used, the codebooks for instruments such as standardized surveys and interviews and questionnaires should be ordered more or less according to the question order on the instrument. When the codebook is constructed in hard copy, it is a good idea to leave space here and there for addition of variables and codes, just in case the process of analysis generates new options that the researcher thinks are important to consider. Electronic programs will automatically include and print new codes.

It is a good idea to code all numerical data—or data whose codes are numeric—on coding sheets before the data are entered into a computer. It usually is better to use coding sheets than to do direct entry from the instruments or field data itself because mistakes in coding are more difficult to locate in the surveys. The coding sheets also can be a valuable backup if disks or data tapes are destroyed or lost, so they should be saved with the codebook and other valuable data, and coding sheets and hard copy surveys should be kept in separate locations for security. Ethnographers should verify coding by outputting text associated with codes to check their consistency before conducting more elaborate analyses. They should also verify survey data entry by running frequencies to evaluate the data for accuracy of input before continuing with steps in data analysis.

SUMMARY

The preceding chapters have spelled out how researchers move from raw data to chunked data. In this chapter, we have taken the analytic process one step further by describing the cognitive processes researchers use to create codes for various kinds of data and how they use those codes to crunch the multiple kinds of data customarily collected in ethnographic research. In the subsequent chapters of this book, we describe how to use computers in the organization and analysis of data and then discuss how crunched data are assembled into more complete portrayals of cultural phenomena, complete with explanations of their meaning, as well as why these, and not other, portrayals have emerged.

8 ❧─◆─◆─◆─❧

MANAGING QUALITATIVE AND QUANTITATIVE DATA WITH COMPUTERS

Up to this point, we have been discussing generic ways of organizing and managing text and numerical data. We have not, however, addressed specific strategies for managing the enormous masses of data compiled in ethnographic studies. We also have not talked in detail about the specific kinds of quantitative data that ethnographers use in the many surveys they conduct. We address these issues in this chapter, first by discussing the use of computers in ethnography. Then, in this chapter and chapter 9, we review the primary ways of organizing, managing, and analyzing quantitative data collected through ethnographic surveys.

HOW COMPUTERS FACILITATE THE ORGANIZATION AND STORAGE OF TEXT DATA

As mentioned in the previous chapter, computers can make an ethnographer's life much easier. Below, we list some of the principal ways that computers can assist in the organization and analysis of qualitative data.

TASKS COMPUTERS CAN PERFORM FOR RESEARCHERS

- Produce copies of raw data
- Collate or partition data files or documents
- Store "head notes," memos, and researcher musings in a separate document file
- Store and organize photographs, videos, and records of material archives
- Search for words or phrases in interviews, field notes, and other data documents and retrieve text portions that include those words or phrases
- Attach identification labels to prestructured units of text, such as responses to a questionnaire, and then sort the data by each label
- Divide data into researcher-determined or naturally occurring language analysis units, such as sentences or paragraphs
- Help in preliminary coding prior to the creation of a more refined classification system
- Sort, collate, and print out coded data segments (or units of analysis) into preliminary categories to facilitate their comparison and refinement into a more developed classificatory scheme
- Insert researcher-developed codes into data files or memos as the researcher reads through data
- Enter final codes into data and then sort, assemble, and print out data segments (or units of analysis) according to the researcher's categories
- Count the frequency of coded segments or units in each category
- Identify coded data segments as relevant to two or more categories, which helps researchers discover linkages and associations between and among coding categories
- Count the frequency of co-occurrence of segments or units in two or more categories

- Retrieve coded data segments or units from subsets of data—for example, "females only"—in preparation for contrasting them with other subsets
- Search for and identify segments in the data that appear in a certain sequence, such as chronological sequence
- Search for groups of related codes within data files in preparation for exploring linkages among the categories
- Create graphic displays of hierarchical or temporal relationships between and among categories of data
- Transfer data segments in the form of quotations into research reports (from Tesch, in LeCompte and Preissle 1993, 280–81)

Computer-assisted data analysis software for qualitative data also can do the following:

- Conduct content analysis of publication reports and media to identify themes and word frequencies and represent them graphically
- Carry out analysis of text data in email messages, blogs, and free text archives
- Index and describe publications, conference papers, abstracts, and other collections of written materials
- Facilitate analysis of elicitation data collected for cultural consensus analysis
- Conduct spatial analysis

Prior to the existence of relatively inexpensive and powerful desktop and laptop computers, all of the above tasks had to be performed by hand or by clumsy means such as using carbon paper, scissors, tape, and glue or by large university or commercial computers using punched cards. This made data organization and analysis inefficient and very time consuming. Even though it now is much easier, using computers is not an entirely simple matter. Researchers must decide whether it is worthwhile to utilize a computer program for the management of text data and determine which kind of program they will find most useful. Four important considerations in this decision are:

1. *How much data will be collected.* Using a computer to code a database with fewer than one hundred pages of text data or fewer than twenty interviews probably is not worthwhile because coding it with a computer would require too much time.

2. *Whether codes can be entered directly into the text or whether the text will be coded later.* Entering codes directly into the text so that they can be found later using search commands requires that the coding system be fully developed in advance. Entering the codes later gives researchers latitude to allow the final coding system to evolve from the data. Entering codes directly into the text is very inefficient and, therefore, usually never done.

3. *Whether qualitative and quantitative data should be integrated in the same data set.* Some software programs allow researchers to integrate SPSS files with text files, convert text-based categorical or continuous variable data to Excel or SPSS files, and include spatial and network data. For researchers who are interested in collecting different kinds of data on the same topic, these programs can be very helpful.

4. *Whether audiovisual data will be incorporated into the data set and coded.* Until recently, it was not possible to combine audio and visual data with text data in desktop or laptop computer hardware-software configurations. Now new programs enable researchers to code audio and video data on the screen and to search text, audio, and video databases simultaneously for coded segments. Like text-only computer software, they organize the segments into a single file that researchers can then scan, organize, analyze, and interpret.

WHAT COMPUTERS CANNOT DO

It is important for novice ethnographers to remember that though some computer programs may code data automatically, they do not do it well, and by themselves, they *cannot* analyze data—though they may include various tools that facilitate analysis. Computer programs are designed to help expedite these operations when researchers are working with moderate to large bodies of text or visual data. *The process of coding, retrieving, and subsequently mulling over and making sense of data remains a laborious process* completely controlled *by researchers.* Computers cannot do this. Even if a computer is used, researchers still must go through the process of computer coding each bit of text or other material as they read through their interviews and field notes. *Computers are only extremely fast at labeling, organizing, and managing codes, retrieving and viewing blocks of text, and assisting in comparative exercises. Researchers must remember that only* they can "tell" or *program the computer to retrieve and count data in specific ways*; the machines do not do it automatically. Fortunately, a number of computer programs now exist that make this process relatively straightforward—always, of course, under the direction of the researcher! One early discussion of such computer programs can be found in Renata Tesch's chapter in LeCompte and Preissle's text, *Ethnography and Qualitative Design in Educational Research* (1993). A thorough review of computer programs for analysis of qualitative data as well as good suggestions for ways of proceeding with data analysis can be found in Weitzman and Miles (1995), *Computer Programs for Qualitative Data Analysis*. In addition, there are many websites and listserves to help researchers assess which software packages to purchase and what steps to take to analyze their data using computer software.

Key point

Key point

USING COMPUTERS TO CODE, MANAGE, AND ANALYZE QUALITATIVE TEXT DATA

Most text-based computer coding and analysis programs include a variety of different functions that make the job of developing codes, applying them, and manipulating

them relatively easy. All of them require careful preparation and organization of the data set or sets to be analyzed.

 Key point *It is critical that coding be carried out thoroughly and systematically so that the operations performed on the data
are truly representative of the complete data set.* It does
take time and concentration to code the complete qualitative data set, even if only a few codes are applied, but it is
well worthwhile to do so. Later on, as researchers become
involved in analysis of the data, they will find that computerized and coded qualitative data sets are less than useful if
they are only partially or incompletely coded.

There are three main types of text-based computer-
based software: "code and retrieve" programs, code-based
theory-building software, and text retriever–text manager
programs. Code and retrieve software programs allow
researchers to code and retrieve blocks of text, facilitate the
discovery of variables and items for survey research, and
help to identify themes within factors and domains. EZ-
Text (freeware downloadable from the CDC), for example,
is meant specifically for focus group or other forms of
simple, semistructured data sets. Inputs for EZ-Text are
organized by question, and data input consists of respondents' answers to each question. Responses to questions
are "output" or retrieved, reviewed, compared, contrasted,
and discussed in terms of dominant and secondary themes
and subthemes. Most programs, however, include and go
beyond simple search-and-retrieve capacity.

Code-based theory-building software and text retriever–
text management programs serve different research purposes. Code-based theory-building software offers the primary functions most useful for the interactive development
of social science theory and interpretation using a qualitative
data set. They allow for coding data at levels ranging from
specific to abstract, extraction, searching, and various types
of writing that facilitate interpretation. In addition, they offer
the ability to explore associations among variables, to merge
variables or concepts into higher-order themes and patterns,
to identify items for surveys or description, to quantify data,
and to explore data visually.

Text retrievers and text-based managers are useful for
searching for trends and themes in very large amounts of

text data—for example, in media, archival, or Internet content analysis. They offer ways of searching for words and word sequences, word frequencies, word lists, indexing, and key word and key phrase searches and are able to consider word associations, proximity plots, and quantitative displays. Researchers interested in semantic analysis may find such programs very useful. For the most part, though, ethnographers seldom use these programs, but researchers interested in semantic analysis and quantitative identification of thematic meanings identified through word associations may find them useful.

Lewins and Silver (2004) describe several basic functions of code-based theory-building software. These include:

- The "structure" of work. This refers to the way the program organizes and provides links to the data files. Data files may be located inside or external to the program unit. Where data files are located determines how data can become portable and shared with others. Table 8.1 shows the content of a print screen, displaying how all the data and files for a study of the drug MDMA was stored for use on a computer.
- Interactivity with the data. All programs offer instant access to all data files and analysis functions.
- Text searching. Most programs offer the ability to search the data for key concepts, words, and word strings. This capacity permits rapid perusal of themes reflected in the vocabulary of the text data as well as presence/absence of specific behaviors, statuses, and so on. For example, a text search using the combination word "pregnant/pregnancy/fertility/child/children/baby" would allow a researcher to review a set of interviews to identify in short order those women who were pregnant and then search their ideas about pregnancy, history of pregnancies, and information about fertility history and health of their babies.
- Code and retrieve functions. These include easy coding or text blocking and a variety of ways of

TABLE 8.1 Example of a Computer Data File: MDMA Study

Directory 1:	Biannual reports and continuation grant
Directory 2:	Focus Groups—Community experts
Directory 3:	Focus group materials—forms and consents
Directory 4:	Focus group notes
Directory 5:	Focus group interview log
Directory 6:	Community expert—forms and consents
Directory 7:	Community expert interviews and notes
Directory 8:	In-depth interviews—materials, forms, and consents
Directory 9:	In-depth interviews notes and transcription logs
Directory 10:	MDMA field notes
Directory 11:	Pilesorts
Directory 13:	Guidelines for fieldwork
Directory 14:	Literature and literature reviews
Directory 15:	SPSS data
Directory 16:	Study papers and associated materials

extracting and outputting blocks of text for specific codes or code interactions.

- Project management and data organization functions. These organize and store data sets for analysis and offer options for creating subsets, organizing and reorganizing data (documents, codes, quotations, and other writing) to facilitate analysis on an ongoing basis.
- Writing capacity. All programs offer ways of writing about the data on an ongoing basis through memos, comments, and other additions. These facilitate analysis and communication with other members of a research team.
- Querying and recording capacity. This includes ways of examining and recording the intersection of codes, both descriptively and analytically/theoretically.
- Output. Programs offer multiple types of output, including lists, comments, codes, textual extracts, combinations of codes, codes/comments, memos, spreadsheets, and quantitative data files.

Most code-based theory-building software programs include the following specific components that reflect the general functions described above:

- A software unit in which the data are kept along with some forms of preliminary analysis that is named. (For example: "SLT_KI_Interviews_final" would refer to "smokeless tobacco key informant interviews final version.") In ATLAS.ti, this is referred to as the Hermeneutic Unit.

- A location in the unit where the "primary" documents, videos, photographs, and other materials that constitute the basis for analysis are stored. Each document is assigned its own ID number and stored in a location standardized so that all computers using the software can access it using the same configuration. Usually, though not always, this is the "C" drive, which is standard in all desktop and laptop computers.

- A location where all bits of text or blocked sections of videos and such are stored. These may be coded using a standardized coding system or simply identified as important and labeled with a general description for future reference.

- A location where codes and code definitions are stored. Computer programs make it easy to create (and to delete, rename, differentiate, and merge) codes in the process of coding. Every code that is created should be defined and only those codes kept that constitute the study's primary coding scheme. We recommend working with no more than thirty to forty codes.

- A location where memos can be stored that contain researchers' thoughts and ideas about what themes, patterns, and other associated ideas are emerging in the data as they code. These memos can be shared, printed, compared, combined, and used for higher-level analysis and interpretation later on.

- Ways of writing comments that can be associated with specific blocks of text, a document, or the entire archive.

- One or more means of searching the database for specific coded blocks of text or interacting codes, which can then be printed and compared.

- A variety of ways of counting dimensions of the data, for example, word counts, code counts, and case counts (the number of cases or primary documents that are labeled and described (e.g., by age, marital status, whether or not they use a particular drug, whether teacher and student have an exchange of ideas or not).
- Ways of organizing codes and documents that facilitate comparison. For example, documents can be organized into comparative categories (pregnant or not pregnant; in-school event versus out-of-school event). Codes can be organized into groups or "families" or factors, which can be used for within and across-code comparisons within the factor.
- A filtering mechanism, similar to that in quantitative data analysis programs, that allows researchers to select specific groupings of cases or examples, or groupings of codes (variables) for consideration/comparison; for example, in a study of situations in which women use tobacco, the filtering facility allows for the selection of the codes associated with *one* factor (stress) for PREGNANT WOMEN only, or to filter for stress, but not cause of stress, so as to examine differences in experiences of stress in both pregnant and nonpregnant women.

Cross Reference:
See Books 1, 2, and 3 and chapters 9 and 10 in this book for discussions of how to identify and construct such groups or factors

Some programs have additional, very useful functions that make it easier to understand how and how often different codes interact in the data. One program, for example, shows the intersection of each code with all others with which it is cross-coded in the data. This function helps in seeing what codes appear together and how frequently and to generate hypotheses. It also takes readers back to each of the citations or blocks of text where the two codes appear together so that their intersection can be viewed, understood, and interpreted. A similar function shows the presence or absence of all codes in each "case" (for example, a person, organization, observation, site, or document). This allows readers to select only those cases for comparison and analysis where specific configurations of codes appear.

Another useful function available in most text software programs is the word count. This function produces counts of the frequency of words in the data set and will output the data in matrices. Categories of words (for example, all words referring to mental health problems, or types or names of tobacco, or leisure time activities) can be identified, extracted, and classified to give a broad idea of how these topics are reflected in the data set.

Most text software programs will output codes into Excel or SPSS. The outputs generally consist of a matrix that includes the ID numbers of the "cases" in the data sets against the frequency of a selected code in the case. For example, in a data set on interviews about smokeless tobacco and reproductive health, the code "reason for use-tooth pain" may appear five times in one case and once in another. Each of these consists of selected coded variables. Standardization of "reason for use-tooth pain" as a categorical (presence/absence) variable rather than a code count is required before that variable can be used in an Excel or SPSS analysis. Researchers must have good reasons to perform the transformations necessary to make a data set ready for descriptive quantitative analysis, as it is quite time consuming and may produce no more insights than a qualitative examination of the way the same variables configure or pattern across cases.

SELECTING DATA ENTRY AND ANALYSIS HARDWARE AND SOFTWARE

Once upon a time, a calculator and a pad of columnar or ledger sheets sufficed as tools for analysis of most data. They still might be good resources when researchers need to conduct analyses rapidly, have small databases, and, as often happens, are far from computing resources. Most of the time, however, we recommend that all survey data and large data sets consisting of numerical data collected through structured (precoded and enumerated) observations be computer analyzed.

Many quantitative software packages exist to help new and experienced data analysts. The most popular desktop software packages are SAS (Statistical Analysis Software) and SPSS. Both universities and nonprofit organizations prefer to use SPSS (Statistical Package for the Social Sciences) for desktop or portable computers because it is readily accessible, menu driven, and less expensive than SAS. Both packages are sold on the basis of **site licensing**. Epi Info, a data analysis software package developed in association with the World Health Organization, is used by epidemiologists and researchers in other disciplines, especially in the developing world. It can be downloaded and is free. There also are simple data analysis packages appropriate for novices, teenagers, or younger children.

Definition: Site licensing refers to the purchase of a software program for desktop computer use at an initial cost per person and an annual registration fee

A statistical software package allows researchers to enter data or import it from other data management programs such as Excel or Access, perform transformations on variables, use a variety of different statistical procedures, demonstrate results in different visual formats, and prepare and print reports. Graphic results from the two packages mentioned above can be transported into word-processing software such as Word and WordPerfect or directly into presentation software such as PowerPoint.

Electronic data can now be tailored for use with ethnographic survey (precoded quantitative) data using electronic data entry hardware and software. However, high-powered desktop computers with good memory and storage capacity, a high-resolution scanner, and software for creating data entry forms specific to each study's survey instrument are needed for such purposes. Data are collected and coded using these forms. When scanned, the data on the forms are entered directly into statistical software databases, which must be conceptualized and prepared in advance.

Hardware and software for desktop electronic data entry currently are still quite expensive, although they are priced to be purchased by university departments and centers and larger nonprofit organizations. Some data entry software is available free of charge. Free or not, it still takes some time to create data entry forms that can be scanned and read accurately into data analysis software. Once the form is created, however, the entry process is swift and efficient. Those who once entered data by hand can then spend their valuable time correcting any entry errors and cleaning data. The microcomputer electronic data entry market also has high appeal for ethnographers who are conducting surveys with large (over four hundred) sample sizes because it is efficient and accurate.

DEVELOPING A DATA ENTRY SYSTEM

Electronic data entry requires the creation of a coding system along with the survey instrument because data are scanned or entered directly from the instrument into a database. Though all variables are quantified in a survey, they are not necessarily precoded. That is to say, the variables in the survey are not given names and defined—as were the variables described in Tables 7.2 and 7.4 in the previous chapter. Thus, the first step in organizing ethnographic survey data is the development of a coding system that establishes and defines the basic set of variables that constitute the database. Novice researchers, in particular, usually create surveys without defining and naming most of the variables for analysis in advance. This is a mistake, because in so doing, they create for themselves a very big job later on, once their surveys are administered and collected.

As we have demonstrated in chapter 7, the best way to create a codebook is to imagine what it will look like as the questionnaire with which it will be used is being constructed. The coding system generally follows the questionnaire sequence. It is important to remember that questions in a questionnaire do not always translate directly into single variables. Some "questions" may include multiple variables, for example, when they are composed of a list of "yes/no" responses or a set of Likert scales. In such instances, each response is represented by a separate variable in the codebook. The codebook may be enhanced later by amalgamating these responses into composite variables or scales and naming and describing them briefly. The survey instrument thus can be transformed into a codebook or guide to variables in the SPSS or SAS file. Steps in developing a codebook for quantitative data are similar to those listed for qualitative data in chapter 7.

ENTERING DATA

Depending on the scope of the project, size of data entry staff, and time constraints, data can be entered by the research staff or by employees of data entry firms. Survey data can be keyed in by hand or read electronically. If data are entered by hand, they should be double-entered or checked to ensure accuracy. It is increasingly common to use computer-assisted data entry (QDA). QDA computer programs facilitate data entry in the field as well as in the "office." Survey questions and response alternatives can be preprogrammed into handheld or desktop computers and data entered by researchers or the respondents themselves, especially if the program has an audio component in which the questions are read to the respondent as the respondent enters the data on the computer screen. QDA involves initial costs to purchase the equipment and program the software, but it has the dual advantage of self-correction. It thus avoids incorrect responses, and it downloads data into an SPSS, Excel, or SAS file, thereby avoiding the tedious and often inaccurate job of data entry.

In studies carried out across sites, data are usually entered in one central location and shared with other sites. Regardless of who enters the data, the process should be overseen by a data manager, who must provide quality control over the entire process. Not only must the data manager arrange for the data entry to be done by competent individuals, he or she also must:

- review the completed instruments to make sure that each instrument is filled out completely, that the data are coded correctly, and that there are no missing data;
- send incomplete instruments back for review and completion;
- make copies of all completed instruments prior to data entry, because accidents can happen and data can be lost; and
- run frequencies on all data regularly as the data are being entered to make sure that there are no inap-

propriate entries (entries outside the appropriate numerical range) and to assess how much missing data there might be.

CONSTRUCTING NEW VARIABLES

Researchers entering data will do so from a codebook that has been created as described in the previous chapters and translated into an SPSS, SAS, or other quantitative data entry system. However, researchers rarely work only with the responses to items in the ethnographic survey. Instead, they transform these variables for purposes of data reduction, analysis, and more effective representation, or even for new analyses later on. The following example illustrates how new variables can be created from existing ones.

EXAMPLE 8.1

TRANSFORMING ONE VARIABLE INTO ANOTHER THROUGH RECODING

Table 8.2 illustrates the age range of youth in a youth program of the Institute for Community Research. This table produces a curve skewed toward older youth, as illustrated in Figure 8.1.

TABLE 8.2 Age Range in a Youth Group

		Frequency	Percent	Valid Percent	Cumulative Percent
Valid	13	8	10.4	10.4	10.4
	14	2	2.6	2.8	13.2
	15	5	6.5	6.7	19.9
	16	8	10.4	10.2	30.1
	17	4	5.2	5.4	35.5
	18	22	28.6	28.8	64.3
	19	16	19.5	19.7	84.0
	20	12	15.6	15.1	99.9
	Total	77	100.0	100.0	100.0

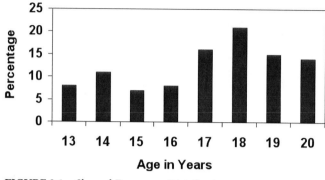

FIGURE 8.1   Skewed Frequency Distribution

For some analyses, it may be better to reconstruct age as a nominal variable, recoded into two categories. Figure 8.2 recodes age into two categories, ages seventeen or below and ages eighteen or above, coded as "0" or "1."

The histogram in Figure 8.3 is more "normal" than the one in Figure 8.1; that is, the distribution of the two categories is roughly equal. It displays a normal curve (evenly distributed data) for a continuous variable, age, from twelve years to twenty years.

Combining, collapsing, and transforming variables facilitates a more efficient, and often more accurate, display of the data. Other reasons for creating new variables include:

- creation of scales and indices, for example, scales that rank order or count the number of correct answers to AIDS knowledge questions;
- clustering variables (see the section on factor analysis below); and
- combining two variables to create a new variable, for example, subtracting "respondent's ideal age at first sex" from "reported age at first sex" to yield a new variable called "discordance between real versus ideal age at first sex."

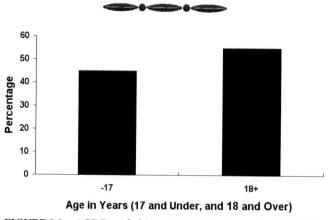

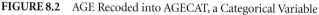

FIGURE 8.2   AGE Recoded into AGECAT, a Categorical Variable

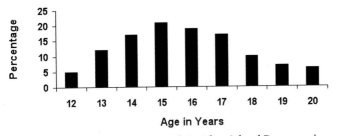

FIGURE 8.3 Normal Curve: Youth in After-School Programs in Hartford

Another example from data on young women in the Mauritian workforce demonstrates the utility of combining two or more variables into a third. The procedure involved subtracting the age of the respondent from number of years worked in the industrial sector. This created a new variable, "age of entering the industrial workforce." By creating this new variable, we were able to discover that 13 percent of the sample had entered the workforce prior to fifteen years of age, the legal age for entry into the workforce. This new variable, then, raised interesting policy questions regarding the degree to which child labor regulations were being observed; it also highlighted how very young workers were at risk of being exposed to sexual activity.

We estimate that in a typical ethnographic survey data set, many variables in the original data set eventually will be transformed into new variables for analysis. It is important to label and define new categories and keep comprehensive notes on the construction of the new variables. If this is not done, the database will become clogged with a number of potentially useful variables rendered useless because no one can remember how they were constructed or defined.

DEVELOPING THE STRUCTURE FOR A QUANTITATIVE DATABASE

Quantitative databases are basically of two types:

a. *Simple databases*, sometimes called "flat files," which consist of a matrix with "cases" vertically arrayed along the side (persons or other units) and variables horizontally arrayed across the top. Most databases created by ethnographers working with **cross-sectional survey data** will be of

Definition: Cross-sectional refers to data collected at one point in time only

this type. Cross-sectional data is that which is collected for only one point in time.

b. *Relational databases*, which consist of multiple databases linked to each other by a common identifier. For example, spatial analysis usually involves overlaying different types of data (for example, crime rates, income, population age, physical and geographic features, education level, number of toxic waste sites, etc.). One file includes the computerized spatial boundaries of the units to be compared in the spatial analysis (for example, census tracts or neighborhoods). Each neighborhood is assigned an identifier, for example, 001, 002, and 003. Crime rates, income, education level, and toxic waste sites are separate databases that contain data on these topics for each of the neighborhoods. The databases are linked by neighborhood identifiers; for example, the crime rate for neighborhood 001 will be stored along with the neighborhood designator. The same applies to the other sources of data. In this way, data on each neighborhood in each related database is linked by neighborhood identifier and can be called up in spatial analysis software to compare neighborhood variation and interactions among variables across neighborhoods. Relational databases allow different "levels" or types of data to be kept and analyzed separately. Sections of each data set consisting of groupings of variables can be selected later, along with the unique identifier, and joined with each other to form new databases. Longitudinal studies, which collect the same data at two points in time, often are kept in this way. For example, a study of adolescents in a participatory action research-based intervention study at the Institute for Community Research tracked participants over three time points. The data for the sample of ninety teens were kept in a relational database in which each teen had the same linking identifier. The data for each time point were kept in separate databases but linked for the final analysis to identify changes in individual and group outcomes (e.g., patterns of substance use) over time. Network data also can be kept in this way. Network research calls for collecting information about the individuals in one person's network. Network data sets often are very large. When demographic, household, and psychosocial data are collected on an individual as well as network data, a flat file could be enormous and

 Cross Reference:
See Book 4, chapter 5 on types of network data and examples of data collection matrices

time consuming to manage. Thus, it is efficient to organize the network data collected from each individual in the study into a separate file. This allows the network data to be analyzed separately, consolidated or "crunched," and then linked to the index person's demographic/household database.

It is important to make decisions as to which type of database will be needed for a study early in the process of conceptualizing the database. This is because the type of database will affect the number of sub- or smaller related databases that must be established, the mechanisms through which they should be related, and the software that will be most useful in establishing and connecting them. For anything more than a flat file, a relational database management system such as Access is much more efficient because it allows data from two or more linked data sets to be extracted and merged much more easily. We refer readers to the manual for the Statistical Package for the Social Sciences (SPSS) for more information on conceptualizing and constructing databases.

As noted, using an electronic data entry system requires setting up electronic data entry forms. These forms follow the format and content of the questionnaire, providing boxes for data codes. Some scanning programs read numbers only; others have the capacity to read script. It is important to make sure that data entry personnel using electronic forms to record their data have been trained to do so carefully so that scanners can read their entries accurately.

Once data are entered, the data manager should make several backup copies of the original data set. These should be kept in separate locations, in locked cabinets for safety reasons. Nothing is worse than losing a data set. Raw data should always be stored and kept until a study has come to an official end. Some researchers follow the seven-year rule, keeping their raw data stored for at least that length of time before destroying it.

DATA MANAGEMENT

Data cleaning and tidying up, which we describe in detail in chapter 3 of this book and in Book 3, is required for effective quantitative data analysis and management. We have noted the tasks that the data manager must complete to make sure that instruments have been completely and correctly filled out.

Cleaning Up by Producing Frequencies

 Definition:
A frequency distribution shows the number and percentage of cases responding to each of the attributes or descriptors for a variable and the number of cases that are missing a response for that variable

 Definition:
A quantitative outlier is an entry whose value is less than or more than the proper range for that variable

Once data are cleaned, the first step in data crunching is to produce **frequency distributions**. A frequency distribution shows the number and percentage of cases responding to each of the attributes or descriptors for a variable and the number of cases that are missing a response for that variable. For the purpose of identifying problems with individual cases or the data set, frequency distributions should be produced regularly during the time the data are being entered. Producing frequencies assures that data are entered accurately and there are no unusual **outliers**. For example, entries of 4, 5, and 7 would be outliers for the variable "sex," in which 1 = male and 2 = female; any other option would not make sense. Where there are unexpected numbers or where the distribution of a variable does not look right (for example, it does not conform to known characteristics of a population or is skewed or biased in an unexpected direction), it is important to return to the raw data to see whether there are mistakes in data entry or, if necessary, to return to the original questionnaires. Computerized and electronic data entry systems help to save time at this stage because they set limits to the range of numbers that can be entered for any given variable. Thus, it is impossible for data entry personnel to enter a code that does not fall into the range of acceptable responses for variables.

Outliers can be eliminated from the variable descriptors by recoding them as missing data or "other"; or the variable can be redefined to incorporate the outlier in some reasonable manner. For example, in a data set on injection drug users, two individuals who self-reported as injecting over 250 times a month were viewed as outliers and removed. Furthermore, the questionnaires for these cases were reviewed to see whether they produced outliers on other variables. If a case demonstrates a number of outliers, the data may be incorrectly reported or recorded, or the case may be unusual, warranting a review of the original data and treatment as an example of an extreme case. It is also possible to adjust for outliers by normalizing a distribution through log transformations. Figure 8.3, "Youth in After-School Programs in Hartford," is an illustration of a normal curve.

As we have discussed in other books in this series, ethnographic surveys are based on both random and systematic sampling procedures. As such, assumptions can be made about what should be the proper shape of the curve in such a population. The production of a non-normal curve in a randomly sampled population may have to do with the characteristics of that population (e.g., what kind of adolescents were included, and excluded, from the population). Producing frequency distributions can illuminate whether there are problems or unusual skewing. Once the reasons for the skewing have been discovered, decisions must be made regarding whether **parametric** or **nonparametric statistics** should be used for analytical purposes. Parametric statistics are those procedures that can be used to show relationships among variables in a random sample. Nonparametric statistics can be used with nonrandom samples. Parametric statistics require impeccably drawn random samples, which, as we note in Book 3, are difficult to create in many field situations because the requirements for constructing them appropriately cannot be met, including the existence of normal distributions of characteristics within the population. With nonrandom samples, however, nonparametric statistics can be used. Nonparametric statistical techniques parallel parametric statistical techniques; they permit researchers to consider relationships among variables in nonrandomly selected samples. We will explain this distinction further in the last section of this chapter and refer readers to introductory statistics texts for more advanced discussion of these issues.

Cross Reference:
See Book 1, chapter 5 and Book 3 on sampling

Cross Reference:
See Book 1, chapter 5 for a discussion of research designs, units of analysis, population selection, and sampling, and Book 3, chapter 10 for discussions of random and systematic sampling

Definition:
Parametric statistics are those procedures that can be used to show relationships among variables in a random sample. Nonparametric statistics can be used with nonrandom samples

CONSOLIDATING QUANTITATIVE DATA (DATA REDUCTION OR "CRUNCHING")

Ethnographers tend to collect large amounts of survey data because they are interested in seeing the way in which many social, cultural, or environmental factors influence individual behavior or beliefs. This produces a large number of variables. Ethnographers are not unique in this preference, however. Multivariable epidemiological surveys, panel studies, national surveys, and cross-site studies with many cases often produce very large data sets. Just as we consolidate or crunch text data to reduce pages of field notes to a manageable number of concepts, we can also engage in reduction of quantitative data into a more manageable data set that may show relationships more clearly. There are several common procedures used in the social sciences for consolidating quantitative data. These are:

- constructing indices;
- constructing scales;
- creating Guttman scales; and
- using factor analysis.

All of these are ways of combining several related indicators into a composite variable.

Constructing Indices and Scales

Indices and scales are similar to one another in that they order people or other units into a sequence with respect to the selected variable. For example, a material style of life scale that includes seven items (rent/own home, mud/cinderblock walls, thatched/tin roof, garden plot/no plot, presence/absence of electricity, presence/absence of piped running water, presence/absence inside bathroom) yields a score of 0–6. As composite variables, indices and scales can often provide a better or broader range of variation than a single variable that may range from 0 to 1 (yes, no) to 1 to 5 (a five-point Likert scale). Furthermore, indices can sometimes give a better or more comprehensive indication of a variable than a single item. When added together, the material style of life items listed above give a better indication of material wealth than, for example, information about rental or home ownership alone.

 Definition: An index is created by summing the scores of two or more variables in a set

An **index** is constructed simply by adding up scores assigned to attributes or indicators in a related set of variables into a total score. The index range is from the lowest to highest possible score. Each attribute in an index has equal weight in relation to the others. To construct an index from the items in the material style of life listing above, an ethnographer would assign 1 to the presence of each item and add the total. Table 8.3 displays overall ranked frequencies, and the number and percentage of people who have from 1–8 items.

Indices can also be composed of summed Likert scales. Likert scales range from three to five points. All the subscales or items in an index composed of summed Likert scales should have the same number of points (three, four, or five

TABLE 8.3   Items in the Material Style of Life Index for Sri Lanka

Items	% of the Population Possessing Them (N = 615)
Wall clock	94
Electricity	84
Television	83
Sewing machine	74
Bicycle	50
Motorbike	23
Car	14.7
Telephone	8.8

Material Style of Life Index for Sri Lanka: Ranking Frequencies (Ranks range from 0 to 8 items)				
Ranking	Frequency	Percentage	Valid %	Cum. %
(0–8 items)				
0.00	11	1.8	1.8	1.8
1.00	21	3.4	3.4	5.2
2.00	56	9.1	9.1	14.3
3.00	98	15.9	15.9	30.2
4.00	196	31.9	31.9	62.1
5.00	115	18.7	18.7	80.8
6.00	69	11.2	11.2	92.0
7.00	30	4.9	4.9	96.9
8.00	19	3.1	3.1	100.0

This index approximates a bell-shaped curve in which the median, the mean, and the mode overlap.

points). An index composed of five related three-point Likert scales would have a range of scores from 3 to 15. Indices are used more frequently than scales because they are easier to construct from the available data. But the construction of a good index is not always easy. The most important things to keep in mind in constructing an index are the following:

- The items in an index must have face or logical validity. They must logically be indicators of the concept indicated by the variable. The indicators in the material style of life index are material items. Although these material items are probably purchased with cash, cash income is not an indicator of material style of life because this scale concerns material items, not available cash resources.

- The index must be unidimensional. The items in the index or scale all must relate to the same domain. An index of drug use risk behavior, for example, should not include items related to sex risk, even though risky drug use may be associated with risky or unprotected sexual behaviors. The variable should be clearly defined so as to avoid including in the index irrelevant or tangentially associated indicators.

- The items should demonstrate variability. If everyone answers an item in the same way (either yes or no), there will be no variance, and the item will not add anything to the index. An item can be selected if responses are split equally (50 percent/50 percent or in equal thirds if it is a three-point Likert scale) or if items differ in amount of variance (some may be split equally and some unequally).

- **Bivariate and multivariate relationships** among items should be established. Items in an index should be associated with one another using percentages or correlation coefficients, but the relationship should not be perfect. If there is a perfect relationship between two items, one can assume that both are indicators of the same thing and can stand in for each other in an index. This is important, because redundant items unnecessarily increase survey length, which is undesirable. It is important to

 Definition: Bivariate refers to displaying the relationship of one variable to another in a two-by-two table. Multivariate refers to the relationship of two or more variables to a third variable

examine the relationships among all the items in an index, first one by one and then together, since two items may relate to each other but one of them may not relate to a third.

■ A way must be found to handle **missing data**. Missing data can be handled by eliminating the case or inserting a value based on judging the general pattern of response for the total sample or the pattern of response for the individual. For example, an individual may only check items with "yes" responses, leaving some items blank. Researchers could then erroneously assume that the blanks really meant "no" responses.

> **Definition:**
> Missing data refers to missing responses to a question

By considering the relationships of the responses "don't know" to "no" or "yes" with other variables, it may be possible to impute or attribute a value to "don't know." For example, if both relate in the same way to two other important variables, they may be considered similar; in such instances, "don't know" can be recoded as "no" for the purposes of further data analysis. Missing data can also be inserted as proportional by assigning the mean or assigning the range of response values at random. The most effective approach is to construct the same index using several strategies to see whether the same correlations can be found with each.

■ The index must be validated. Validating the index can be done by seeking a correlation of each item to the entire index (Chronbach's alpha is a statistic that measures the degree of correlation or association among items in an index or scale) or by seeking a correlation between the index and another external and widely accepted measure of the same variable. For example, one could correlate estimated caloric output based on number and type of activities carried out during the week against an electronic instrument for measuring energy outputs.

Constructing Scales

Scales are ordinal rankings of cases composed of different items that represent a range of intensities. For example, a

TABLE 8:4　Examples of Scale Items for Scale of Acceptance of Nontraditional Occupations for Women: Masonry (Likert Scales 1 = don't agree; 5 = completely agree)

—Girls in this community can become masons	1	2	3	4	5
—The masonry work of girls is as good as that of men	1	2	3	4	5
—Girls will be hired to do masonry work in this community	1	2	3	4	5
—I would allow my daughter to become a mason	1	2	3	4	5
—I would hire a girl to do masonry work on my house	1	2	3	4	5

scale of acceptance of nontraditional employment (carpentry, electrical wiring, car engine repair, metal work, masonry) for women in Senegal includes the items in Table 8.4.

Logical sequencing by intensity or weight in an ethnographic survey is based on understanding the significance of each of the items in the cultural context of the community or population for which the survey is being designed. Identification of scale items can take place in the survey construction stage, with validation in the data management phase; alternatively, scales can be constructed after the fact from items already included in the survey that logically relate to one another based on the study itself and knowledge of the cultural context in which it is taking place.

EXAMPLE 8.2　

BUILDING SCALES FROM SURVEY ITEMS BEFORE AND AFTER DATA COLLECTION

In an ethnographic survey of factors associated with AIDS risk in Sri Lanka, indicators of knowledge of AIDS risk were identified based on previously conducted semistructured ethnographic interviewing. These items were included in the survey under "knowledge of AIDS risk." Scale construction was carried out during the data management period. In the same study, however, a scale of "sexual risk behavior" was constructed after the fact from items located in several different sections of the survey.

Building a Guttman Scale

Guttman scaling is a useful scaling technique that lends itself readily to ethnographic data. Guttman scaling is based on the idea that items in a set or sequence can be arranged so that the presence of the last (the greatest or most intense) predicts the others. In addition, the items accrue in order (of strength, intensity, risk, etc.) so that the last not only predicts the *existence* of all the others but also the *order* in which they accrue. Guttman scales are based on nominal measures (presence/absence; yes/no).

HOW TO BUILD A GUTTMAN SCALE

Building a Guttman scale requires that the researcher first identify the items that logically and culturally fit into a single cultural dimension. Items that often scale using the Guttman technique include specific sexual behaviors (from least to most intimate or risky), items reflecting economic status (land, house style, etc.) or material style of life (items purchased with cash income), and community infrastructure (roads, electricity, health and educational resources, etc.). Attitudes also may scale. Babbie (1995), for example, notes that three items indicating support for abortion—if the woman's health is endangered (92%), if pregnancy is a result of rape (85%), and if the woman is not married (45%)—probably form a Guttman scale.

Guttman scales can be constructed by hand or by using a computer program (for example, ANTHROPAC or SYSTAT; both include Guttman scaling programs). The scale is created by arranging each case in sequenced order of item accrual. The arrangement takes into consideration the likelihood that there will be exceptions to the pattern and looks for the best fit. Items are arranged across the top and cases along the side. Each group constitutes a scale type. The prototype design is shown in Table 8.5.

The strength of the scale is determined by the number of "mistakes" or incorrect predictions in the cases. The

TABLE 8.5 Guttman Scale of Social Organization: San Juan de Lurigancho

Community	Asistentes Sociales	Services Chefe de Deportes	Chefe de de Manzana	Secretaria de Economia	Scale Type
Huascar	X	X	X	X	V
10 Octubre	X	X	X	X	
9 Octubre	X	X	X	X	
Arriba Peru	X	X	X	X	
Las Violetas	X	X	X	X	
Proyectors Esp.	X	X	X	X	
San Fernando	X	X	X	X	
Caja de Agua	X	X	X	X	
San Hilarion	X	X	X	X	
Santa Elizabeth	X	X	X	X	
Byovar	X	—[a]	X	X	
Azcarunz Alto	X	—	—	X	
Valle Sharon		X	X	X	IV
Los Angeles		X	—	X	
Macchu Picchu		X	X	X	
Las Casuarina		X	X	X	
Villa Hermosa			X	X	III
Los Alamos			X	X	
Ayacucho			X	X	
Los Pinos				X	II
El Ejemplo				X	
Chacarilla de Otero	X[b]			X	
Santa Fe	X			X	
Santa Fe 2					I

Canto Rey					
Mariscal Luzuriaga					
Canto Grande					
La Huayrona					
La Libertad					
Pueblito					

Coefficient of Reproducibility = .95

[a] The dash represents a scale error. In this scale type, Chefe de Deportes should be present.
[b] The X in the case of Chacarilla de Otero and Santa Fe are scale errors. In Scale Type 4, Asistentes Sociales should not be present.

percentage of correct predictions is referred to as the coefficient of reproducibility. It is a ratio, arrived at by placing the number of *empirically derived* correct responses (the numerator, or the checks in the scalogram) over the number of *predicted* correct responses and dividing the numerator by the denominator (the predicted correct responses).

In Table 8.5, there are eighty-four possible correct answers. The scalogram is 100 percent correct. If there were cases in which Xs were present, or if they were absent where they should be present (and thus these cases could not be placed in a perfectly predicted logical order), the number of incorrectly placed Xs constitute the errors, which are then subtracted from the total to create the numerator.

The scale types can then be entered as a new variable. In Table 8.5, there are five scale types, representing different stages in the evolution of women's health organizations in communities in the northeast quadrant of Lima in the mid-1980s. The variable "women's health organizations" would be coded from 1 (scale type I) to 5 (scale type V). Scale type V would be considered to represent those communities that are most evolved or complex in terms of women's health organizations.

In addition to the fact that it is a useful data reduction technique, the value of Guttman scaling in ethnographic research lies in two important characteristics:

1. It depends on categorical data that are very useful in qualitative ethnographic analysis. This is because it is difficult to use qualitative data to determine the precise degree or amount of variation in a variable. Ethnographers find

it useful and easy to note whether something is present or absent, or even where there is "more" or "less" of it (high or low).

2. Items in a Guttman scale emerge empirically from field research in the setting. They generally cannot be transferred from one site or study to another, even though similar cultural domains tend to scale in this manner. This means that they usually are quite valid measures of phenomena in a specific site.

Using Factor Analysis

Factor analysis is used to discover patterns among the variations in values of several variables. This generates statistically constructed dimensions or factors that correlate highly with several of the real variables and are independent of one another. The researcher then attributes meaning to the underlying dimension associated with each statistically determined factor. Factor analysis is appropriately used *only* with data from random samples. The following example is adapted from Forslund, 1980 (in Babbie 1980, 428–29).

EXAMPLE 8.3

USING FACTOR ANALYSIS TO IDENTIFY PATTERNS OF DELINQUENT ACTS AMONG HIGH-SCHOOL STUDENTS

Morris Forslund conducted a study of delinquency among high-school students in Wyoming. He used a list of twenty-four delinquent behaviors included in his questionnaire to create a typology of delinquency. A factor analysis was conducted with this list; the result was four factors. The first factor included eleven items with highest factor loadings of between .45 and .66; these items accounted for 67 percent of the variance in acts of delinquency among the students. The eleven items seemed to be related to destruction of property, so factor 1 was named "property offenses." The second factor included six different items, with highest factor loadings of between .44 and .64, all of which had to do with acts against the norm or disobedience. This factor was called "incorrigibility" and accounted for .13 of the variance. The third factor consisted of five additional items related to drug use, with highest factor loadings ranging from .31 to .75. These items accounted for 11 percent of the variance; the factor was named "drugs/truancy." A fourth factor, which included only two items related to physical fighting, with .84 and .60 factor loadings, respectively, accounted for only 8 percent of the variance. Variances added to 100 percent. Forslund defined these constructed factors with their attributed meanings as delinquency profiles.

The advantages of factor analysis are its ability to integrate and "crunch" a large number of noncategorical items believed to be at least somewhat related, and its quality of inductivity, which resembles the cognitive discovery processes that ethnographers utilize to organize, analyze, and interpret text data. The disadvantages of factor analysis include its inability to predict factor loadings, the consequent lack of previously assigned meaning to predicted factors, and the often high loadings for unrelated items.

SUMMARY

In this chapter we have reviewed many of the central concepts in the organization, management, and initial crunching of both qualitative text data and ethnographically based survey data and discussed some computer-based options and issues related to both. In the next chapter we shift to quantitative analysis and introduce procedures for analyzing quantitative data and integrating or triangulating results with other data sources in a comprehensive ethnographic study.

9 ━━•━━•━━•━━

ANALYZING ETHNOGRAPHICALLY BASED SURVEY DATA

INTRODUCTION: WHY DO ETHNOGRAPHERS USE SURVEYS?

In chapters 7 and 8, we reviewed the steps required to organize and prepare qualitative and quantitative data for coding and analysis. As we have said throughout the *Ethnographer's Toolkit*, we believe that ethnographers *must* use survey methods, simply because the data collected from small groups of key informants is insufficient evidence to substantiate claims made about a larger population. In this chapter, we will walk readers through the steps in the analysis of quantitative ethnographic survey data. The quantitative data obtained from standardized and structured observations can be treated in the same manner as standardized and structured survey data, so we will not discuss analysis of observational data separately.

HOW ETHNOGRAPHIC SURVEYS DIFFER FROM OTHER SURVEYS

Quantitative surveys are not what many people think of when envisioning what ethnographers do. However, ethnographers *do* make frequent use of surveys—but with certain caveats. While these data are as amenable to organization and manipulation by computers as any other quantitative data,

Cross Reference:
See Book 3, chapter 9 on structured data collection and ethnographic surveys

ethnographically informed surveys (cf. Trotter and Schensul 1998) differ from other surveys in several significant ways:

- They are based, at least to some extent, on a "locally derived theoretical model" that may or may not be linked to more general theories of behavior and culture.
- Scale items are usually derived from prior ethnographic research that has identified which domains, factors, variables, and items are locally significant and important to the study.
- They are usually (although not always) administered face to face.
- The survey questions interface naturally with coded text data since the coding system used to organize text data originates with the topic of the study on the one hand and the primary domains structuring the study overall, and the questionnaire on the other.
- They are not likely to include a large number of nationally validated scales or other measures; and those that are chosen for inclusion are likely to have been tested with similar populations and locally validated in the specific research site.

These kinds of considerations mean that the way such surveys are developed and the derivation of questions and terminology for an ethnographic survey differ significantly from that of other kinds of standardized and structured instruments. These differences also have implications for the way ethnographic survey data are analyzed and integrated with other types of data in an ethnographic study. Below, we discuss how ethnographic surveys are constructed from the formative theoretical models developed prior to a study.

LOGICAL PROCESSES: RETURNING TO THE ORIGINAL RESEARCH QUESTIONS AND FORMATIVE MODEL

As we always have done in the *Ethnographer's Toolkit*, in this chapter we begin our discussion of ethnographic surveys by returning readers to the original problems or questions posed by researchers and to the formative theoretical models that guided the development of quantitative survey instruments in the first place. Analysis of survey data proceeds from these models. In the last section of the chapter, we review approaches to analysis of other types of quantitative data, including elicitation data such as listings and sortings, network data, and socio-geographic mapping.

Throughout the *Ethnographer's Toolkit*, we have paid close attention to:

- where research questions come from;
- how research questions guide the development of research methods;
- the importance of formative ethnographic theories and how they are generated; and
- the scientific importance of linking research questions, theory, models, and methods to data collection, analysis, and interpretation.

In Book 1, we referred to research design as a "road map" or blueprint that researchers develop and follow to arrive at a destination; we have elaborated on what research designs and research models do in Book 2. Here, we remind readers that in ethnographic research, the destination we are attempting to reach is an answer to the research questions we asked in the first place. Analysis of ethnographic survey data, like the analysis of text data, returns us to our original research questions. These original questions usually are somewhat broad or abstract. Questions such as *"What is the range of variation in the energy outputs of Latino children of preschool and elementary school age?" "How do family, peer, school, community, and media influence adolescents' drug-related behavior?"* or *"What accounts for the apparent success of the Arts Focus program?"* are typical of the questions that initiate studies. Quantitative data collected with respect to such questions usually are related to some explicitly formulated hypotheses developed on the basis of prior knowledge or exploratory research. These hypotheses are embedded in the questions included in the survey and the ways the responses are formulated and coded. Hypotheses may be phrased in the following ways:

- "If X, then Y."
- "X will be more likely to be associated with or to predict the problem than Y."
- "Y 'causes' or predicts X."

In Table 9.1 we have provided some examples of statements based on the above logical equations. Although the equations are slightly different, the logical construction of all the hypotheses is basically the same. Column 1 of the table states the formal hypothesis. The second column translates it into ordinary English as it is likely to emerge at any point during the study. It is easy to see how the hypothesis, when translated into "ordinary English," can be used to guide both qualitative and quantitative analysis. The third column provides an initial "interpretation" of the hypothesis. Only one or two ideas are expressed in this column. When researchers are seeking to identify and interpret results, they must return to the initial explanation for the hypothesis and verify it in both the literature and the text or qualitative data gathered in the study. We will say more about this in the chapter on interpretation in this book.

The initial formulation of the research question(s) is stated in the form of questions and subquestions related to a "problem" or conceptual domain. The idea of a problem and its conceptual domain refers to exploratory research that leads to formulation of an empirical question or to a more formalized formative predictive model that identifies dependent and independent variable domains and the relationships among them with respect to the "problem" or phenomenon to be explored. Ethnographic surveys help researchers determine the distribution and strength of relationships between variable domains as those relationships are expressed in a particular group of people under study. We now turn to a review of just what variables are.

TABLE 9.1 Ways of Framing Hypothetical Questions Guiding Analysis of Ethnographic Survey Data

Hypothesis	Translation	Possible Explanations
If-Then Statement		
If formal education is high, **then** employment status will be high	More formal education results in better employment	Formal education results in more skills; formal education results in more contacts necessary to improve potential for employment
If mothers' activity outputs are high, **then** children's activity levels will be high	Mothers who engage in more activities will have children who do the same	Mothers act as role models for children; mothers are the ones who make decisions about whether or not the activity levels of children are high or low
If one or both parents have health problems, **then** young women are more likely to engage in risky behavior	The health problems of parents will contribute to the involvement of daughters in risky behavior	Sick parents create emotional and financial tension in the household, which leads girls to seek relationships outside
If parents are involved in the program, then it is more likely to be successful	Parental involvement in a program will contribute to its success	Parental involvement results in more academic and social supports for children; parents involved in program activities will be more invested in children's participation and performance

(continued)

TABLE 9.1 (*continued*)

Hypothesis	Translation	Possible Explanations
Statements of Association or Correlation		
Girls **are more likely** to engage in activities inside the house than are boys	The gender of a child will play an important role in determining the location of the child's activities	Parents are more protective of girls and do not allow them to play outside unsupervised
Social influences **are more likely** than psychological characteristics to be associated with adolescent involvement in illegal activities	Social influences are more important than psychological ones in predicting teens' behavior	Older teens and young adults involved in illegal activities will have an important influence on their peers and will socialize them into illegal activity
Causal or Predictive Statements		
Low self-esteem **predicts** dropping out of school	Low self-esteem is the most important factor in determining whether a student will drop out of school	Students who have low self-esteem will not do well in their schoolwork and will not seek out help when they need it
Exposure to media influence **predicts** "sex at an early age"	Youth who have more exposure to the media (television, movies, music videos) will initiate sex earlier than their peers	Media portray the benefits of sexual engagement without communicating the disadvantages; youth unsupervised at home after school have a lot of time to watch media with their friends
Inability to recognize and report symptoms of diabetes **predicts** late diagnosis and treatment	People who cannot identify symptoms of diabetes and do not have easy access to health care are less likely to report symptoms, be properly diagnosed, and start treatment early	Two of the biggest problems in the management of adult type 2 diabetes are lack of knowledge of symptoms and consequent late reporting to health-care providers

WHAT ARE VARIABLES?

Variables are the building blocks of domains in formative research models, which in turn structure the components in ethnographic and other surveys. Variables "fit" in the organization of both qualitative and quantitative schema at the lower end of the continua, and the items of which they are composed approximate, represent, or act as "proxies" for observed or understood local "facts." In our approach to formative modeling, qualitative methods provide the background material that enriches our formative theory and begins to illustrate issues related to our research questions. These methods also provide the data from which items to construct questions eliciting information about survey variables can be culled.

Variables are measured by descriptors, elements or "facts" that indicate whether the variable is present or not (qualitative and quantitative measures) and to what degree (quantitative measures). For example, the variable "intimacy with one's adult parents" can be measured by the presence or absence of elements or descriptors such as "writing letters to parents," "visiting parents," "calling parents on the telephone weekly," "living near one's parents," and "living in the same house as one's parents." These in turn can be quantified by determining how often letters are written, how long they are, and how much information they cover; or how often parents are visited and for what duration; or how close in miles or kilometers one lives in relation to one's parents. In ethnography, as we have said elsewhere, we conceptualize variables both qualitatively and quantitatively. Both qualitative and quantitative data analysis proceed by building up from items and variables (units) to factors (patterns), domains (structures), and paradigms as follows:

- Units—*variable* level. Units can range from simple alternate attributes (for example, yes/no responses) to more complicated sets of attributes (rankings or combinations of items).
- Patterns—*subfactor and factor* level. Patterns are relationships among variables measured or assessed either qualitatively or quantitatively.

Definition:
A variable is a characteristic, descriptor, or idea that can be found in a study population in differing, or varying, degrees or amounts

Cross Reference:
See Book 2 chapters 4–7

Cross Reference:
See Book 3, chapter 1

Key point

Cross Reference:
See Book 1, chapter 2 for a discussion of units of analysis

■ Structures—*domain* level. Structures are relationships among patterns (consisting of clusters of variables).

In Table 9.2, which readers will remember as Table 1.1 from chapter 1, we illustrate these relationships again.

In chapters 4, 5 and 6 of this book, we have discussed how we construct variables (units) qualitatively from items. In the next section we describe how we construct variables quantitatively as the basic building blocks of theoretical or explanatory statements, as well as of survey construction and analysis.

Structuring or Building Variables

Survey questions and quantitative data analysis utilize one of four different types of variables. In quantitative research, these are referred to as "measures" because they measure variation in the variable in terms of numbers. The kinds of measures are:

■ nominal (categorical) measures
■ ordinal measures

TABLE 9.2   Linking Theoretical and Operational Levels in Ethnographic Research

	Structure	*Pattern*	*Unit*	*Fact*
Domain	**Family dynamics** and **life achievement**			
Factor		**Parental discipline** and **job performance**		
Variable			**Modes of parental punishment** and **ability to supervise employees**	
Item				**Frequency of spanking** and **frequency of evaluative feedback to employees**

- interval measures
- ratio measures

Nominal Measures. **Nominal measures** are variables whose attributes are exhaustive (i.e., complete) and mutually exclusive (i.e., there is no overlap of meaning or definition among items or attributes that compose the measure). Nominal measures do not vary in terms of *amount*, only in terms of *quality*. We can say that they are categorically different; that is, they can be differentiated by name or label only, not by "quantity." For example, in an international training program that brings together people from different countries, people could be grouped by country. The variable would be "country of origin." All people from Zimbabwe, Ireland, Peru, and Indonesia would differ by one characteristic: "country of origin." All those from Zimbabwe would share the same characteristic "Zimbabwe as country of origin." People can be arranged in the same way by gender (male versus female), food preference (vegetarian versus nonvegetarian), home tenancy (home ownership versus rental) or meeting attendance (present versus absent). However, the differences between these attributes cannot be ranked. They are simply categorically or qualitatively different. The following are examples of questions based on categorical variables:

Definition: Nominal measures are variables whose attributes differ in terms of quality but not quantity

- Do you belong to a church? Yes___ No___
- Are you: Female___ Male___
- Choose the after-school activity you spend the most time with:
  ___Sports ___Clubs ___School Newspaper ___Hanging Out
- Are drugs sold in your neighborhood? Yes___ No___
- Do you have a boyfriend/girlfriend? Yes___ No___

In these questions, there is no "degree" of response.

Ordinal Measures. Variables with attributes that can be said to possess "more" or "less" of something are referred to as **ordinal measures**. Rank ordering means that different attributes have relatively "more or less" of the variable when compared with each other, but the differences are not

Definition: Ordinal measures have attributes expressible in terms of quantity

measured in absolute terms. A list of educational levels can constitute an ordinal measure:

- Some elementary school
- Completed elementary school
- Some intermediate school
- Completed intermediate school
- Some high school
- Graduated from high school

These items are mutually exclusive and are ranked in terms of "amount of education." Yet the specific "amount" of education, as measured by classes, or years, is not indicated. The specific amount of education would be measured as exact years or grades of education completed. The so-called distances between levels do not have any meaning other than "more or less than," especially since the categories may differ from one community or person to another (e.g., high school may consist of three, four, or five years depending on city, state, or nation). Likewise, elementary schools in the United States may range from kindergarten to eighth grade with every permutation in between.

Table 9.3 displays another kind of ordinal measure, one that uses a Likert scale. These measures, named after the researcher Rensis Likert, ask respondents to rate a preference or opinion from one to five. For example, we can say that teachers can be "more or less" satisfied with a new curriculum, but the units or degrees of satisfaction are qualitative, not absolute. The specific amount of satisfaction cannot actually be measured in degrees of equal weight. The so-called distances between levels do not have any meaning other than "more or less than," especially because the way in which individuals interpret categories may differ. Each of the responses, A through E, in Table 9.3 is a measure of how a teacher assessed her students' response taken from a curriculum satisfaction survey used with teachers to assess receptivity to a new social development and AIDS curriculum. The survey, which measures degrees of agreement, an ordinal variable, required teachers to choose only one response from the possible five answers to the statement, "My students have done very well in mastering . . ."

TABLE 9.3   Teachers Rate Their Student Performance

My students have done very well in mastering...					
	A 90–100%	**B** 80–89%	**C** 70–79%	**D** 60–69%	**E** Below 60%
Facts about AIDS transmission					
AIDS prevention methods					
Research strategies for learning about AIDS					
Techniques for discussing sex and sensitive topics					

Other examples of questions based on ordinal variables include the following:

- How often have you seen freaky dancing in music videos?
  ___never ___rarely ___often
  ___always (a Likert scale)
- How widespread do you think verbal harassment is in your workplace? (a Likert scale)
  ___very widespread ___somewhat widespread
  ___not very widespread ___not at all widespread
- Rank from 1 (highest) to 6 (lowest) the importance of the following reasons for dropping out of school (a ranking)
  ___taking care of a baby
  ___working to support a child
  ___"getting lazy" (feeling tired during pregnancy or after birth)
  ___low self-esteem
  ___poor grades
  ___working to support your household (parents, brothers and sisters, or other relatives)

Interval Measures. **Interval measures** are defined as variables in which the distance between attributes or different conditions of the variable can be measured with a standard

Definition: The distance between attributes in interval measures have meaning as standard units of measurement

unit of measurement. Height, weight, and temperature are interval measures. It is difficult to find true interval variables in social science research that are not based on a real or assumed zero start point. Some authors give the example of IQ or other intelligence scores in which the distance between a score of 100 and 120 is considered to be the same as the distance between 90 and 110, but for a living person, the start point could not be zero because no living person could be considered to have no intelligence functions at all. Even if a person were brain-dead, the presence of some bodily functions would indicate intelligence, even if it could not be measured. Similarly, if asked a question based on an interval measure, such as, "How much do you weigh?" no respondent would ever answer "nothing."

Definition:
Ratio measures are based on a true zero point

Ratio Measures. **Ratio measures** are based on a true zero point. Ratio measures include actual age, absolute income in monetary units, numbers of people in personal networks, or spatial units such as miles or kilometers. Questions reflecting a ratio measure are:

- How old are you now? years_____ months_____
- What is your estimated monthly income from all sources?
- How many people live on this block?
- How far is it from this house to the nearest elementary school?

Question formats should reflect the nature of these measures; researchers should be clear about why particular question formats are chosen and generally how they are going to be utilized in data analysis. This is important because the range of variation in each of these measures is calculated differently. Further, different statistical procedures are utilized to establish relationships among measures of the same and different types. Having defined the variables to be used and having chosen appropriate formats with which to elicit information about them, researchers then must "describe" the numerical characteristics of the varying conditions for each variable.

For the most part, ethnographers will use a computer to carry out the next steps in the analysis. In order to do this, some preliminary housekeeping is necessary. Organizing ethnographic survey data so that it can be analyzed calls for selecting appropriate computer analysis software, establishing a process of entering data, making sure that all variables have been defined and named, and most important, making sure that the entry process is quality controlled. Once the data are entered, they must be **cleaned** and all data errors repaired or removed to prepare for data analysis. When these issues have been attended to, actual description of the data can begin.

STEPS IN DESCRIBING ETHNOGRAPHIC SURVEY DATA

The first step in describing quantitative data, the focus of this chapter, as well as qualitative data, the focus of previous chapters, involves examining the domains as they existed in the initial research formulation. For quantitative data, this requires creating descriptive statistics. The second step involves considering the relationships between and among each of the independent variable domains and the dependent variable domain(s). This process requires bivariate analysis. The third step involves considering the relationships among the independent variables in relation to the dependent variable domain, which calls for multivariate analysis. In Table 9.4 we summarize the statistical procedures used in describing quantitative data. Each of these procedures is described more fully in the pages that follow.

Step One: Descriptive Statistics

Descriptive statistics permit the researcher to display

- the distribution of the variable (range of variation);
- the typical value of the variable (mean, median, and mode);
- the variation around the typical value (variance and standard deviation); and
- the shape of the distribution (a histogram).

Cross Reference:
See chapter 8 in this book for illustrations of how to make sure data are formatted appropriately for computer analysis

Definition:
Cleaning data refers to making sure that data have been entered correctly and that data entry errors have been repaired

Cross Reference:
See Book 2, chapter 3 on building formative ethnographic theory

TABLE 9.4 Statistical Techniques and Their Uses

Procedure: Descriptive Statistics	Purpose	Description	Uses
Frequency distribution (includes the definition and description of subgroups within the population)	Portrays modal pattern and range of variation	Raw scores ranked from low to high; grouped scores; frequency of appearance of scores	Decide on types of variable transformations; describe profiles and variation in the population
Central tendency: mean	Defines **average** of a set of "scores"	Add scores and divide by number of scores	Describes the predominant trend at the interval or ratio level
Central tendency: median	Defines the **midpoint** in a range of scores	Rank scores. Find the midpoint. Divides a distribution of scores exactly in half	Describes the predominant trend at the ordinal, interval, and ratio levels
Central tendency: mode	Defines the **most frequent** score	Scores or group scores are ranked and frequencies established. The modal score or group score has the highest frequency	Describes the predominant trend at the nominal, ordinal, interval, and ratio
Range	Difference between **highest and lowest** scores for a variable	Highest and lowest scores	Describes the spread of scores to show the extent of variability in the population
Variance	**Variance** is the average of the summed squared deviation of each score from the mean	Standard deviation squared	Used instead of standard deviation in inferential statistical analysis
Standard deviation	A measure of the **spread of scores** around a mean	Square root of the variance	Summarizes variability in a population; used for descriptive purposes instead of the range

Procedure: Inferential Statistics	Purpose	Description	Uses
T-test	**Compares means** for two **unrelated** samples (interval and ratio)	Compares means	Used to determine whether there are statistically significant differences in the means of two independent, or two related populations
Paired T-test	**Compares means** for two **related** samples (pre- and posttests)		
Chi square	Determines whether the **relationship between two nominal variables** is greater than chance	Bivariate (2 × 2) table with independent or predictor variable at the top and dependent variable or variable whose variance is to be predicted along the side	Explanation of the relationship between these two variables such that one is logically seen as "causing" or "predicting" the second; tests covariation between two nominal variables
Fisher's exact test	Determines whether the **relationships between two nominal variables** is greater than chance	Identical to Chi square	For use with 2 × 2 tables where frequencies for any cell in the table are less than 5; used most often with small samples; does not suggest direction of relationship
Gamma	Measures the association between two **ordinal variables**	3 × 3 table; formula is same as for ranked pairs – opposite ranked pairs/same ranked pairs + opposite ranked pairs	Tells whether knowing the ranking of a pair of people on one variable enhances capacity to predict ranking on a second variable
Pearson's product moment correlation (r)	Determines whether there is a statistically significant relationship between two **interval or ratio** measures	Based on guessing the value of one variable by knowing the other	Can be used with interval/interval variables; interval and ordinal variables; ratio/interval/ordinal variables

(continued)

TABLE 9.4 (*continued*)

Procedure: Descriptive Statistics	Purpose	Description	Uses
Eta (n)	Considers the relationship between groupings of means within a population and a continuous dependent variable	Groups means based on researcher opinion; establishes means of subgroups; relates means to outcome or dependent variable; arrives at a total probability score	Used to test covariation between nominal and interval variables and between ordinal and interval variables. Is the only statistic that addresses nonlinear relationships with interval variables.
ANOVA	Tests the hypothesis that the **means** of two or more populations on a single variable are not equal to one another	Compares means of two or more independent populations on a single variable	Inferential: Used to compare group means in two or more groups within the same population or between two different populations at two points in time (for example, random samples of a target population at times 1, 2, and 3)
Factor analysis	Assesses associations among continuous variables to determine statistically defined variable groupings (factors)		A means of "data reduction"; can reduce many variables to scales, consisting of similar continuous variables. Factors are usually not predetermined, but allowed to emerge from the data
One-way ANOVA	Explores the effect of **one** categorical independent variable on a continuous dependent variable	Requires a predictive model with at least one categorical independent variable and one continuous dependent variable	Inferential: Used to determine relationships between categorical and continuous variables
Two-way ANOVA	Tests the effect of **two** categorical independent variables on a continuous dependent variable	Requires a predictive model with at least two categorical independent variables and one continuous dependent variable	Inferential: Used to calculate relationships between categorical and continuous variables

MANOVA	Tests the effects of **more than two** categorical independent variables on a continuous dependent variable	Permits an examination of the effects of multiple independent categorical variables on a continuous dependent variable
	Requires a predictive model with more than two categorical independent variables and one continuous dependent variable	
Regression analysis	Association between two interval or ratio variables: Y is a function of X	Regression analysis establishes the regression equation representing the geometric line that comes closest to the distribution of points on the XY axis. With values of X we can predict values of Y
	X "causes" Y, so the value of X determines the value of Y	
Multiple regression analysis (simple, stepwise, and hierarchical linear modeling, or HLM)	Association among multiple interval or ratio independent (antecedent) variables and a dependent variable	When a dependent variable is affected simultaneously by several independent variables
	Multiple independent variables account for more of the variance than a single independent variable	
Path analysis or structural equation modeling	Assumes that the values of one variable are **caused** by the values of another	Considers patterns of relationships among variables, and calculates the strength of the relationships in a multivariate model
	Must identify independent, intervening, and dependent variables (cause and effect)	

Range of variation is displayed with a frequency table. A frequency table gives the actual numbers and percentages of cases by variable value. The table for each variable will look different depending on whether the variable is a nominal, ordinal, interval, or ratio measure. Examples 9.1 through 9.4 demonstrate frequencies for each of these different measures.

EXAMPLE 9.1

VARIATION IN ATTRIBUTES OF THE VARIABLE *GENDER* AMONG LATINO ADULTS WITH DIABETES (A NOMINAL MEASURE)

Value	Count	Cumulative Count	Percentage	Cumulative %
Female	66	66	66.0	66.0
Male	33	100	33.0	100.0

Example 9.1 demonstrates that in this study of diabetes, women constituted two-thirds of the group studied, while men constituted only one-third.

EXAMPLE 9.2

RANGE OF VARIATION IN THE ATTRIBUTES OF THE VARIABLE ENTITLED *HOUSEHOLD SOCIOECONOMIC STATUS* (AN ORDINAL MEASURE) FOR A POPULATION WITH A SAMPLE SIZE OF 130

Variable Value	Count	Cumulative Count	Calculating Percentage	Cumulative %
Low	27	27	27/130	22
Medium	67	94	67/130	50
High	36	130	36/130	24

Example 9.2 shows that half the respondents fell into the medium socioeconomic status range while about one-quarter fell into the low-status category and another quarter fell into the high-status category.

EXAMPLE 9.3

RANGE OF VARIATION IN THE ATTRIBUTES OF THE VARIABLE *SAT SCORES*
(SCHOLASTIC APTITUDE TEST: AN INTERVAL MEASURE) WITH A SAMPLE SIZE OF 550

Variable Value	Count	Cumulative Count	Percent	Cumulative %
900–1000	120	120	21.9	21.9
1001–1100	100	220	18.1	40.0
1101–1200	90	310	16.3	56.3
1201–1300	87	397	15.8	72.1
1301–1400	63	460	11.4	83.5
1401–1500	54	514	09.8	93.3
1501–1600	36	550	06.5	99.8

Example 9.3 displays the number and percent of test takers whose scores fell into one of seven possible score ranges, from the lowest (900–1000) to the highest (1501–1600). The largest number of respondents, 120, received scores in the lowest category, while only 36 test takers received the highest scores.

EXAMPLE 9.4

RANGE OF VARIATION IN THE ATTRIBUTES OF THE VARIABLE *AGE OF INITIATION OF ALCOHOL USE*
(A RATIO MEASURE) WITH A SAMPLE SIZE OF 120

Variable Value	Count	Cumulative Count	Percent	Cumulative %
9 years	12	12	10.0	10.0
10 years	15	27	12.5	22.5
11 years	22	49	18.3	40.8
12 years	31	80	25.8	66.6
13 years	15	95	12.5	79.1
14 years	13	108	10.8	89.9
15 years	12	120	10.0	99.9

Example 9.4 shows that the largest number of individuals in the study began to use alcohol at age twelve. The youngest initiators were age nine, while the highest age of initiation in the group was age fifteen.

The following example shows how frequencies can be used to describe certain characteristics of the family structure of young women respondents in the Mauritius industrial sector.

EXAMPLE 9.5   ◆━◆◆━◆◆━◆

USING FREQUENCIES TO DESCRIBE FAMILY STRUCTURE OF YOUNG WOMEN IN THE MAURITIUS INDUSTRIAL WORKFORCE

The first step in analysis of the qualitative and quantitative data from the Mauritius study of young women, work, and AIDS was to describe the variables in each of the domains in the original formative theoretical model—family, peer, and work. In the analysis of the ethnographic survey, the following subfactors were grouped into a factor referred to as "family structure": father's role in the family (absent or unhealthy), mother's role in the family, and sibling structure. Frequencies were obtained for variables identified in each of these subfactors and explained with ethnographic text data. Fathers were explored first. Frequencies for variables including presence/absence of father in the household and physical health of father in the household included the following:

Cross Reference: See chapter 5 of this book for a discussion of the domains in this theoretical model

Presence of Fathers in the Household (Total number, 498)

	N (total)	Percentage
Absent	165	33.1
Present	333	66.9

Physical Condition of Fathers Present in the Household (Total Number, 333)

	N (total)	Percentage
Unhealthy	158	47.4
Healthy	175	52.5

From the frequencies derived from these two categorical or nominal variables, researchers Schensul and Schensul determined the total number of fathers who were either absent or unhealthy to be 323, or 64.9 percent.

A similar analysis was conducted for mothers and siblings. Mothers were present in 464 (93.2%) of the 498 households from which young women were inter-

viewed. Of these, 219 mothers were working (47.1% of those present), and 158 (31%) reported having health problems. In 60 percent (296) of households, at least one sibling was also working in the industrial sector. Since adult men make twice as much as women, households in which fathers and at least one child are working are likely to be better off than households in which siblings only, or mother plus siblings, are working.

We will return to this hypothesis later in this chapter when we discuss the role of bivariate analysis.

    Central Tendency. **Central tendency** is a measure of the typical value of the variable. It is a measure that *sums up* the variable for the population. There are three measures of central tendency, the mean, the median, and the mode.

Definition: Central tendency is a measure of the typical or general value of a variable

MEASURES OF CENTRAL TENDENCY

- Mode: The *mode* is the attribute that occurs most often. In Example 9.4, the mode is 12 years of age.
- Median: The *median* is the midpoint in the scores in a distribution. In Example 9.4, the median is also 12 years of age.
- Mean: The *mean* is the average of values for a variable. The mean age for initiating alcohol use in Example 9.4 is 12.5 years, a figure obtained by multiplying the number of respondents in each category by the category number (age at onset), adding up each of these products, and dividing the total by the number of age categories—seven.

EXAMPLE 9.6

MEAN SCORES OF REASONS FOR GOING TO WORK AMONG YOUNG WOMEN IN MAURITIUS

The ethnographic survey utilized in this study asked 498 women respondents to rank six reasons for going to work from the most important, 1, to the least important, 6, reason. The reasons had been derived from exploratory and semistructured data collection. The ranked mean scores for each of the reasons are the following:

Reason for Working	Mean score
To support the family	2.0
Financial independence	2.6
To be away from home	3.2
To avoid boredom	3.7
Friends were working	4.6
Family problems	4.7

These data indicate that the two main reasons for working given by this population of young women were, first, to support the family, and second, for financial independence. Ranking from high to low means that respondents rated each of these reasons against every other. The mean scores suggest that *most respondents* (the central tendency) chose the first two items as either their first or second choices. These two reasons for work are potentially contradictory if the young woman must use most or all of her salary to support the family, when in fact she anticipated gaining some economic independence from the family. The proximity of ranking of these two reasons suggests that many young women may experience considerable conflict both internally and with family members with respect to their work and their income.

⬤▬●▬●▬⬤

The above example indicates how the mean, as one measure of central tendency, can be used to describe an important dimension of a sample and how the data may be discussed and tentatively interpreted at this stage of the analysis.

Measures of central tendency all portray a general picture of the main pattern or trend in the target population. The median is a more stable measure than the mean because the mean can change dramatically with one or two outliers, whereas the median remains approximately the same regardless of outliers. If the distribution is symmetrical, however (Figure 9.1), the mean is the best measure of central tendency to use.

Measures of Dispersion. Measures of dispersion provide information on the degree of variation in the sample. They include the variance and standard deviation. Different patterns of dispersion in distribution of data or scores result in

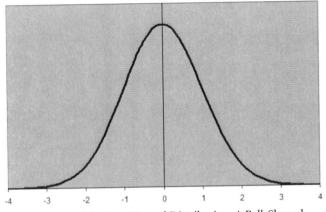

FIGURE 9.1 Univariate Normal Distribution: A Bell-Shaped Curve

different shapes in the distribution curve. A symmetrical distribution of values results in a bell-shaped curve (where the median, mean, and mode coincide with the top of the curve). Asymmetrical distributions may be positively or negatively skewed. A positively skewed distribution is determined if the mode is located to the left of the median. A negatively skewed distribution is determined when the mode is located to the right of the median. A bimodal distribution occurs when there are two modes or primary patterns.

Standard Deviation. Standard deviation is a statistic that tells researchers how much the scores in a distribution vary or deviate from the mean score. Standard deviation is a measure of variation in the distribution of scores from the mean score. It is calculated by taking the *square root of the variance.* The amount of deviation from the mean lets you know how homogeneous or heterogeneous a population is. A large standard deviation indicates that the population is very heterogeneous.

To arrive at the standard deviation, we must first calculate **variance.** Variance is the average squared deviation from the mean of each of the scores for a continuous (ordinal, interval, or ratio) variable (Table 9.5). To calculate the variance for each variable of concern, researchers must follow these steps:

1. Find the mean for the variable (e.g., age of population).

Definition:
Variance is the average squared deviation from the mean of the scores for a continuous variable

TABLE 9.5 Finding the Variance for Age of Youth Population (Total $N = 120$ cases)

Value	N	Mean Age	Difference	Squared
9 years	12	11.9–9 = 2.9	2.9 × 12 = 34.8	1211.04+
10 years	15	11.9–10 = 1.9	1.9 × 15 = 28.5	812.25+
11 years	22	11.9–11 = .9	.9 × 22 = 19.8	392.04+
12 years	31	11.9–12 = –.1	–.1 × 31 = 3.1	9.61+
13 years	15	11.9–13 = –1.1	–1.1 × 15 = –16.5	272.25+
14 years	13	11.9–14 = –2.1	–2.1 × 13 = –27.3	745.29+
15 years	12	11.9–15 = –3.1	–3.1 × 12 = –37.2	1383.84+
Total	1429			4826.32
Mean (Total/N1429/120)	11.9		Variance (Total/N4826.32/120)	40.21

Formula

1. Obtain the total number of years/case (e.g. (9 × 12 + 10 × 15, etc.).
2. Subtract each observation or case score from the mean.
3. Square the difference for each result.
4. Add all the squared differences.
5. Divide the sum by the sample size—the N.

2. Add each case.
3. Subtract each observation or case score from the mean.
4. Square the difference for each result.
5. Add all the differences.
6. Divide the sum by the sample size or the N.

Step Two: Bivariate Statistics

Frequencies, measures of central tendency, and measures of dispersion allow us to describe the characteristics of the overall sample in terms of the primary variables in which we are interested, but they only allow us to speculate as to how variables might be related to each other within subfactors, factors, and domains. One purpose of bivariate and multivariate analysis is to help with this because it can explain as much of the variance in a selected variable as possible. **Bivariate statistics** make it possible to explore statistically the relationships among the variables and groups of variables that have been proposed in an original theoretical model. They are used to find, describe, and test the significance or strength of the association between two variables at a time. Most ethnographically informed surveys contain many variables. Theoretically, analysis could go on

Definition:
Bivariate statistics permit researchers to examine the relationships between two variables at a time

forever, which is why it is important to work with a conceptual road map or puzzle design. For guidance, researchers return to their formative theoretical framework. By the
time that researchers arrive at this stage of the research
process, the number of variables with which researchers
are working will have been reduced by using some of the
"data crunching" strategies outlined in chapter 8. Further,
researchers will have developed additional hunches based
on the emergence of patterns from frequencies and means.

As researchers define and characterize the domains
in the study's model, more pieces of the puzzle will have
been identified. If the study is primarily descriptive
or inductive, the domains of primary interest will have
emerged and been defined and other domains will have
been linked to the central domain in logical ways. If the
model was fully developed prior to the implementation
of the study, the main variables included as dependent
and independent domains in the survey will have been
measured or operationalized beforehand. With text and
quantitative data (frequencies and means) already partly
crunched, researchers also will have begun to fill in a more
elaborated description of each of the domains in the conceptual or explanatory model. Now the task becomes one
of exploring (a) the relationships among the main variables in each domain, and (b) the associations between
selected independent and dependent variables.

Some researchers argue that since life is complex, we
should turn directly to considering the interaction of many
variables all at once. While this may be the most sophisticated statistical approach to data, we believe that it is better
to use our accumulated understanding of the study situation
by examining, one by one, the relationships among variables
that previous fieldwork indicates might be important. We
therefore suggest that the next step in data analysis should be
to examine the relationships among *pairs of variables*. Bivariate associations can be explored with directionality using
Pearson's R correlation or without directionality using other
statistics of association. These statistics permit us to know:

- how strong the association or covariation is;
- whether an association can be attributed simply to
  chance or rather to something specific (i.e., something

recognized in a study or program intervention) that is "causing" it in our sample;

- whether the association is positive or negative; and
- whether the shape is linear or nonlinear.

Any given two variables can have:

- no relationship (e.g., there is no direction to the relationship between income and educational level);
- a positive linear relationship such that one variable predicts another in the same direction (e.g., the higher the income, the higher the education level);
- a negative linear relationship such that one variable predicts another in the opposite direction (e.g., the higher the income, the lower the education level); or
- a nonlinear relationship in which the direction changes at a specific point for predictable reasons (e.g. the higher the income, the higher the education level until income reaches a certain point, at which education level begins to drop because after a certain point, inheritance or general business skill supersedes education level as a predictor of income generation).

The most frequently used measures of association are Chi square or Fisher's exact test for small cell size (for nominal level data), gamma or Kendall's tau (for ordinal data), and the Pearson's R correlation for interval and ratio data, unless the relationship is nonlinear. Bernard suggests using a statistic called eta when the relationship is nonlinear or for establishing relationships between interval/ratio (for example, age) and nominal (for example gender; yes/no) data (Bernard 2011, 523–24). Eta enables researchers to separate interval data into nominal groupings, which are then correlated with a nominal measure. Eta measures the strength of the association between two variables when one of the measures is nominal and the other is interval (e.g., male/female in relation to number of days cigarettes are smoked in the past thirty days). If the relationship is significant, the two variables are associated and not independent of each other.

Tests of Association Based on Comparison of Means. A number of statistics are used to assess the strength of asso-

ciation between variables. Below we discuss those most commonly used. The **t-test** is a descriptive statistic that compares two means to determine whether they are different enough to show "real," that is, statistically significant, differences between two populations. If it is possible to predict the direction of the difference in advance, a *one-tailed test* should be used. If researchers are only interested in whether or not there is a difference, but not in the direction of the difference, a *two-tailed test* is used. For example, in a study of drug and AIDS risk among youth in Hartford, researchers hypothesized that males would consume more alcohol than females and that Latino and white youth would consume more alcohol than African American youth. A one-tailed t-test was used to determine whether there was a significant difference in *amount of alcohol* (a continuous variable, measured by number of drinks consumed in the past thirty days) used by girls versus boys, by ethnicity.

Pairwise difference t-tests are used to test the difference in means between related populations (for example, pre- and posttest means obtained from the same target group of students). This procedure was used in an intervention study at the Institute for Community Research designed to reduce risky behaviors among female preadolescents by improving communication between mothers and daughters. A one-tailed t-test was used in comparing an intervention group with a matched sample to determine whether improvements had actually occurred from baseline assessment to immediately postintervention as measured by a self-report communications scale (Romero and Berg 1997). In a similar assessment of a risk prevention intervention with youth in Sri Lanka, the t-test was used to determine whether participants' knowledge of sexual risk prevention, as measured by an AIDS prevention knowledge scale (an interval measure), improved subsequent to the intervention (Nastasi et al. 1998/1999). Statistical software packages allow researchers to choose which t-test to use and whether or not it is one-tailed or two-tailed.

ANOVA, or analysis of variance, tests the hypothesis that the difference in the *means* of two or more populations (for example, test scores) is statistically significant, that is, not due to chance alone. One-way ANOVA explores the effect of one categorical independent variable on a continuous dependent variable. Two-way ANOVA explores the effect of two

Definition: The t-test compares two means to determine whether they are statistically different

Definition: ANOVA (*analysis of variance*) is a statistic that is used to determine whether differences in the means of two or more populations are statistically significant or not due to chance alone

categorical independent variables on a continuous dependent variable. The following example shows how one-way ANOVA can be used to display statistically significant gender differences in friendship patterns among youth in Sri Lanka.

EXAMPLE 9.7

USING ONE-WAY ANOVA TO ANALYZE GENDER DIFFERENCES IN FRIENDSHIP PATTERNS IN SRI LANKA

In a study of youth and AIDS risk in the central province of Sri Lanka, a total of 615 young people were interviewed. Approximately half were drawn from an urban low-income community and the other half from the undergraduate student body of the University of Peradeniya, an arm of the national university system. Participants were asked to specify the number of same-sex and opposite-sex friends with whom they discussed personal matters. One-way ANOVA was used to consider gender differences in mean number of friends for the overall sample and then for community versus university students. In the overall sample, females reported a smaller number of friends (8.5) than males (12.3) (One-way ANOVA, P > .001) (Silva et al. 1997). When the total sample was disaggregated by gender and community, however, the results were as in Table 9.6.

TABLE 9.6 ANOVA: Gender and Residence as Associated with Same- and Opposite-Sex Friends

	DWM	DWF	UPM	UPF
Mean number of total friends	11.5	8.3**	13.0	8.7**
Mean number of same-sex friends	7.9	6.2	9.7	6.3**
Mean number of opposite-sex friends	3.5	1.7*	3.3	2.4

*Difference significant at .05 level (one-way ANOVA)
**Differences significant at .001 level (one-way ANOVA)

Sample Code:
DWM = Deyannewela community male
DWF = Deyannewela community female
UPM = University of Peradeniya male
UPF = University of Peradeniya female

Pearson Correlation Coefficient (Pearson's R). This statistic indicates the degree of linear relationship between two variables measured on an interval scale. The Pearson's R assumes values between +1.0 and −1.0. A value of +1.0 indicates a perfect direct linear relationship between the two variables. That is, one predicts the other directly. For example, a Pearson's R correlation coefficient of +.73 indicates a direct relationship between educational status and household income (high/high or low/low). A value of −1.0 predicts a perfect inverse linear relationship; for example, a Pearson's R correlation coefficient of −.73 indicates an inverse relationship between occupational status (low) and health problems (high).

Step Three: Multivariate Analysis

Multivariate analytic techniques are used to establish relationships among multiple independent or predictor variables and dependent variables. The most frequently used general procedure for multivariate analysis is multiple linear regression. Multiple linear regression allows researchers to examine the relationship of a set of continuous independent or predictor variables, for example, age, years of education, and socioeconomic status, with a dependent continuous variable, such as school performance (e.g., grades or attendance) or drug use (frequency of use of cigarettes or alcohol). Preferable conditions for multivariate analysis are a random (or at least systematic) sample, a normal distribution of the variable (see normal curve above) and continuous independent and dependent variables.

Researchers describe these procedures by saying that for continuous variables or measures (ordinal, interval, and ratio), general linear models (GLM) are used and that the standard procedure is "multiple regression of independent variables onto the continuous dependent measure." In other words, researchers "regress age, years of education, and socioeconomic status of the household (the independent variables) onto grades (the dependent variable)." The primary interest is in finding out which independent variables account for the most variance in the dependent variable.

A commonly used statistical procedure is hierarchical multiple regression (Cohen and Cohen 1983) because it calls for entering independent variables into the regression equation sequentially in order of their hypothesized chronological order or perceived importance in predicting variance in the dependent variable. In the example above, if the researcher believed that socioeconomic status was the most important predictor of grades, that variable would be entered into the regression equation first, followed by the other two in order of hypothesized importance. In this way, the researcher controls the analysis. If an entry step is statistically significant and at the same time accounts for a reasonable amount of the variance (i.e., 1 percent or more), we describe this as a variable that will be considered for inclusion in the statistical model we are trying to build. Ironically, statistically significant findings often account for less than 1 percent of the variance in many studies. Researchers should remember that statistical significance does not always mean that a result has practical significance. Hence, we recommend that both criteria—having a statistically significant entry step *and* the ability to account for a reasonable amount of variance—be utilized. The ability to account for variance is called the *effect size*.

There are other forms of regression analysis where groupings of variables defined by major independent variable domains were entered into the regression equation as blocks. This strategy was utilized in the analysis of the data collected from young women in Mauritius.

EXAMPLE 9.8   ◀▬●▬●▬▶

ENTERING VARIABLES INTO A MULTIPLE REGRESSION EQUATION: AN EXAMPLE FROM MAURITIUS

The formative ethnographic theory guiding a study of young women, work, and AIDS risk in Mauritius stated that a combination of factors associated with the independent domains PEER, FAMILY, and WORK would be important in predicting outcomes in the dependent variables. Outcome or dependent variable domains were SEX BEHAVIOR, VALUES REGARDING PREMARITAL SEX, AIDS KNOWLEDGE, and CONDOM KNOWLEDGE.

Variables from each independent domain were identified using stepwise regression analyses. Stepwise regression analysis allowed researchers to specify independent variables that might be important in determining variance in the dependent variables. SPSS was used to identify those independent variables that correlated best or accounted for the greatest amount of variance in each of the dependent variable domains listed above. The program then entered all other identified variables. The results were different in terms of predicting each of the dependent variables. Below we explain how we arrived at the results.

First, each of the major domains was disaggregated into "blocks of variables" that made conceptual sense according to the model informing the study. The end result was a refinement of the formative model. Below, we show how these blocks were organized, first by independent variable domains and then by dependent variable domains. Each of the variables named in the column to the far right was created and defined. Variables for which there was no variation were eliminated. *Independent variable domains, factors, variables, and variable names are displayed in Table 9.7.*

TABLE 9.7   Independent Domains, Factors, and Variables for the Young Women, Work, and AIDS Risk Study (Predictors of HIV Risk)

Domain	Factor	Variable	Variable Name
FAMILY	Family structure	Father's role in family	(FA_ROLE)
		Mother's role in family	(MA_ROLE)
		Sibling structure	(SIB_ROLE)
	Family environment	Family approval of work	(FMAPPR)
		Family traditionality	(FTRAD)
		Family violence/restriction	(FVIOL)
		Family problems	(FPROB)
		Hours of housework/wk.	(FCHOR)
		% of month's salary given to family	(FCONT)
		No. of activs. with family	(FAMACT)
		Work to suppt. fam.	(FAMSUP)
WORK	Characteristics	Work seniority	(WSEN)
		Education of respondent	(RED)
		Salary of respondent	(RSAL)
		Age on entry to work	(EPZAGE)
	Work environment	Knowing men at work	(KNOWMEN)
		Satisfaction w. income	(SATINC)
		Trust of female workers	(FEMTRST)
PEERS	Peer structure	Size of female peer net	(FEMNET)
		Activities with fem. frnds.	(FEMACT)
		No. of male friends	(MALENET)
		Activities with m. friends	(MALEACT)
		Boyfriend	(BOYFD)
		Fiancé	(FIANCÉ)
		BF/GF/fiancé activities	(FBCOMM)
	Peer environment	BF/fiancé control/violence	(FBVIOL)
		BF/fiancé communication	(FBCOMM)

TABLE 9.8 Dependent Domains and Variables for the Young Women, Work, and AIDS Risk Study (Risk Outcomes)

Domain	Factor	Variable	Variable Name
Sex Behavior		Count of sex behaviors	(SEXCT)
Premarital Sex		Values /premarital sex	(VPMSEX)
AIDS Knowledge		Level of AIDS Knowledge	(AIDKNOW)
Know Condoms		Know of Condoms	(CONDKNOW)

 Definition:
Stepwise regression analysis is an exploratory analytic procedure used to identify sets of variables within preidentified conceptual/cultural domains that predict variance in the dependent variable. Forced stepwise regression is used to test hypotheses regarding which variables predict the greatest amount of variance by entering variables into the regression equation in the order of their hypothesized importance, based on researcher experience and prior data analysis (Cohen and Cohen 1983)

As an example of the way in which each variable was defined, FA_ROLE and MA_ROLE were ordinal scales constructed after the survey data were collected, each with three levels: mother/ father absent, mother/father present but unwell, and mother/father present and well.

Dependent variable domains, factors, variables, and variable names are displayed in Table 9.8.

All of the independent variables were regressed in blocks on each of the dependent variables. Those that were significant predictors were entered into a final regression analysis (in which all independent variables are considered in relation to each other as well as the dependent variable). Some were significantly associated with specific dependent variables, and others were not.

Table 9.9 shows which variables drawn from the seventy-two-question survey instrument were correlated with the four dependent variables. Some variables from all of the main independent domains and factors were significantly correlated with the dependent variables.

The next step in the analysis involved entering into a **forced stepwise regression**. Those variables are ones hypothesized to be important or demonstrated to be important by the strength of the correlation or by the amount of variance they predicted in each of the dependent variables. For sexual activity (SEXCT), *six* variables were entered, starting with the one predicting the greatest amount of variance. *Five* variables were entered from the peer domain, and *one* from the work domain. *No variables* were entered from the family domain. For attitudes toward sex (VPMSEX), *six* variables were entered, *two* from the family domain and *four* from the peer domain. For AIDS knowledge (AIDKNOW), *five* variables were entered, *three* from the work domain and *two* from the family domain. Finally, for condom knowledge (CONDKNOW), *three* variables were entered, *one each* from the work, peer, and family domains.

TABLE 9.9 Regression Showing Significant Interactions between Dependent Variable Domains and Variables (family, work, and peers) and Independent Variable Domains (number of sex behaviors, values about premarital sex, AIDS knowledge, and condom knowledge)

PREDICTOR SET	SEXCT	VPMSEX	AIDKNOW	CONDKNOW
FAMILY DOMAIN				
Family structure	NS	NS	FAROLE	NS
Family work	FCONT	FMAPPR	FAMSUP	FAMSUP
	FMAPPR			
Family environment	FTRAD	FAMACT	FAMACT	
	FTRAD	FBVIOL		
	FACT			
WORK DOMAIN				
Work structure	Q 18	NS	R_AGE	R_AGE
	WSEN		EPZAGE	
Work environment	KNOWMEN	NS	KNOWMEN	NS
PEER DOMAIN				
Female friendship network	FEMACT	FEMNET	FEMACT	FEMACT
	FEMNET			FEMPRI
Male fd. Network	MALEACT	MALENET	MALEACT	MALEACT
BF/fiancé network	FIANCE1	FIANCE1	FIANCE1	FIANCE1
BF/fiancé environment	FBOMM1	FBVIOL1	FBCOMM1	NS

The results were the following. Only variables from the peer domain predicted sexual activity. They included size of male and female network (FEMNET), activities with peers (FBACT), learning more about male peers at work (KNOWMEN), better communication with boyfriend or fiancé (FBCOMM), and more restrictive behavior from boyfriend or fiancé (FBVIOL).

Variables from the family and peer domain predicted values held about premarital sex. In the family domain, the *less traditional* the family (FTRAD) and the *more the family disapproved* of work in the EPZ (FMAPPR), the *more positive the attitude toward premarital sex*. In the peer domain, larger male network (MALENET), greater range of activities with boyfriend or fiancé (FBACT), and better communication with a boyfriend or fiancé (FBCOMM) predicted a *more positive attitude toward premarital sex*.

Variance in AIDS knowledge was predicted by variables in the family and work domains but not in the peer domain. In the family domain, the presence and health of the father (FAROLE) and more activities with the family (FAMACT) predicted more AIDS knowledge. In the work domain, higher education (R_AGE), knowing more men through work, and older age at entry into the industrial work-force (EPZAGE) predicted more AIDS knowledge.

Most of the variables did not predict variance in condom knowledge. Only one variable from each of the domains was entered into the regression equation, R_AGE (WORK), FBACT (PEER), and FAMACT (FAMILY). This completed the hierarchical and stepwise regression analyses. The coding tree for the qualitative text data for this study includes most of the same variables so that patterns of association could be explored in the text data while they were also being investigated in the quantitative data. These results, coupled with the examination of blocks of text coded with the same variable names, provided the basis for interpretation, which we will discuss in the next chapter (Schensul et al. 1994, 86–128).

The last form of multiple regression analysis to be mentioned here is *logistic regression*. Logistic regression is used when *dependent variables* are dichotomous or when they have been transformed from a continuum to a dichotomy because the curve is not normal. Logistic regression requires that independent variables also be converted to categorical variables subsequent to entry into regression equations. Logistic regression is viewed as increasingly useful by researchers who have come to believe that most variables in which we are interested in social science research are ranked (ordinal) rather than absolute (interval or ratio). A description of logistic regression and instructions regarding how to use this analytic technique are beyond the scope of this book. For assistance in deciding whether to convert dependent variables into categorical variables and how to conduct logistic regression, readers are advised to refer to the work of H. R. Bernard (2011). There are many other more sophisticated procedures used to analyze quantitative data that we have not discussed here. To learn about and apply more advanced techniques, readers are referred to the appropriate statistical texts.

The case study above describes how a statistical model was constructed from ethnographically informed survey data based on:

- an initial formative ethnographic theoretical model;
- the elaboration of the model into factors and variables based on exploratory and semistructured data collection;

- the transformation of the revised model into an ethnographic survey; and
- returning to the model for analysis of survey data.

In the final section of this chapter, we suggest ways to integrate with ethnographic survey data qualitative (text and observation) data, survey data, and data collected via other means such as network research, social-spatial mapping, and elicitation techniques described in Books 3 and 4.

INTEGRATING QUALITATIVE AND QUANTITATIVE DATA

By this time, readers will probably recognize that ethnographic survey data are not likely to be collected unless considerable exploratory work has been done. There are a number of ways in which other forms of data can be integrated with survey data:

- Using qualitative data to inform the development of theoretical models. We have discussed in detail both in this book and in Book 2 ways of using ethnographic text data to inform the development of the theoretical model guiding the survey. We refer readers to Books 1 and 2 for more information on this topic.

Cross Reference: Book 1, chapter 4; Book 2, chapter 7

- Using qualitative text data to explore quantitative associations or correlations qualitatively. This step requires that the coding system for text data be developed in advance of the survey and that at least the major coding categories (domains, factors, subfactors, and even variables) be used for both purposes. To maximize the interface between qualitative and quantitative relationships, researchers would then search coded text for blocks of text that display multiple codes consistent with the correlations being pursued quantitatively.
- Using the study in the case example of AIDS risk above, researchers could search the coded text databases for the intersection of text blocks coded as FAMILY and SEXCT to find descriptions of the relationship in the text data. Or, with a more refined coding system, they could search for the interac-

tion of family activities (FAMACT)—a variable—and SEXCT. Programs such as NVivo or ATLAS.ti allow for up to twelve or more codes to be applied to a single block of text. Thus, at least theoretically, depending on the detail with which coding categories are applied, it is possible to find text blocks that reflect qualitatively or descriptively the most complex quantitative equation.

- Using text data to develop new conceptual guidelines. This can be done by exploring text data using methods outlined in earlier chapters of this book to develop new conceptual models that can guide data analysis in new and unpredicted ways. This approach is useful even when the formative theoretical model is well developed because, when read thoroughly, high-quality text data often reveal new insights. They have the potential for generating interesting ideas and questions that can be tested with matched survey data in ways never anticipated in the original study.

- Using quantitative results to guide additional qualitative investigation. Unexpected correlations and associations found in the survey data can raise important issues that can be addressed and understood better by returning to the text data for interpretation (Schensul, Munoz-Laboy, and Bojko 1998; Schensul et al. 1994). For example, in a study of health needs and health-care utilization in the Puerto Rican community of Hartford, ethnographer Stephen Schensul and activist Maria Borrero made the unanticipated discovery, via quantitative data analysis, that high numbers of Puerto Rican women of childbearing age were turning to sterilization as a form of birth control. This led to further analysis of in-depth interview and narrative data, new focus groups with women, and a review of the history of fertility control among Puerto Ricans in Puerto Rico to discover the reasons for this unexpected pattern. Research indicated that it was rooted in the history of the development and testing of new forms of fertility control among Puerto Ricans (Schensul et al. 1982).

Other forms of data can be utilized in conjunction with survey data in the same ways. Quantitative data collected on a focal individual's (ego's) personal networks can be entered into data files as information about ego's network. Such data can include, for example, information seeking, help in accessing resources, financial assistance, child care, drug and tobacco use, participation in clubs, or other activities. Ethnographic descriptions of observed networks in action can help to quantify network questions, confirm network data obtained through questionnaires, or describe the context within which ego-centered networks function. Similarly, networks discovered through in-depth interviews and observations can help to explain the history and functioning of components of full relational networks identified quantitatively through survey research.

Elicitation techniques described in Books 3 and 4 capture information on the way people organize and think about cultural domains. Data obtained through listings, for example, offer an important opportunity for identifying cultural "items" or "units." When obtained in a focused group interview setting, they also provide the framework for detailed discussions about cultural domains that enrich both further analysis and other dimensions of the study. Finally, like frequencies and measures of central tendency, multidimensional scaling and cluster analysis performed on sorted items are designed to identify cultural consensus and at the same time reveal intragroup variations that are important to explore further, both qualitatively and through survey research.

Cultural consensus data can confirm other study results. Our explorations of sexual knowledge among teens in Hartford, Connecticut, had given us reason to believe, for example, that AIDS was not a salient subject for teens there. Listing exercises confirmed that it was not mentioned in most groups that performed a listing exercise that required them to identify major areas of concern to urban teens. Items drawn from the listing exercise, sorted and subjected to multidimensional scaling and cluster analysis, revealed that AIDS was located in a cluster of its own, apart from other issues, including those related to sexuality and sexual health (Schensul 1998/1999).

Cross Reference: See Book 4, chapter 5 on network research

Cross Reference: See especially Book 4, chapter 3 on elicitation techniques and consensus analysis

Cross Reference: See Book 3, chapter 8 on on focused group interviews

The activities and behaviors of social network members, patterns of accessing health care and other community resources, and school choices at a time of diversification and privatization are examples of issues often addressed through survey data. The location of individuals in relation to social activities and institutions is critical to understanding how and why they use resources. GIS and other forms of mapping, described by Ellen Cromley in Book 4, chapter 4 in the *Ethnographer's Toolkit*, are tools that help researchers to array their data in space, revealing patterns otherwise not noticeable.

Cross Reference: See Book 4, chapter 4 on spatial mapping

RESOLVING DIFFERENCES BETWEEN QUANTITATIVE AND QUALITATIVE RESULTS

Different approaches to the collection of data may produce different as well as complementary results. Information obtained from in-depth interviews and observations may expand what we can learn from surveying, for example, but they often tell a slightly different story. For example, survey research results from a random sample of five hundred young women surveyed in the Mauritius study produced somewhat lower rates of penetrative sex and higher counts of oral sex than counts from the ninety women who were interviewed using a semistructured interview (Schensul et al. 1994; Schensul et al. 1995). This finding led researchers to conclude one of two possibilities: either women were more comfortable reporting oral sex on a survey than in person because it was a very intimate behavior, or there were slight differences between women in the two samples. Similarly, data collected in field observations about whether safety measures such as bleach were used to protect against HIV infection sometimes contradicted results obtained from surveys with the same people who had been observed in the field. Respondents were more likely to *report* safe behavior (i.e., to tell interviewers what they wanted to hear), even when they knew the interviewers and interviewers had actually observed them engaging in risky drug use in the field (Broomhall et al. 1998). As we stated earlier, putting together the results of ethnographic data collection is like completing a puzzle.

In the instances mentioned above, some pieces of the puzzle do not quite fit. We would not suggest that they must always fit. Instead, we urge ethnographers to continue their data collection until some explanation for the differences emerges. In the case of bleach use among injection drug users, the explanation was that drug users tried to portray themselves in a better light to researchers by *saying* they used bleach to sterilize needles, even when observations proved they did not. Often, explanation will provide greater insight into cultural patterning.

Further, to understand differences (and similarities) in results, researchers should also consider:

- the purpose of the data collection method (explanation through collection of in-depth information versus explanation through the collection of the most valid data possible with a large sample, through ethnographically informed surveys);
- the nature of the information being collected, for example, how personal or embarrassing it is for people to discuss it openly in the setting;
- who is collecting the information, and therefore how the status of the data collector might affect what he or she is being told by respondents;
- how well the researcher is able to collect the information (e.g., are tape recordings made in a noisy environment that interferes with acuity? Are other people present who affect how the respondent answers? Are there barriers of language or jargon that interfere with the researcher's full understanding of what the respondent is saying? Was the researcher unable to record information at the moment of interview so that recording is based on recall done after the fact?);
- how well the researcher is able to establish a relationship with respondents; and
- how well the particular form of data collection is suited to collecting that particular form of data.

SUMMARY

In the previous chapter we reviewed a variety of ways to organize, manage, and begin to "crunch" or reduce the complexity and number of variables in an ethnographic survey data set. In this chapter we have suggested that many steps in quantitative analysis parallel those in qualitative analysis as researchers examine the intersection of items and variables and move toward establishing patterns in the data. We have conveyed the importance of returning to the original study model when taking the first steps to analyze survey data, which may be in tandem with or triangulated with qualitative data reflecting the same or similar variables. Quantitative data analysis proceeds in logical steps from frequencies to bivariate analysis, followed by multivariate analysis of the integration of a number of variables in relationship to a single dependent variable. Many anthropologists will not move beyond multiple regression analysis or structural equation modeling (a form of sequenced regression analysis that shows pathways through which some variables predict others that in turn mediate or have an effect on the final outcome variable). There are many ways of exploring and combining variables that we have not covered in this chapter; readers are referred to statistics courses and textbooks as well as the Internet to learn more about them. In the final chapters of this book, we discuss how to assemble all the analyzed parts of an ethnographic data set, how to display them for various audiences, and how interpretation provides deeper meaning and various levels of the portrait created in the ethnographic study.

10 ◆━◆━◆━◆

CREATING PRELIMINARY RESULTS: PUTTING PARTS TOGETHER

CREATING MORE COMPLEX DATA PATTERNS AND EXPLANATIONS

Up to now, we have been talking about how to break down a stream of behavior and what it means to participants and researchers into its constituent parts. We have also shown how we can begin to examine the relationships or associations among these parts in order to begin building a broader picture or story of what the data are telling us. The laborious process of developing and applying coding procedures and manipulating quantitative data described in the previous chapters will generate information about the constituent parts of a phenomenon and the range of variation within it. It also can illuminate the relative size, importance, or density of elements in a database. It now is time to begin reassembling elements into a coherent story that is informed or explained by formative theories and well evidenced with data. Readers will remember the former—theories—as the vertical dimension that builds a framework of explanation from locally relevant rationales to summative theory, and the latter—data—as the horizontal dimension from concrete (items) to abstract (domains). In chapters 5 and 6, we discussed how to address relatively concrete items or units that are easy to identify and well differentiated from each other; we have associated them with clearly localized theories or rationales for their existence. Many of these items are like the specific codes we defined earlier; they have clear boundaries and are the easiest to find, code, and enumerate; the relationships among them also may be fairly clear. Similarly, local theories often are readily articulated by research participants. One could call these "lower-level" patterns and rationales as "just the results," or local-level phenomena. However, other important kinds of data and rationales are more elusive. These are data and rationales that illustrate phenomena that are more abstract and harder to operationalize or explain, except in terms of multiple discrete behaviors (see the example of "respect for Native American culture" in chapter 1), which do not have clean beginnings and endings and which may have multiple meanings and origins. They include such things as meanings, motives, themes, explanations, causal links, complex activities or belief structures, and patterns of interaction, practices, or norms and values. Often these must be identified in terms of some cover term or category name that "stands for" a complex of behaviors or ideas, as is the case of "disciplined creativity" in the Arts Focus study (see Example 10.4 and Table 10.3), "respect for Native American culture" in the Learning Circle study (see Example 1.3), or gendered "ways of knowing" about sex and sexuality in the Sri Lanka study (Schensul et al. 1994).

Cross Reference:
See Example 10.5

In the pages that follow, we discuss how these complex phenomena are created. By now, the reader should have discerned that the process of identifying patterns of behavior or things in a person's lived world is similar to the process of identifying factors that explain why people say they behave as they do and what their behavior means to them. It also will become clear that these processes do not operate independently of one another. In fact, experienced ethnographers actually engage in the processes of identifying both patterns and factors (or phenomena in the horizontal dimension and meanings and rationales in the vertical dimension) more or less simultaneously.

Once patterns and factors have been identified and the relationships among them established, researchers move to the final stage of assembly of an ethnographic portrayal:

structural or constitutive analysis. **Structural or constitutive analysis** involves linking together or finding consistent relationships among all of the various components or constituent parts of the study (factors and other conceptual domains) and the theoretical hunches or explanations that tell why they are related. Perhaps the most important point to remember at this stage of the process is that researchers can assemble constituents and the theories explaining their assembly deductively (from the top down), inductively (from the bottom up), and recursively, which involves a combination of moving back and forth between the two. Regardless of how researchers initiate their work, there is always interaction among what we have earlier referred to as "levels of abstraction." The cognitive or intellectual processes involved in analysis are similar for inductive, recursive, and deductive approaches, though the steps involved in analysis are somewhat different depending on the study's start point and how much is known about the topic prior to its initiation. These cognitive processes also are informed by theory, whether the theories consist of the formative theoretical model informing the study from the outset, additional theories not anticipated in advance but that have emerged as relevant, or substantive theories that have been generated from field data during the investigative process.

As the outlines and contents of structures and constituents and the relationships joining them become more and more distinct, they become part of a clear portrait of the phenomenon under study. It is this portrait that constitutes the story to be told and is what will be displayed in the write-up of the ethnographic report. In this chapter, we discuss the mechanics of assembling the portrayal; in chapters 11 and 12, we present strategies for writing up the story and interpreting what it means.

Definition: Structural or constitutive analysis integrates all of the various components or constituent parts of the study and embeds the result in an overall set of theories explaining their relationships

THE PATTERN LEVEL OF ANALYSIS: LINKING RELATED GROUPS OF ITEMS AND UNITS TOGETHER AND IDENTIFYING RELATED EXPLANATORY VARIABLES AND FACTORS

Once data are coded, researchers can begin to examine collections of codes to see how they are related to each other. We call this stage the *pattern level* of analysis.

Key point

Cross Reference:
See also Table 5.4 for a summary of these levels of analysis

Pattern level analysis involves organizing related items (or indicators of a variable) into higher-order patterns and creating explanations for these relationships from conceptual factors and subfactors. These conceptual subfactors were displayed in tabular form in chapters 4 and 5. Eventually patterns are organized via constitutive analysis into structures, explained by theories, hypotheses, and other rationales, and finally, linked to larger-level theories from various paradigms that help to explain their existence.

Pattern level of analysis is something like the middle stages of assembling a jigsaw puzzle; once the player has found all the orange pieces and all the blue pieces, for example, or all the pieces with a particular pattern on them, he or she then can begin to assemble those pieces into a coherent chunk of the design portrayed in the completed puzzle. The canons for "coherence" reside in both how the player believes the picture should look and what logically seems to make sense. Further, the player can begin to see how the orange chunks are related to the blue chunks, or where they fit into the overall picture, by looking at the little dents and hooks in the individual pieces, examining their relationship to other chunks already assembled, noticing shadings of color, and identifying pieces of the overall design. Ethnographers sometimes talk rather intuitively about how patterns "emerge" from the data; while the process *does* involve a bit of intuitive thinking, there are, in fact, some rather systematic ways of looking at data that facilitate the process—just as puzzle players also approach their task systematically.

HOW DO PATTERNS EMERGE FROM DATA?

Patterns emerge in ways that can include the following.

Patterns emerge by:

- Declaration
- Frequency
- Omission
- Similarity

- Co-occurrence
- Corroboration
- Sequence
- A priori hypothesizing

Below we discuss in more detail what researchers do when they are using the above strategies to identify patterns in their data.

Patterns Emerge by Declaration

Sometimes, informants will tell a researcher that a pattern exists; in those cases, researchers can look for data that confirm or deny the informant's declaration. For example, a key informant in Jean Schensul's 1999–2003 study of hard drug use among teens and young adults told a member of the research team that he preferred to continue his association with street life while at the same time working in a regular job so that he could "keep his feet in both worlds." The pattern of maintaining connections in two or more sectors emerged early in the study and constituted a focal point for further exploration. The pattern linked two factors—"connecting with street life" and "connecting with a regular job." Together they constituted and explained a structure called "keeping feet in both worlds," which in turn was linked to strategies for maintaining "connex" (the series of social relationships that allow an individual to span multiple worlds and buy and sell drugs through these personal social connections), a factor crucial to sustaining the informant's multiple roles in his world. Thus, this study not only mapped out the way the informant lived, but also provided his own set of reasons or local theories for why he behaved as he did.

Patterns Emerge Because of the Frequency with Which They Occur

One very common way to identify patterns is in terms of the frequency with which specific items, events, responses, kinds of persons, or themes occur. When a particular unit, theme, or idea appears over and over in the data, then researchers can feel fairly certain that a pattern may exist. A case in point is LeCompte's repeated observation that some or all of the four behaviors (units) that illustrated parents' involvement in Learning Circle schools were frequently linked. After observing these associations repeatedly, she eventually decided that taken together, they constituted a pattern that she referred to as "respect for Indian parents." In brief, to Indian parents, being "respected" not only meant being treated with as much deference as white parents were, but also required having their own customs, values, and practices inform the activities of the program— just as those of white parents did.

Cross Reference: See Example 1.5 in this book

Patterns Emerge Because of Omission

Another common but often overlooked form of pattern recognition is one where something notable is *missing*. For example, despite the fact that women and men in the field of public education attain the same amount of education and training, men still dominate all forms of leadership in schools and women are almost totally absent from the ranks of large-city school superintendents. Or, in a study exploring supports and barriers to asthma compliance in young children, omission became apparent when researchers sought but did not find the community-based informational resources on asthma management for families that they had thought existed.

EXAMPLE 10.1 ⬥•⬥•⬥

PATTERNS IDENTIFIED THROUGH OMISSION: NOTICING GAPS IN SPECIAL EDUCATION INFRASTRUCTURE IN A SUBURBAN ELEMENTARY SCHOOL

In a study of parental involvement in placement decisions for children with special needs, one important first step was to identify the "places" (meetings and other settings) where informal as well as formal decision making regarding special education placement took place. The second was to study the roles of the various participants in this decision-making process. The third was to consider the facilitators and barriers to parental participation in the process. During the second stage of the study, researchers Schensul and Robertson noticed that parents who were well informed and outspoken came to both child study team and pupil placement team meetings,

and those who remained relatively silent came only to the child study team meetings. With further probing, they discovered that the more frequent attendees lived in the "hills" outside the town in the wealthy suburbs, and those who came only the first time or not at all lived in the "flats" near the school. They attributed this pattern to social class differences (Yoshida, Pelto, and Schensul 1978).

In this example, what was missing was the presence of a group of people whose attendance had been assumed. LeCompte noticed a similar omission when she did not find in the classrooms she studied an emphasis on achievement that she thought should be there. The problem is that explanations for behavior or theories to explain them also can be missing, despite the researcher's expectations. As indicated in Example 1.3, medical researchers could find no "reasonable" physical explanation for why Hmong refugees suddenly became blind. That omission led them to a search for nontraditional but still acceptable explanations in the Hmong's experiences with wartime atrocities.

Patterns Appear Because of Similarity

Often items, events, responses, persons, or themes appear to clump together because they are similar to one another. LeCompte and Holloway first noticed that the theater teacher in the Arts Focus program frequently addressed the students as if they already were actors. The teacher repeatedly would utter statements like "Now, this line is supposed to be funny. You all are actors; you know how to put humor across." The researchers later not only noticed that this particular teacher used a variety of other ways to refer to students as actors, but that all four of the Arts Focus teachers referred to their students as if they already were artists. For example:

- ■ "Now, composers always sign the music they write. So put your name at the bottom of your score."
- ■ "Artists always keep their brushes clean. Make sure that yours are washed out before you leave."
- ■ "Let's brainstorm some ways to get the work of all you writers published."

Frequency counts first identified this pattern of address in the theater teacher's class; the existence of similarity then established a pattern of other ways to address students as artists both in her own classroom and in those of the other teachers as well.

Patterns Emerge Because of Co-occurrence

Patterns also can be identified by the fact that items, events, responses, kinds of person, or themes occur at the same time or in the same place; that is, they appear to be "correlated." LeCompte and Dworkin (1991), for example, noticed that schools where teachers had high levels of burnout and feelings of entrapment also had higher percentages of students who dropped out of school (LeCompte and Dworkin 1991). Example 10.2 documents another case of co-occurrence.

EXAMPLE 10.2

PATTERNS IDENTIFIED THROUGH CO-OCCURRENCE: ASSOCIATIONS BETWEEN AGE AND USE OF HIGH-RISK DRUG USING SITES

In a study designed to determine whether it would be useful to locate HIV prevention activities in urban sites where drug users were injecting drugs and sharing needles, researcher Kim Radda identified sites that ranged from outside, public and exposed, to inside, in private apartments or behind the locked doors of public bathrooms. She then asked whether different types of people might prefer one kind of site over another. Based on observations and preliminary ethnographic survey data, the first choice for most drug users consisted of public sites, which were less safe but easier to access. Older drug users also selected outside public locations as their first choice but did so in smaller numbers. Their second choice was the apartment of someone they knew. A much larger percentage of older drug users made this choice than did than younger users. Radda theorized that the discomforts of using drugs outside coupled with the fear of being caught by the police prompted older drug users to look for safer and more private locations, even if they had to reduce the frequency of their drug use (Radda et al. 1998).

Patterns Emerge as One Piece of Data
Is Corroborated by Others

The process of triangulation often can unearth patterns as responses, items, events, or themes from various sources of data begin to corroborate one another.

EXAMPLE 10.3

PATTERNS IDENTIFIED VIA TRIANGULATION AND CORROBORATION

Barbara Medina discovered a pattern of social-class differentiation among Navajo teachers and teacher aides when she compared field note data collected from three different types of educational settings: a camping trip on a remote mesa at the end of the school year for elementary schoolchildren, their teachers, and the teachers' classroom aides; activities in daily classrooms; and interactions in meetings of the bilingual program's staff. Medina noticed that in all three settings, teachers asked aides to do all kinds of menial tasks and felt uncomfortable when aides demonstrated knowledge superior to theirs in some specific areas. For example, on the camping trip, some of the teachers came dressed in the same good clothes they wore to work, systematically requested the aides to prepare and serve coffee to them, and left the job of sleeping in the tents with children to the aides. The teachers, meanwhile, slept in their nearby and comfortable campers and recreational vehicles. In the classrooms, aides usually were asked to work with the most difficult and least able students, those to whom the lowest social status was attached. And in the bilingual meetings, teachers expressed discomfort when it became obvious that they sometimes had to rely on aides who, despite their lower social status, were more fluent in Navajo than the teachers themselves. Triangulating data from these three types of settings indicated that teachers seemed to feel that aides needed to "pay dues" by performing less pleasant tasks—as the teachers themselves felt they had done earlier in their careers. Medina reasoned that the teachers, with their college degrees and higher salaries, felt that they had attained a status level higher than that of the aides, who sometimes had less than a two-year associate of arts degree. Medina was able to link the behaviors she observed in educational settings to more pervasive systemwide patterns of status discrimination and exercise of power within and between groups in the community with varying degrees of education and affluence (Medina 1998).

Patterns Appear as Sequences

Patterns also appear as a sequence, usually temporal, of items or events. Rituals and repeated practices often show up as an invariable sequence of behaviors, as Holley and Doss (1983) found when they noticed—contrary to common belief among teachers and school administrators—that young women who became pregnant did not drop out of school when they got pregnant or when their pregnancies became noticeable, or even when the babies were born. Rather, the sequence that predicted dropping out of school was: *first*, the young women gave birth. *Next*, the young mothers' child-care arrangements failed, and only *then* did they drop out of school. Dropping out, then, was a child-care issue, not one of motherhood alone. Dropouts stayed home because they had to care for their babies. However, this sequence of factors associated with dropping out was revealed only after many observations over time.

Patterns Appear Because of Congruence with Prior Hypotheses

Even before their actual fieldwork begins, researchers often do hypothesize that patterns exist; these hypotheses are embodied in the formative models that inform initial fieldwork. Based on their prior experience, readings, and the theories that informed their work, researchers decide in advance that a specific pattern *should* exist, and they then look for confirming or disconfirming evidence. LeCompte proceeded in this fashion to look for a pattern of teacher behavior that encouraged student achievement *for its own sake*, thus supporting the intrinsic value of learning. This pattern, however, was found only in the behavior of one of the four teachers in the Learning to Work study. Similarly, LeCompte and Holloway hypothesized that arts instruction *should* involve a variety of strategies for inducing students to think in imaginative ways; they structured both their observations and their data analysis so as to identify this kind of instruction. Silva and colleagues (1997) hypothesized that there *should* be significant differences in risk behaviors between urban lower-income and university youth, and that because of the emphasis on maintaining female virginity, gender *would* play an important role overall and within these socio-geographic groupings. Both semistructured and ethnographic survey questions were formulated to test this hypothesis. Data analysis using both sources of data confirmed the predicted differences among groups in attitudes toward sex- and substance use–related risk behaviors, with urban young men most likely to engage in smoking, drinking, and risky sexual behaviors, followed by university males, urban women, and finally, female university students (Silva et al. 1997).

Patterns Can Emerge as the Study Progresses

Patterns can become more and more elaborated during the life of a study. New subcomponents of the patterns can emerge at any time during the study, and these can be added to guide further data collection and analysis.

GROUPING PATTERNS WITHIN DOMAINS TO CREATE STRUCTURES AND SUBSTANTIVE THEORIES

Once researchers have isolated a stable set of patterns, they can investigate how two or more of the patterns actually may be linked together. A number of linked empirical patterns then can be seen to constitute a *structure*; the explanations given for why these patterns group together within a structure constitute emerging substantive *theories*.

➤•➤•➤ **EXAMPLE 10.4**

LEARNING THE DISCIPLINE NEEDED TO BECOME CREATIVE ARTISTS

In the Arts Focus study, LeCompte and Holloway (1997, 1998) began their exploration by examining a domain that they called *learning how to become artists*. They linked this idea to a series of teacher activities that the researchers thought had the potential to change how students thought about themselves and their artistic endeavors. One of the key ideas was that being an artist was not simply a matter of doing whatever you liked and calling it "creativity." Rather, students had to learn difficult techniques, acquire serious work habits, and learn both the norms and the skills required in their trade. This key idea led to a structure that came to be called "disciplined creativity." The patterns that constituted this structure included:

- Watching professional artists at work
- Learning norms and rules of professional behavior
- Learning the concepts and language of specific arts disciplines
- Acquiring the tools of the discipline
- Learning to use the tools of the discipline
- Learning "tricks of the trade"
- Identifying mentors

◆━●━◆━●━◆

These patterns categorized the aspects of discipline teachers felt students needed to learn in order turn their creativity into real artistry; in turn, the patterns dictated "what teachers do" to help students learn. These patterns were associated with the teachers' rationales for why they taught as they did. Each category contained multiple concrete acts, statements, and activities that teachers did, said, and organized to illustrate the pattern in which they had been placed. These patterns were applicable to each of the four teachers, even though they respectively taught writing, theater, visual arts, and instrumental music. LeCompte and Holloway also examined what the students did, said, and organized to demonstrate that they were, in fact, "becoming artists" under their teachers' guidance. These, too, could be categorized according to the same patterns as teacher behavior.

LeCompte and Holloway began the Arts Focus study with some initial hunches and ideas about the impact of arts education on students, based on their reading of research literature and theory prior to beginning the study and their own experiences in music and creative writing. They felt that the arts would have an important impact on students' identity and that both role modeling and opportunities to practice the discipline would be factors reinforcing such an identity. These hunches were informed by theoretical work on role learning and acquisition by Erving Goffman, Robert Turner, and Pierre Bourdieu. Using the work of these theorists to guide their development of coding categories, LeCompte and Holloway tried to imagine how each of these concepts would look in practice, an exercise in operationalization. They developed a preliminary set of patterns and units with concrete examples of the behavior each unit and pattern represented. They also linked these to related conceptual domains and subdomains that helped to explain why these activities occurred. Table 10.1 displays some of these initial patterns and examples of the behavior they subsumed. Blanks in Tables 10.1, 10.2, and 10.3 indicate that specific behavioral indicators for that domain still needed to be isolated from the data. Note that "IM" stands for "instrumental music," "TA" for "theater arts," "VA" for "visual arts," and "LA" for "literary arts"; the other initials represent the names of specific teachers.

Cross Reference: See Book 4, chapter 3 for a discussion of cultural domains

At the end of the first year of observations and interviews, the researchers began a systematic review of their data, looking inductively for themes that seemed to be the most important emphases in the program in terms of what the teachers themselves articulated as goals for their students and what they seemed to stress in their classrooms. The results, which *emerged* from the data after a laborious process of reading and rereading field notes, transcripts of interviews from students and teachers, and documents from the program, was a set of additional patterns linked to *learning to become an artist*. In a sense, these patterns were surprises, not anticipated by the researchers initially but perfectly congruent with other theories about the impact that participating in the arts has on people. These were built into the emerging theory informing the study. Two of these are displayed in Tables 10.2 and 10.3.

LeCompte and Holloway had not anticipated that risk taking, portrayed in Table 10.2, would play such a large role in the program—until they realized that each of the arts programs required students—and their teachers—to perform publically and to "think outside the box." Sometimes the thinking involved nothing more threatening than a new color scheme or costume, but assignments that required them to embody a different sex or species or to imagine themselves or the world as other than it seems to be could be threatening indeed. Further, the act

TABLE 10.1 Proceeding Inductively and Deductively: Chunking Data into Conceptual Categories of Role Modeling, Learning Skills, and Acquiring an Identity

Structure: Learning to Become an Artist	*Pattern: What Teachers Do*	*Units: Types of Behavior or Activity*	*Items: Concrete Examples*
	Teach the physical tools of the discipline	Provide lists of artists' tools and equipment to buy	Theater arts: "We're going to have a makeup man come in, and the first thing he'll tell you is to have your own makeup kit. For $30 you can get a start-up kit."
		Organize practice sessions for using tools	Theater arts: "Our stage combat expert is coming tomorrow and we'll practice swordplay with broomsticks. So bring in a broomstick. Make sure you sand it smooth or you'll get splinters in your hands."
			Visual arts: "Next week, come with your smocks. We'll do clay modeling and it's messy."
		Demonstrations	Instrumental music: "You first have to set up your keyboard like this."
	Provide role models	Visit artists' studios, backstage, go to foundry, book fairs	Visual arts: "OK, remember that your assignment for this weekend is to visit Open Studios. You have to visit two studios and take notes on what you saw."
		Guest artists and writers	Visual arts: "Our guests are two of the most renowned contemporary Pueblo potters. They're going to be showing you how to hand build a pot."
		Teachers *are* artists; talk about their own art practice	Literary arts: "I wrote my autobiography as a fictionalized biography because the publisher didn't think kids would buy an autobiography."
	Teaching the proper behavior and norms of the art discipline	Procedures for establishing creatorship of an artwork	Visual arts: To the class: "Sign your painting in cursive. Remember how we do that?"
			Instrumental music: "As a composer, you always put your name on your piece."

		Learning the ropes, tricks of the trade	Visual arts: "Wash your brushes or they'll get hard and useless." Theater arts: "No jewelry; it reflects from stage." Theater arts: "Maurita demands quiet backstage because the audience can hear backstage noise."
	Teaching the concepts and language of the specific discipline		Visual arts: "I want you to understand these terms: 'realism' [explains]; 'photorealism' [explains]; 'abstract and nonrepresentational.'" Visual arts: "Lots of people think that abstract and nonrepresentational art are the same, but they're not." Visual arts: "Pop art is about shape." Theater arts: On how to act out T. S. Eliot's poem: "Don't think about the poem. Be cats! Don't get into your head. What do cats DO?"

of risk taking linked both to Vygotskian notions of learning and development, which require learners constantly to take on challenges just beyond what they can do easily by themselves, and to writings by Lev Vygotsky (1978), John Dewey (1934), and Maxine Greene (1995) about the riskiness inherent in the nature of the artistic enterprise. The ideas articulated by these learning theorists provided more general theoretical roots for explanations of the kinds of activities emphasized in the Arts Focus program. Table 10.3 portrays yet another emergent structure in the Arts Focus database: disciplined creativity.

The structure that LeCompte and Holloway ultimately named "disciplined creativity," displayed in part in Table 10.3, embodied the important emphasis in the program that creativity is not a magical gift for the isolated few. It can, in fact, be nurtured, systematized, and honed in very specific ways. For students who were not accustomed to thinking of themselves as creative all the time, learning about these strategies was a revelatory part of their

TABLE 10.2 Adding Patterns and Structures Inductively in Arts Focus: Risk Taking

Structure: Risk Taking	Pattern: What Teachers Do	Units: Types of Behavior or Activity	Items: Concrete Examples
	Solicit criticism or feedback	Teacher offers own work or behavior for critique	Literary arts: Teacher asks students to write letters telling him how they feel about his leaving for New Zealand at semester's end.
		Models how groups can safely critique each other's work	Visual arts: "Gather round this easel, far enough away to get a perspective. Not too far away. Now: Let's all examine the brushwork. The uses of color. Does it fit with the mood of the subject? Is the lighting convincing?" (The painting is a Vermeer reproduction.) "Now, let's look at our own work."
		Requires students to critique each other's behavior or practice	Theater arts: "OK, everybody. Last night's play. What worked well? What could we have done better?"
		Uses "debriefing" sessions	Visual arts: Teacher, after students attended an exhibition: "So why wasn't the exhibition very successful?"
	Publically confront controversial or sensitive subjects	Bring in controversial speakers or guests	Social studies teachers invite Socialist Worker Party candidate to address class
			Visual arts: Teacher takes students to university museum where artwork portrays full frontal male nudity
		Assume a nontraditional role	Theater arts: Teacher recruits girls to play male roles in *Romeo and Juliet*; teaches them how to walk and sit like men
	Performance	Teachers require of themselves the same kinds of performance demands that they ask of children	Theater arts: Good-looking assistant principal plays the part of the prince in *Romeo and Juliet*—his first-ever theatrical performance
		Invites assessment of teacher's own behavior or practice	Literary arts: Teacher engages in a reading of his own novel at a local bookstore
			Visual arts: Visual arts teacher invites students to attend her own first piano recital

TABLE 10.3 Adding Patterns and Structures Inductively in Arts Focus: Disciplined Creativity

Structure: Disciplined Creativity	Pattern: What Teachers Do	Unit: Types of Activity	Item: Concrete Example
	Teach how to stimulate creativity, get started	Brainstorming	Language arts and Instrumental music: Encouraging students to come up with new ideas and interpretations for their compositions
		Looking for resources	Theater arts: To a student who can't figure out what to do with his flawed painting: "Remember your resources. Go to the books. Look at other landscapes. That's what resources are for. Either you can come up with ideas on your own or you have to use resources to help you get ideas."
		Going to experts	Visual arts: Viewing multiple versions of *Romeo and Juliet* and reading the play itself before helping theater students design the sets
	Teach students how to get unstuck	How to get a new perspective	Visual arts: "Put your work up on the easel and step back from it."
		How to stop the jitters	Theater arts: "OK, we now are going to practice stage fright exercises." Language arts: "If you can't get started at the beginning of your story, start in the middle. Read other work in the same genre to get ideas."
	Internalize or "fossilize" the rigors of everyday practice (Vygotsky)	Multiple rehearsals	Theater arts: "Diction is something you work on all your life. If you have braces, it's harder."
		Daily practice	Language arts: Students wrote multiple drafts. They had to write every day Instrumental music: Students created multiple drafts of their compositions. They practiced their instrument daily Visual arts: "Start with a sketch. Then rough out a color scheme. Try it on the sketch. Then do another one. See which works best."

experience; for the researchers, this structure was linked closely to the practice theory of Pierre Bourdieu, whose theories informed the study. Taken together, both the initial (Table 10.1) and the subsequent analysis (Tables 10.2 and 10.3) created an overall coding and analytic scheme for the data, especially since each pattern was concretely associated with a number of the specific behaviors and statements from teachers and students that exemplified what the researchers meant by the specific cover terms and included terms (Spradley 1979) they used. This scheme was used in two ways: first, to code data already collected—field notes and interview transcripts; and second, as a focus for subsequent observations in classrooms. At the end of the second year of fieldwork, it also was used to classify information about the responses or reactions of the students to what the teachers were doing and information about what the students said they were getting out of the program.

At this point, LeCompte and Holloway found that they needed to add units and items to the original existing domain categories—including some of those developed in the Learning to Work study regarding use of time, patterns of keeping busy, and accountability. These, in turn, were used as codes for data that were then classified and manipulated. Overall, the scheme developed initially for the Arts Focus project served well for analysis of all of the kinds of data collected during the project's duration: field notes, unstructured interviews, standardized surveys, test scores and school-level data on students, artifacts and documents, and archival material. The process described here is parallel to the development of formative theory or theorizing as we describe it in Books 1, 2, and 3 and earlier in this book, although there are a variety of ways of engaging in it, as Book 2 illustrates.

In Book 2, we provide additional examples of the ways in which patterns emerge from both qualitative and quantitative analysis. We describe the interaction between the creation of a formative model, the collection of qualitative/ethnographic data that guide survey generation, and the ways in which data from both qualitative and survey/quantitative data intersect, using the formative model as

 Cross Reference:
See Book 1, Book 2, chapters 4, 5 and 6, and Book 3, Chapter 1

 Cross Reference:
See Book 2 for a more detailed approach to the intersection of qualitative and quantitative data in development and analysis

guidance. We also pay close attention to the ways in which a combination of formative (derived locally) and literature-based theory explain the relationships among study domains. The following example illustrates this approach.

EXAMPLE 10.5

DISCOVERING A PATTERN OF GENDER DIFFERENTIATION IN FACTORS PREDICTING SEXUAL RISK OUTCOMES AMONG MALE AND FEMALE ADOLESCENTS IN SRI LANKA

The example in chapter 9 from a study of youth and sexual risk in Sri Lanka (Silva et al. 1997) shows the association between the variables in each of the key domains—family, work, and peers—that were associated with four different, though related, dependent variables associated with sex risk. All the variables were identified in the formative qualitative work that preceded the survey, and the items were amalgamated into the measures incorporated in the survey. The links among them were hypothesized to exist in the study model, but they did not actually appear until the associations among the variables in the independent and dependent domains were examined quantitatively using the entire study sample. Because the formative qualitative data and other literature suggested that girls might be at increasing risk, the researchers decided to examine the role that gender played in predicting outcomes. The explanation for the independent variable/outcomes associations emerged when the data were reanalyzed by gender. The reanalysis showed that males were more independent of their families, had a wider network of friends and were more likely to engage in a wide variety of activities with them, had more access to information on sexuality from more sources, and were less geographically constrained in the work environment. Girls were more socially and geographically constrained by their families and at work had narrower, primarily female, friendship networks and also had limited access to information on sexuality and sexual risk. The researchers referred to this pattern as "women's ways of knowing" and illustrated the limitations that gender conferred on women's experiences and resources that prevented them from protecting themselves more effectively against sexual risk.

As mentioned earlier, theorizing such as occurred in the example above occurs throughout the life of an ethnographic study, and it is only at the end that the study's explanatory model is fully developed.

SUMMARY

In the previous chapter, we detailed the ways quantified data from standardized ethnographic surveys are organized, managed, and analyzed. In this chapter, we have discussed the way ethnographers use all of their crunched and coded data to identify the patterns and structures that constitute the cultural portrait they are trying to assemble. Next, we devote chapters 11 and 12 to the display and interpretation of analyzed data.

11 ━◆━◆━◆━

FINE-TUNING RESULTS AND BEGINNING THE WRITE-UP

As noted in chapter 10, James Spradley calls the process of putting together all the pieces of a study *structural or constitutive analysis*. Constitutive analysis, however, does not produce the final ethnographic product. The assembled pieces have to be transformed into a full "story"—a process that many ethnographers find difficult. To solve this problem, ethnographers have developed many strategies for getting started, ranging from the rather mundane and routine to the artistic.

STRATEGIES FOR GETTING STARTED

Perhaps the most important thing to remember at this stage of the process is that the entire story does not have to be told all at once. Essentially, since they know that it is impossible to write up an entire story all at once, ethnographers usually start with a single piece of the story. And if they cannot begin at the beginning, they begin to write about whatever place seems feasible.

Researchers can begin chipping away at the task by first assembling some constituents deductively, from the top down, or inductively, from the bottom up, or using some recursive combination of moving back and forth between

Describe the
Functions or
Organizational
Structure of a
Group

Write Up
the Critical
Events in
Chronological
Order

Make a List
of the Most
Important
Empirical Facts

Create a Display,
or, When in
Doubt, Draw a
Picture!

Summary

induction and deduction. They also can use the conceptual framework developed in the formative stages of a study to begin writing up rationales and explanations for phenomena at the item, variable, factor, and domain level of theorizing. All of these strategies involve identifying a chunk of the story to be told and writing up a piece of it.

Ethnographers also can create a rough outline by simply closing their eyes (metaphorically), thinking about their original research questions and what they have learned in the field, and writing up the best story they can about what they think they have found—without looking at the data. Such a story can provide a basic outline for figuring out where to begin and how it seems the story unfolds, although it never should be used as a substitute for real, evidenced research results. Below we describe a number of strategies for beginning to organize partial results and conceptual musings into a full-fledged ethnographic portrait.

REEXAMINE THE THEORETICAL FRAMEWORK

If researchers began their investigations with an initial, relatively well-developed formative ethnographic theory, the process of assembling and integrating components would, to some degree, be informed by this model. A review of this formative theory can structure the beginning of the write-up. A study that began with such a deductive approach based on a formative theoretical framework but then shifted to bottom-up induction was the Schensuls' study in Mauritius, presented in Example 11.1. In this case, getting started involved the following:

**Cross
Reference:**
See Book 2 for
a discussion of how
to operationalize
variables in a model

- making sure that all the relevant independent domains or "causal factors" were included in the model;
- making sure that both the independent and dependent (problem) variable domains were well understood and operationalized;
- exploring and confirming, disconfirming, or developing a broader understanding of the relationships among these independent variables and between them and the problem or dependent variable; and
- explaining these relationships both qualitatively and quantitatively.

EXAMPLE 11.1

WRITING UP RESEARCH BY BEGINNING WITH A FORMATIVE THEORETICAL MODEL:
SEX RISK IN MAURITIUS

In the formative theoretical model for research on young women, work, and risk in Mauritius, the process of domain modeling identified three domains—family, peers, and work—that researchers believed would be important in shaping sexual beliefs, attitudes, and behaviors. Exploratory ethnography **Cross Reference:** See Figure 5.2 and Table 5.1 in chapter 5 of this book resulted in an elaboration of these domains into a coding tree or taxonomy (see Figure 11.4) that was developed further through semistructured interviews with a sample of ninety unmarried young women and thirty unmarried young men. Results from investigation with these two data sources contributed to a further elaboration of the coding tree and the identification of items and variables that were included in a structured interview schedule. The process of assembling components and writing up the data followed the guide established by the coding trees. For example, one section of the monograph the researchers produced summarized both qualitative and quantitative data related to "family." Paragraphs or larger sections of the write-up focused on different items and factors in the taxonomy, and the section as a whole covered a description and analysis of all the items included in the coding tree for that domain—family structure, family health, family work history, family activities, family socialization practices, and so on—with greater emphasis on those that seemed to be related more specifically to sexuality. The quantitative analysis identified statistically significant associations among variables, and the qualitative data illustrated those examples and helped to explain why the associations existed. This process was recursive—proceeding both inductively and deductively.

In contrast, some exploratory or descriptive research begins with questions rather than concepts. Researchers first identify a problem, question, or topic as the central domain. At least initially, some of the variables or conditions associated with the central domain or problem may be identified or predicted in advance of the study, but many more may emerge in the course of data collection. Furthermore, it is likely that many additional new domains associated with the original set will be identified and explored as the study progresses. The purpose of the study, then, becomes to identify new domains associated with the topic or problem, describe them, find associations among them, and interpret the relationships. One such study that began with questions, rather than with a formative theoretical framework, is described in Example 11.2.

EXAMPLE 11.2

UNDERSTANDING CHILDREN'S ACTIVITY LEVELS: WRITING UP EXPLORATORY RESEARCH

Researchers Schensul, Diaz, and Woolley were interested in finding out what activities Latino children ages seven to ten were involved in and what might account for the patterns that were expected to emerge. To find out, they conducted listing exercises with classrooms of children in the target age group. They asked children to brainstorm all the activities in which they were involved. Researchers probed for the times when and the locations where these activities occurred, asking such questions as, "What about weekends?" or "What about at home, or in the back yard, or on the back steps?" This exercise produced a listing of sixty-two items ranging from helping with housework to athletic exercises after school. These activities then were reconstituted into an "activities recall" instrument in which nearly eighty young students and their primary caregivers participated; they also took part in a semistructured interview.

The recall activity provided information on the central concept: children's activity outputs. The interview schedule provided additional data on a variety of factors associated with differential involvement in activities and perceived differential output. The results were descriptive, although researchers also generated some predictive hypotheses, including the idea that mothers' activity patterns established norms for daughters but not for sons.

REVIEW THE RESEARCH QUESTIONS

One of the most important—and often forgotten—ways to begin the write-up of ethnographic data is to go back to the research questions and focus on the most important questions that the study was intended to answer. This provides critical clues and directions as to what parts of the study can and should be written up first. This is the approach that LeCompte took to the Learning Circle study.

EXAMPLE 11.3

WRITING UP RESULTS FROM THE RESEARCH QUESTIONS: THE LEARNING CIRCLE STUDY

Initially, LeCompte was stymied when faced with mountains of data from the Learning Circle study. Then she remembered that the original questions to be addressed in the evaluation portion of the study had to do with the impact of the program on student achievement and self-esteem. These data were crucial to the program for refunding. LeCompte began by assembling all the results they had amassed for student performance, including teacher grades, standardized tests, classroom teacher-made tests, and the developmental records maintained by the Learning Circle teachers, and she wrote a section of the report summarizing this information. Subsequently, after describing the results of the study with respect to the outcomes—or dependent variables, student achievement and self-esteem—LeCompte had many choices. She could (1) review the remainder of the data to identify and describe the causes—anticipated or unanticipated—of the outcomes as defined above. She could (2) try to determine why these causes were plausible explanations for the student outcomes. She could (3) consider what other aspects of the setting and activities might relate to student achievement and self-esteem and describe these. Or she could examine the data to determine whether there were differences in perception of parents, teachers, and students with regard to what satisfactory "outcomes" might be, thereby (4) offering alternatives to the standard student outcome measures itemized above. These possible directions are appropriate for most studies.

━●━●━●━

In summary, LeCompte chose to address all three of the ways that results can be written up:

- Explain why the particular results had the described effect.
- Describe what other circumstances, not anticipated, explained the phenomenon studied.
- Offer alternative theories or measures to explain why events transpired as they did.

CREATE SOME VIGNETTES

A look at the initial research questions also can give hints as to how an initial portrayal could be formulated. One very specific strategy is to begin by creating **vignettes**. Vignettes often are snapshots or short descriptions of events or people that evoke the overall picture the ethnographer is trying to paint. There are other kinds of vignettes that describe what we call dramas and critical events. Van Maanen (1988) refers to all vignettes as "impressionist tales"; they are stories that can be told quickly and that "mark and make memorable the fieldwork experience because they

Definition: A vignette is a short dramatic description, some of which typify by creating a composite of all the people or events studied. Others dramatize a person, act, event, or activity so as to catch the attention of the reader; still others summarize a biography, event, or other phenomenon

reconstruct in dramatic form people or events the ethnographer regards as especially notable" (ibid.) and hence
reportable. Van Maanen divides material suitable for
vignettes into "realist tales," "impressionistic accounts," and
"confessional tales." Realist tales are descriptions of everyday events, daily or regular routines, or average people.
Impressionistic accounts resemble the personal journal
of a researcher, as they include the researcher's own value
judgments and impressions. Confessional tales are accounts
of the ethnographer's own behavior in the field and often
include quite intimate revelations about the ethnographer's
own mistakes and successes in the field.

Our own categories of vignettes are somewhat different from Van Maanen's, though they serve the same
descriptive purposes as his. One significant difference is
that we do not include the confessional category except
under special circumstances in which the ethnographer's
actions—deliberately or inadvertently—changed the
course of events or highlighted particular practices. We
categorize vignettes as follows:

TYPES OF VIGNETTES

- *Normative depictions* that portray typical phenomena
- *Dramas* that portray a sharp break from typical events
- *Critical events* that change the course of events

Normative depictions are similar to what Van Maanen
(1988) calls "realist tales." Normative depictions present
in a forceful and succinct way a description that the ethnographer considers to be an authentic cultural representation. They usually are written in the third person; many
of them describe "normal" behavior, such as "a typical day
in the life of the persons I am studying," "a typical person of the type I am studying," or "a typical performance
of the activity I am interested in." In Example 11.4, Elias
Martinez creates such a normative vignette to describe the
daily activities of Latino immigrant schoolchildren in a
mountain community.

EXAMPLE 11.4

A NORMATIVE DEPICTION: THE DAY BEGINS AT SNOW MOUNTAIN ELEMENTARY SCHOOL

Mornings dawn crisply in the high mountain valleys. The whole valley seems energized with the expectation of a new day of work for many of the inhabitants of a trailer city, La Sierra Trailer Court, located about two miles from the edge of town. Soon the school busses would be arriving and the children would begin another day of school. The trailer park is abuzz with sounds of cars warming up or others having the ice scraped from their windshields. Parents, older siblings, or relatives make sure that the children are up in the darkness of winter mornings and are prepared for another day of school. Mornings at the bus stop are quiet. The children, still sleepy from the night before, begin to arrive from their respective trailers. The trailer park is large, and some have walked nearly a quarter of a mile from their trailer. As the bus arrives, hurried goodbyes are exchanged and the children's mood seems to change; their energy level increases and they begin to chat with each other in anticipation of another day at school. This morning, as on most mornings, the parking lot of the school is teeming with activity. Automobiles, minivans and sport utility vehicles line up to discharge children as directed by a teacher or the principal. Up on the hillside, away from the bustle, five busses unload the immigrant children from across the valley. Teachers meet them and escort them to a staging area on the playground so they can await their march into the school building. With backpacks flying, children hurry to their assigned places. Latino children stop to greet whomever happens to be around who can speak Spanish. They seem anxious to maintain continuity with someone who can speak their language. . . . The more ebullient Latino students call out to any Latino person they see and engage in banter. Conversations in Spanish can be heard as the Latino children call out to give each other encouragement for the day ahead. Then begins the separation.

The energy that was created in the short bus ride down the mountain is soon diffused as the children are separated into groups lined up behind their respective teachers. Some are lucky enough to have two or three other Latino children in their class with whom they can talk in Spanish. Others are not so lucky. They join classes where they might be the only Spanish speaker. These students adopt a subdued demeanor or continue to talk with another Latino student in the lines near them, but not for long. As soon as the children have gathered, the teacher marches them to the classrooms to begin another day of learning (Martinez 1998, 237–240).

Martinez's description continues, following the children through the day. He traces how they first are separated from each other and then from regular classroom instruction when they are sent to several kinds of special language instruction, instruction that only infrequently is related to what the nonimmigrant students are being taught. He argues that this process destroys educational continuity and prevents Latino children from developing both social competence and academic skills in English.

Key point　　*Because ethnographers look for patterns and structures, overall themes, and shared meanings, normative depictions—as composites of what people say, do, believe, or are characterized by—can come close to an accurate and full picture of a cultural scene.* By contrast, *dramas* are vignettes that say to the reader, "Okay, now that I've gotten your attention with this exciting story, let me back away from it and tell you about what happened every day in more normal circumstances." Below is such a drama; it describes the violation of an important norm whose existence became very clear because of the violation.

EXAMPLE 11.5

IDENTIFYING AN UNBREACHABLE RULE IN PUBLIC SCHOOLS: TAKING ATTENDANCE EVERY PERIOD

During a faculty meeting in December, the new high school math teacher suddenly blurted out, "So, what do you do with all these little blue slips for student absences? I thought it was too much trouble to hand them in each period, so I've just sort of been taking attendance at the beginning of the day and ignoring the rest of the periods." A shocked silence filled the room, broken after a few long minutes by the Spanish teacher, who said, "You know, these are really important. A child could show up at the beginning of the day. But if they decided to leave at ten o'clock to go to the restaurant across that busy street outside for a snack, and they got hit by a car and hurt, or even kidnapped, we wouldn't know where that child is. And we are responsible. Legally responsible! In fact, the last teacher who saw that child is responsible. If that last teacher were you, it's *your* neck! That's why we take attendance after *every* class. And I suggest you do the same."

Critical event vignettes also catch the reader's attention, but they depict scenes that were turning points in the researcher's understanding or that changed the direction of events in the field site.

A CRITICAL EVENT: THE FACULTY CHANGES ITS STANCE ON ARTS FOCUS

Even after a year and a half, the Arts Focus program at Centerline Middle School was perceived by the non-arts teachers to be something of an intruder. It was received warmly by some and with distrust by others, but it truly was embraced only by the principal, assistant principal, and the four participating arts teachers. A constant source of low morale among the arts teachers was the lack of support, disinterest, and sometimes open hostility they experienced from other teachers. The message seemed to be that though art was nice, it was a frill, and certainly not the responsibility of non-art teachers.

During the first year, the four arts teachers did all of the recruiting of students, all of the media publicity, and all of the visits to parents and other schools in the district, trying to stimulate interest and build enrollment. The faculty's disinterested stance changed dramatically, however, at a faculty meeting in December, just before the open enrollment period was to begin. The old principal had not been very enthusiastic about the arts program. By contrast, the new Centerline principal had been a band director and was convinced that the best thing the school had was its Arts Focus program—and that without it, the school would be in danger of closure because of dropping enrollment. So he proposed that the other teachers help out with recruiting, perhaps by talking about how strong the academic program at Centerline was at the spring parents' meeting. These meetings were an annual community event at which parents chose which public school their child would attend. Each school tried to put on a good "show" to make its program appear irresistible and appealing to parents.

But not a single academic area teacher at Centerline volunteered to help. One person grumbled that art wasn't his responsibility. At that point, the assistant principal stood and began to write on the blackboard. She reminded the faculty members that three years ago, enrollment at Centerline had dropped so precipitously that school district officials were about to close the school. The arts program had been initiated to encourage new enrollment. The assistant principal quickly sketched out the current and projected enrollment figures, with and without the Arts Focus students. Her figures made it clear that the school still was underrolled for the size of the faculty—given that teachers were assigned to schools based on enrollment size—even though the 165 Arts Focus students brought the total enrollment out of danger of imminent closure. Further, though the school building had a capacity of 630 students, current enrollment was only 420 students. With a school board whose mandate was to cut costs, underenrolled schools were being closed and surplus teachers were in danger of losing their jobs, "This means," said the assistant principal, "that each of you will have to bring in at least one new student next year if we aren't going to lose faculty." Silence fell.

Then a sixth-grade teacher who previously had been unsupportive of the arts program blurted out, "You know, our current sixth grade is so small that all of the sixth-grade teachers are teaching part-time this year. Next year, the seventh grade will be small, and the seventh-grade teachers will be part-time, too. And the next year, it'll be eighth grade. The Arts Focus teachers kept our school open for us last year, and we never even noticed. This year, we've got to go out and help them or we won't have *any* jobs in three years!" Another silence fell.

Suddenly, three teachers volunteered the entire team of sixth-grade teachers to make presentations at parents' night. Others volunteered to help in designing newspaper advertisements to publicize the program. The rest of the meeting was devoted to planning ways the whole school could participate in recruiting Arts Focus students. And for the first time in eighteen months, the Arts Focus teachers began to feel as though they had become crucial participants in their school.

◆▬●▬◆▬●▬◆

 Key point   *Dramas and critical event vignettes should be used with caution, since they generally portray extreme, unique, or unusual events rather than patterns, and they are* **not** *typical.* Focusing on extraordinary or extreme events can create a biased picture of the daily life the ethnographer usually attempts to portray, unless it is the existence of such an extreme case that makes the pattern emerge clearly. Sometimes, for example, an ethnographer cannot really learn what the rules are in given situations unless somebody violates them. The dramatic event depicted in Example 11.5 does not portray a typical event, but it does demonstrate clearly what the rules are in the context of a major violation of norms. Similarly, by making explicit the attitudes of teachers before and after the assistant principal's display of enrollment figures, Example 11.6 establishes clearly the cultural norms that originally surrounded the Arts Focus program: the general faculty considered it to be a frill.

Analysis of what these norms were and why they changed helped greatly to explain why the program struggled for its first few years and why, after all the teachers got behind the program, it began to achieve a roaring success.

Too many novice ethnographers think that their analysis and write-up are finished once they have "told the story" of each and every one of their informants. Unfortunately, by themselves, vignettes are not the end product of the ethnography. They merely serve as "advance cognitive organizers" that tell enough of the whole story for the reader to follow subsequent and more complete narratives or arguments demonstrating how the vignette constitutes evidence for, or illustrates, the position the ethnographer is taking or the explanations presented.

WRITE SOME HISTORY

Another way to begin a write-up is to trace the history of whatever has been studied. Often, research results are not very easy to understand unless some of the events that preceded or gave rise to the phenomenon the ethnographer is trying to describe are made clear. Writing down that history is a good way to get some text down on paper and organize both one's own thoughts and the structure of the write-up itself. These can include the history of a program, a culture, or an institution.

EXAMPLE 11.7

STARTING WITH THE HISTORY OF A COMMUNITY

Liane Brouillette began her report of current school reforms in a periurban community in the western United States by describing the growth and change in the community from a frontier agricultural and mining area to the suburban fringe of a major metropolitan area. She used this background to trace the growth of the school district and the changes in educational practice that the philosophies of the three school superintendents the district had had since its founding brought to the district. This historical material formed the background for understanding current conflicts between various community groups over the purposes of education, methods of instruction, ways to finance schools, and administrative styles required for effective leadership in the district (Brouillette 1996).

DESCRIBE A SOCIAL PROCESS

Ethnographers also can begin by describing social processes. LeCompte and Holloway began part of the report for the Arts Focus program by describing the recruitment and enrollment procedures used by Centerline Middle School to fill places in the arts program. When this was completed, the researchers discovered that the description not only documented the target procedures, but it also made considerable reference to bureaucratic snafus that impeded them: areas of conflict and misunderstanding between the school district administration, the school principal, the teachers, and the students' parents, as well as factors that impeded accurate and effective communication about the program to the community at large. These critical areas had not been obvious before; each of them then was written up separately to become a section of the finished report.

Another type of social process is a community ritual that can tell readers a great deal about the structure of a community, the way people organize themselves in relationship to each other and others, and what is important in terms of community identity and positioning. The annual Kandy Perahera is such an event. Each year, Sinhalese people from across Sri Lanka, as well as tourists and nonresident people of Sri Lankan origin, gather in Kandy to celebrate the Esala Perahera. The Esala Perahera, dating to the third century BC, is a ritual enacted to request the gods to send rainfall. The Esala Perahera, a magnificent parade and series of rituals, is believed to be a fusion of two separate but interconnected "*Peraheras*" (processions): The *Esala* and *Dalada*. The Dalada Perahera began when the Sacred Tooth Relic of the Buddha was brought to Sri Lanka from India during the fourth century. The Esala Perahera parade recapitulates the social organization of the traditional Kandian kingdom by caste and occupation. It may be interpreted in many ways—as commodification of a traditional festival, as replication of pre-British Kandian social and caste hierarchy, as a contemporary anticolonial statement, or as an expression of Sinhalese religious and cultural nationalism. Some ethnographers have used such a complex set of rituals as a metaphor for the cultural norms guiding the society overall. Clifford Geertz's "Deep Play: Notes on the Balinese Cockfight" (1973a) uses such a metaphor; by deconstructing and describing the minute details of the cockfight, Geertz actually provided a theoretically informed presentation of the power dynamics, religious beliefs, and a variety of other aspects of Balinese culture.

CREATE SUMMARIES OF INTERVIEW DATA

In the process of in-depth interviewing, researchers generally gain some interesting insights into the processes and issues being addressed in the study. The inclination of many researchers, based on their experiences with quantitative data collection, is to write up the interviews and field notes and wait until the interview sample is completed to review, summarize, and generate trend data or reports. Instead of simply writing up the notes, we recommend that researchers write up a summary of the data regularly. At midpoint, when approximately half of the anticipated data have been collected, it is beneficial to review them, identify themes, trends, ideas, variables, new domains, and other study components, and write them up for sharing with other team members. When data collection is over, these interim reports can be reviewed, while new trends, themes, and patterns are being identified. Such reports, on specific topics defined in taxonomic deduction, as well as on new ideas, can be very beneficial in leading to future analysis.

CREATE SUMMARIES OF TEST SCORE OR PRECODED SURVEY OR QUESTIONNAIRE DATA

We already have indicated that ethnographers sometimes begin their analysis by working with data that are relatively easy to code and tabulate. Similarly, researchers can use computers to rather quickly produce summaries of such data from precoded questionnaires and surveys and educational or other achievement-test scores. These summaries then can be described in narrative form, formatted graphically (see "Create a Display, or, When in Doubt, Draw a Picture!" below), and presented as a significant section of the report.

CREATE COLLECTIONS OF QUOTATIONS FROM DOCUMENTS OR INTERVIEWS

Just as ethnographers can write up summaries of quantifiable data—as described immediately above—ethnographers also can use computers or scissors, tape, and glue to create collections of quotations from texts, documents, or interviews. Placed together, these materials often demonstrate patterns or structures that, when described in narrative form, can be useful first chunks of a report. Computer programs offer easy ways to accumulate such quotations by allowing researchers to mark text and describe it in the program without actually coding it. These noncoded but important text blocks can be returned to, organized, and analyzed for patterns and structures.

EXAMPLE 11.8

STARTING WITH QUOTATIONS FROM DOCUMENTS, INTERVIEWS, OR FIELD NOTES

During the early 1990s, LeCompte and Bennett deMarrais began to notice the wide use of the term "empowerment" by educational reformers. Both researchers had done work on the use of the term, and both realized that although teachers, administrators, policy makers, and public figures all sprinkled the term liberally throughout their speeches and policy statements, there was little consistency within or among these groups as to its meaning. LeCompte and Bennett deMarrais began their research by collecting a list of quotations from public figures from all fields— even military commanders—and educators, each of whom used the term "empowerment" in a different way. Then they reported results from ethnographic interviews asking members of different populations in the school district that LeCompte was studying what they thought the term meant to them. Wide variation in these responses, as well as in the statements from public figures, set the stage for an article presenting the remainder of an ethnographic study examining the term's use in different settings and its current value as a "slogan system" (Apple 1995) in public discourse (LeCompte and Bennett deMarrais 1992).

CREATE OR REFINE A CONCEPTUAL FRAMEWORK AND DRAW A GRAPHIC PICTURE OF IT

Researchers also can create or refine initial or formative conceptual frameworks that consist of categories into which they sort data as if the data were being placed into "bins" (Miles and Huberman 1984) or boxes. Vadebon-coeur's three-category conceptual framework depicted in Figure 5.1 in this volume is a framework with which the researcher began analysis. In her report, she first provided the diagram in graphic form and then followed the diagram with a rather lengthy narrative description that defined the origins of each category and what they represented, iden-tified the kinds of data that she sorted into each category and why they were sorted that way, and then explained how the diagram was related to the reality of the program under study. Later, she created a more complex diagram (Figure 11.1) to display both how her initial model was modified and her analytic strategies. This diagram, too, was written up as above. The process is similar to what we described in Book 2 as "operationalization," or "building formative theory," but it occurs after the data are collected rather than before. As we have explained, however, operationalization can occur at any time during a study, with both qualitative and quantitative data. Further, subdomains within a study can be theorized. Qualitative as well as quantitative data lend themselves to the verification of the formative model, to the creation of subdomains, and to the identification of new domains, factors, and variables that are critical to the study though unanticipated at its initiation.

USE STANDARD NARRATIVE FORM

Ethnographers also often decide in advance to use one of the basic narrative traditions or genres common in West-ern society (see Hayden White, cited in Clifford 1990, 55). Sometimes this involves "telling a story" by structuring it chronologically from the earliest events to the most recent and including in it an abstract form of beginning (such as the "once upon a time" phrase that begins many children's stories); an orientation to the time and place where the phenomenon occurred; presentation of the "cast of char-acters" or persons involved; a description of complicating actions, or what actually happened (analogous to the plot in a story); a coda, or statement of what happened as a result of the complicating action or events; a resolution or

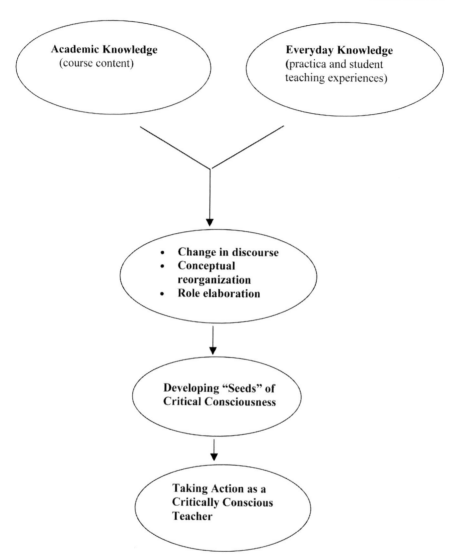

FIGURE 11.1   Revised Analytic Framework from Vadeboncoeur: Self, Other People, and Social Structure, 1998

solution to problems identified or encountered in the plot line; and some evaluative statements, which tell how the writer felt about what was happening or compare the events to others that did occur or might have occurred (adapted from Mishler 1986).

Another form of write-up involves so-called technical writing, which gets to the point quickly. Rather than extensive narrative description, technical writing relies on succinct summaries of data and requires the presentation of a summary of results first, followed by a body of evidence supporting the credibility, validity, reliability, and authenticity of those results. This is then followed by an interpretation and explanation with implications for further research or actions to be taken.

BORROW A NARRATIVE FORM FROM THE PEOPLE BEING STUDIED

The kinds of writing or presentation genres described above have been criticized because of their closeness to Western ways of thinking and communicating. Some researchers argue that presenting non-Western ideas in a Western format destroys their meaning (see Said 1978; Minh-ha 1989; Spivak 1988). Example 11.9 describes how one researcher tried to avoid such a practice.

EXAMPLE 11.9

ANALYZING LAKOTA STORIES USING BOTH WESTERN AND LAKOTA NARRATIVE FORMS

In an unusual ethnolinguistic study, Karen Von Gunten used as data the stories that North American Lakota Indians tell to gain an understanding of how American Indian ways of thinking about knowledge and learning differ from Western European ones. Lakota stories are told on various levels; they constitute entertainment; they are told to teach young Lakota about their religion and preferred practices; and they also are told as a means of social control. Evoking a particular story often reminds the hearers of cultural norms and practices they should be following when they transgress; stories also can serve to reinforce ideals and norms or to present metaphysical interpretations of events. Von Gunten presented her data first in the metaphoric and narrative formats used by the Lakota people themselves because she thought that the standard narrative format of most Western writing—see Mishler's typology described in chapter 5—was absent from and inappropriate for the Lakota stories she worked with. She then reorganized the format to one more comfortable to academics, school administrators, and educational policy makers—people more accustomed to concrete and chronological narratives—who then could use the study's findings to design educational materials more suitable to Lakota children than are the mainstream, European American–oriented ones currently in use (Von Gunten 1999).

DEVELOP A METAPHOR

Ethnographers often begin their write-up by inventing a metaphor or image that captures the sense or evokes the meaning that the writer is trying to convey, using it to create a link between the known metaphor and the more unfamiliar phenomenon the ethnographer is trying to describe.

EXAMPLE 11.10   ━●━◆━●━◆━

WITCHCRAFT IN TENURE AND PROMOTION PROCEDURES

Frank Lutz (1982) used the metaphor of witchcraft to structure his study of university faculty. The analogy suggests that rewards in the university are influenced not by universalistic and well-understood canons for merit, but rather by the evocation of a system of supernatural spirits and powers which, if properly propitiated and attended to by expert practitioners, will produce rewards. Likening the procedures for obtaining tenure and getting promoted to rituals and rites and the documents used to substantiate claims for academic excellence to charms and fetishes, Lutz made an analog between university practices and ways of manipulating people for one's own benefit, inducing them to engage in specific actions, act against others, or engender suspicion toward others so as to affect the course of one's tenure decision.

━●━◆━●━◆━

 Key point *It is important to remember that the metaphor is not the phenomenon itself;* university faculty in the United States usually do not practice witchcraft! However, the practices of witchcraft are well-enough understood—at least at some level—by nonuniversity people that understanding of the arcane and sometimes bewildering procedures undergone by professors can be assisted by comparing them humorously to the equally arcane and sometimes bewildering rituals and procedures used by shamans. A caution should

 Key point be noted with regard to metaphors: *to make sense to the reader, the item that is being used metaphorically must be familiar to the audience whom the ethnographer wants to reach.* A culture that had never heard of witchcraft would find Lutz's metaphor unintelligible. Similarly, a culture in which witchcraft constituted a respected way of understanding and influencing the world and was, in fact, widely practiced, could find the rather humorous way in which Lutz frames his metaphor to be disrespectful or arrogant.

DESCRIBE THE FUNCTIONS OR ORGANIZATIONAL STRUCTURE OF A GROUP

Ethnographers can follow the tenets of functional or eco-logical theorists, who describe the component parts of a group or society and demonstrate how they are inter-related. In this way, they can build the description of the whole society or culture in terms of its functions and the structures that evolve to carry out those functions.

EXAMPLE 11.11

BEGINNING WITH A FUNCTIONAL DESCRIPTION

Hostetler and Huntingdon (1971) studied the Amish, a religious community in the United States whose members follow practices of simple rural living, shun modern urban technology, and adhere to Protestant Christian beliefs and practices generated in the 1800s. Treating the Amish as a "tribe" or self-contained culture, the research-ers examined each aspect of the community's life—family, farming, schooling, religion, and so on—in terms of its relationship with other components of Amish culture and its contribution to the overall harmony and survival of Amish life. The goals of education, for example, were to impart literacy sufficient to read the Bible and to engage in general commerce and agricultural life as the Amish have practiced it for centuries. The Amish believe that eight years of formal schooling is sufficient, and they tend to set up their own schools if they viewed teachings in the public schools in their areas to be detrimental to their beliefs. Thus, the schooling they wanted for their children was one that supported their traditional lifestyle; it was not designed to expose the Amish to other cultures and ways of living or to encour-age them to leave their own community. The Amish, in fact, have a long history of litigation against requirements that they send their children to school for longer than the eight years they feel sufficient for their needs, or to schools whose instruc-tion is inimical, in their view, to their religious teachings.

A functional or structural analysis such as Hostetler and Huntingdon's uses a systems theory approach to iden-tify the basic components in the community, group, or culture; it then describes the operations of each. Further analysis can address how the components support or inter-fere with each other and what the consequences of these relationships are for life within the community and its relationships with external groups and influences. More recently, in her years-long ethnographic study of political economic and ethnic dynamics in the southwestern United States' Four Corners area, Donna Deyhle included as tribes not only the Navajo and Ute Native American residents, but members of the Church of Jesus Christ of Latter-day Saints (Mormons) (Deyhle 2009). Doing so permitted her to compare and contrast the basic components, norms, and objectives of each cultural group and facilitate understanding of the long-standing patterns of conflict among groups in the region.

Ecological modeling is a more contemporary approach to functionalism, but both recognize that sectors or structures in a community or society intersect in a dynamic manner. For the past forty years, anthropologists have used an ecological framework to examine the ways in which individuals and households are affected by and affect policies, regulations, and cultural practices related to human behavior in, for example, malaria control, child development, agricultural management, suburban to urban migration, and other such phenomena. In fact, scientific paradigms that emphasize dynamic systems theory favor ecological thinking because it recognizes that our capacity to predict complex systems is limited. Thus, the best way to understand complex systems is to conduct ethnography that identifies the multiple factors, intersecting in unpredictable ways, that point to emergence of new understandings and directions for theory (Schensul and Trickett 2009; Schensul 2009, 2010; Trickett 2009; Hawe, Shiell, and Riley 2009).

WRITE UP THE CRITICAL EVENTS IN CHRONOLOGICAL ORDER

Ethnographers often begin by linking together in a chronological fashion descriptions of a series of critical events that have occurred during the course of fieldwork. These descriptions of a temporal, usually passing, reality can form the beginnings of a narrative, as is the case of the critical event at the faculty meeting depicted in Example 11.6. In her report on the Arts Focus program, LeCompte created vignettes of several other critical events, including the decisions of the first principal and a key arts teacher to resign and a town meeting in which the community changed its mind about closing the school in which Arts Focus was located. These critical elements or events formed the focal points around which the remainder of the year's report was written. Critical events also formed one component of a study of the introduction of smokeless tobacco products to residents in a low-income area of Mumbai. In this community, the implementation of new forms of packaging (paper instead of plastic packets) for smokeless tobacco and the inclusion of graphic images on packaged tobacco goods changed people's selection and purchasing patterns, at least for a short time (Schensul et al. 2012).

MAKE A LIST OF THE MOST IMPORTANT EMPIRICAL FACTS

Sometimes, the most important results from a study involve a catalog, dictionary, or encyclopedia of empirical facts. These can include an ordered listing of vocabulary in a language or special terms used in a professional field or specialty practice; a taxonomy of behaviors or events such as all the types of locations appropriate for placing hospitals, clinics, schools, coffee shops, residential housing, or other institutions; a taxonomy of all the ways people can contract a communicable disease; or a taxonomy of all the factors associated with students' failure to complete high school. Sometimes these lists or the results of pile sorts or other sorts, explained in detail with rich ethnographic description, are enough by themselves to constitute a report. At other times, the researcher needs to sit down and write a short narrative describing the most important things he or she believes the research or the descriptive listings say, continuing the write-up by giving reasons why these points are important and then elaborating on each narrative by providing evidence in support of those reasons.

CREATE A DISPLAY, OR, WHEN IN DOUBT, DRAW A PICTURE!

With the exception of Vadeboncoeur's conceptual and analytical model diagrams, all of the forms of analysis we have discussed so far involve creating texts. This, however, obscures the fact that one of the most important ways of analyzing data involves figuring out how to draw pictures of what has been found. Miles and Huberman call this the "display" aspect of data analysis; a display is a "spatial format that presents information systematically to the user" (1984, 79).

Contemporary human beings are accustomed to looking at all kinds of displays; the menus on computer screens and websites on the Internet are displays; so are charts and graphs, diagrams showing how to assemble children's toys, and the gauges on automobile dashboards. Miles and Huberman view display as a central component of analysis, and they build it into their research sequence (Figure 11.2). These authors argue that "you know what you can display" (1984, 79)[1] and suggest that presenting analyzed data in narrative text form alone has serious limitations.

First of all, text is dispersed; many pages are required to present what a table can display in one. Many people—especially policy makers and administrators—lack the time to read pages of text, and others find them intimidating. Visually oriented people also find it easier to grasp complex information when it is graphically presented rather than merely as text. Further, because narrative usually is presented in sequential or chronological form, it is difficult for text accounts to consider three or more variables at once—as Vadeboncoeur's figure (see Table 6.4) displaying the change of attitudes over time of teacher training students does. Regardless, a display of some kind often permits

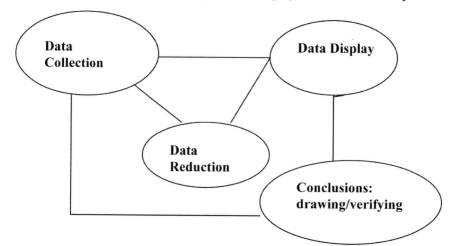

FIGURE 11.2   Conceptual Diagram: Stages of Research

the researcher to look at many kinds of data simultaneously in a focused and systematically arranged format. Displays can permit the researcher to show to an audience the actual process or sequence of his or her data collection and analysis strategies, something which often helps to convince skeptical audiences that the work was done in a systematic and rigorous fashion. Displays also give plenty of opportunity for interesting and vivid graphics, which are becoming increasingly easy to create, given software that creates both black-and-white and color graphics on personal computers and programs that permit computers and projectors to be linked for animated presentations.

How to Start Creating a Display

Displays can begin with the simplest of materials: newsprint and Post-it notes (or tags of paper with glued edges, which can be pasted in place, moved, and repasted), sheets of paper, scissors, glue, and tape to create large spreadsheets or sketches. Key to thinking about displays is flexibility; the researcher has to be able to move pieces of information around, explore different ways of portraying relationships and connections, and revise constantly. Also necessary is a rather large surface on which to compose and assemble ideas, and paper or drawing material that is larger, in general, than a computer screen or standard letter paper. While displays ultimately must be reduced to paper, slide, or photo size, restricting scope in the initial stages also restricts imagination.

Many researchers are tempted to begin to create displays on computers; while the most advanced software graphics can provide much of the flexibility described above, they are expensive, not available to all, and sometimes difficult to transfer to other media. Less sophisticated software tends to enforce two-dimensional, linear, and even boxlike thinking. Our bias is that researchers should not start off creating displays on the computer. We prefer the more traditional newsprint, or better still, a whiteboard or blackboard, which allows for modifying, erasing, and starting afresh without committing to permanent typesetting. The Arts Focus conceptual framework displayed in Tables

10.1, 10.2, and 10.3 involved organizing and reorganizing chunks of data spatially and visually; LeCompte and Holloway began with a pad of 1½-meter by 2½-meter newsprint paper and Post-its or stickers in six different colors (to denote different domains) and in large and small sizes (to represent subdomains and sub-subdomains). The categories of data and specific indicators were written on the Post-its and then organized on the newsprint sheets. Each large sheet constituted a domain; a specific color of sticker represented the subdomains within the domain, the large colored stickers represented the specific subdivisions within the subdomain, and the small colored stickers the behaviors that were indicative of the domain overall. LeCompte spread the sheets of newsprint all over her kitchen and living room tables for several days while she and the research team discussed where various stickers should go. The process moved stickers—and sheets of newsprint—around, sometimes dividing a single sheet into several so that what had appeared to be one domain became subdivided into several separate domains. The physical process of moving, cutting, pasting, and rearranging paper visually reinforced the cognitive processes of comparing, contrasting, matching, modifying, and clarifying needed not only to create a viable set of codes for analysis, but to clarify the conceptual structure of the study overall. While LeCompte found the process described to be useful in organizing masses of data, paper-and-pencil doodling often is the most appropriate way to begin creating conceptual diagrams such as those Vadeboncoeur used in her study or some of the kinds of displays described later in this chapter.

Some researchers may have access to a Smart Board and brainstorming software such as Inspiration; these may well prove useful in the doodling and thinking through involved in assembling displays. Such software can facilitate drawing diagrams and abstract representations. The Healis Sekhsaria Foundation for Public Health in Mumbai has such technical equipment. It permits staff members to model diagrammatic summaries of important meetings on their whiteboard and then copy the summaries from the whiteboard to an embedded image. Images emerge in a standard 8½ × 11-inch size; they provide a rapid way of capturing the main ideas that have been generated in the course of a meeting. Again, however, we caution that the linear and two-dimensional nature of computers and their logic often constrain flexibility and imagination needed in the earlier stages of the process. This is why we suggest beginning with paper and pencil or newsprint and stickers.

Types of Displays: Charts, Graphs, Diagrams, Maps, Taxonomies, Network Diagrams

Contrast or Contingency Tables. Contingency or contrast tables are one of the most common types of display. They generally present a way to represent differences between two or more groups on a given dimension; the differences usually are given in numerical data, but they also can be used to show the presence or absence of a trait, practice, or belief. For example, contingency tables can be used to show differences among males and females in the percentages that patronize credit unions or attend soccer matches. A 2 × 2 contingency table also can be used to display data on the economic status of divorcees in the United States by sex (Table 11.1).

Table 11.1 could be elaborated on, displaying the same data for African Americans, Latinos, European Americans, or Asian Americans and indicating the percentages of males and females of each ethnic group that experience upward and downward mobility.

Event Lists and Time Lines. Event lists simply present a comprehensive list of all the events or activities that have occurred during a given period, without organizing them in any particular way. Such lists can be useful to give a sense of variety; they also can be a precursor for a coding activity that would permit enumeration of the frequency of occurrence of specific kinds of events. A time line, by contrast,

TABLE 11.1   A Contingency Table: Economic Status after Divorce

Sex	*Economic Status after Divorce*
Males	Higher than while married
Females	Lower than while married

arranges such events chronologically. Martinez's normative vignette describing how the day begins at Snow Mountain Elementary School is artful (see Example 11.1), but the entire description of the day requires some ten pages of text. Another way of presenting "a day in the life" is with a time line, as in Table 11.2. Medina used this time line to introduce a much longer narrative description of the specific kinds of instruction offered throughout the day.

Matrices and Scatterplots. Matrices and scatterplots permit a researcher to display co-occurrence, or one piece of information in terms of another. For example, researchers could display the number of responses (one piece of information) given by each of a group of informants (the second piece of information) (Table 11.3). Borgatti and Halgin's chapter in Book 4 on elicitation techniques makes good use of response matrices in the construction of cultural

TABLE 11.2 Time Line: A Typical Day in Room #15

8:30 a.m.: Student Arrival Students came to the classroom from the cafeteria. Students greeted the teachers and each other. They moved the chairs from the top of the tables. Recitation of Navajo Pledge in Navajo followed by the Pledge of Allegiance in English, then a brief period of silence.
8:45 a.m.: Spelling and Basal Reading Groups in English Ability reading groups: low, middle, high
9:20 a.m.: "Building Specials" in English Rotation of art, music, library, PE, and a computer class
10:15 a.m.: Morning Recess
10:40 a.m.: Math Groups and Handwriting in English Ability group instruction in high, middle, low, or whole group instruction of new material. Chapter I time; seven students left the classroom for remedial instruction. Homework "catch-up" time.
12:20 p.m.: Lunch and Recess
1:05 p.m.: Reading in Navajo or English Teacher read aloud or students read library books. Oral story time.
1:35 p.m.: Journal in English
2:00 p.m.: Electives in Navajo Classroom electives: Navajo studies, *Chaa* book,[1] writing, weaving, art. Infrequently, health, social studies.
3:00 p.m.: End of the School Day (Medina 1998, 97)

[1]*Chaa* books were journals, kept in Navajo, of each student's daily activities. They were illustrated by the students.

TABLE 11.3 Matrix: Drinking Frequency Totals

			Less Than Once a Week	Once a Week or More	Total
GENDER	Male	Count	21	21	42
		% within GENDER	50.0%	50.0%	100.0%
		% within Drinking frequency	34.4%	91.3%	50.0%
		% of Total	25.0%	25.0%	50.0%
	Female	Count	40	2	42
		% within GENDER	95.2%	4.8%	100.0%
		% within Drinking frequency	65.6%	8.7%	50.0%
		% of Total	47.6%	2.4%	50.0%
Total		Count	61	23	84
		% within GENDER	72.6%	27.4%	100.0%
		% within Drinking frequency	100.0%	100.0%	100.0%
		% of Total	72.6%	27.4%	100.0%

domains. Scatterplots do much the same thing but require numerical data that can be displayed—or plotted—on the axes of a graph, as in Figure 11.3. Vertical axes represent quantities or locations of one kind of data; horizontal axes represent quantities or locations of another kind of data.

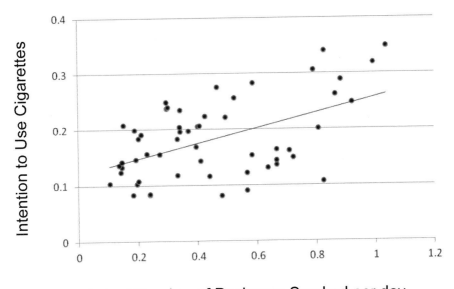

FIGURE 11.3 Scatterplot: Intention to Use Cigarettes by Actual Packages Smoked

Figure 11.3 displays "intention to use cigarettes" on the vertical X axis by the "actual number of packages smoked per day" on the horizontal Y axis. Table 11.3 shows a matrix displaying the frequency of drinking by gender among urban adolescents. The total number of youth in Table 11.3 who report drinking is 84. The matrix includes "row percentages" (reading across within gender) and column percentages reading down within drinking frequency). The matrix shows that it is much more common for boys than girls to drink once a week or more.

Conceptual Diagrams. Conceptual diagrams permit the researcher to map out and display the conceptual and theoretical relationships and structures that guide their study or that they have discovered in the course of the study. The conceptual diagram in Vadeboncoeur's study (Figure 5.1) was constructed at the beginning of her study to illustrate how she initially planned to code or chunk her data. The more elaborate conceptual diagram she created to describe the components in her analysis plan is displayed in Figure 11.1. Conceptual diagrams seldom use numbers; they are a convenient way to portray particular kinds of information that are, in Miles and Huberman's words, "messier and thicker than numbers," and therefore not amenable to counting or graphical representation. Initial and revised formative research models are conceptual diagrams.

Taxonomies or Tree Diagrams. In earlier chapters, we described how tree diagrams or taxonomies can be used to portray the hierarchical structure of coding and analytic frameworks. Such diagrams also can be used to show the hierarchical arrangement of virtually any phenomenon so organized; a typical kind of taxonomy can be found in the organizational charts of virtually any formal organization. Taxonomies usually are organized vertically (as in Table 11.4, which displays children's activities); tree diagrams may be arranged either vertically or horizontally (as in Figure 11.4, which horizontally displays components of the domain "FAMILY").

Pie Charts. Pie charts (Figure 11.5) are circular figures that are divided into wedges whose size denotes the relative importance or proportion of components within a single

TABLE 11.4 Taxonomy of Children's Activities

1. CHILDREN'S ACTIVITIES
1.1. Activities: doing things at home
1.1.1 Sweeping
1.1.2 Dusting
1.1.3 Cooking
1.1.4 Getting groceries
1.1.5 Washing dishes
1.1.6 Washing clothes
1.1.7 Taking garbage out
1.2. Activities: doing things at school
1.2.1 Reading
1.2.2 Writing at desk
1.2.3 Doing group exercises
1.2.4 Recess games
1.2.5 Doing worksheets
1.3 Activities: doing things after school at school
1.3.1 Clubs
1.3.2 Sports
1.3.3 Detention
1.3.4 Tutoring/homework
1.4 Activities: doing things after school, elsewhere (not at school)
1.4.1 Playing in park (not sports)
1.4.2 Playing outside around the house or on the street
1.4.3 Going to an after-school program
1.4.4 Going to the library
1.4.5 Sports program
1.4.6 Informal sports with friends
1.5 Activities before going to school
1.5.1 Brushing teeth
1.5.2 Eating breakfast
1.5.3 Getting dressed
1.5.4 Walking to school

FIGURE 11.4 Tree Diagram: The Domain FAMILY

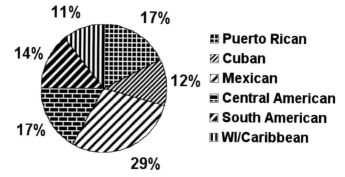

FIGURE 11.5   Pie Chart Showing Distribution of Latino Groups in Worcester

entity. They often are used for displaying such things as the distribution of expenses in a budget, groups within a population, or shades of opinion within a group. Figure 11.5 displays the proportions of specific ethnic groups within a population.

Graphs. Graphs provide another way to represent relative distribution of items. Bar graphs, for example, can display differing amounts of education, drug use, income, or recreational activity among different groups within a population (Figure 11.6).

Venn Diagrams. Venn diagrams show the overlap among items or concepts in a study. Venn diagrams can be presented as overlapping circles, ovals, or other plane figures. Figure 11.7 displays the three principal forms of

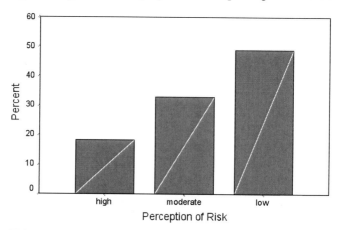

FIGURE 11.6   Bar Graph: Perception of AIDS Risk Exposure among Urban Adolescents

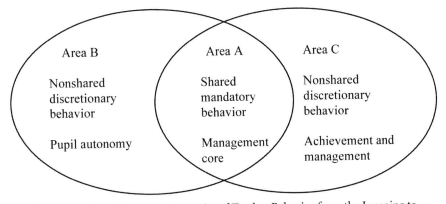

FIGURE 11.7   Venn Diagram: Categories of Teacher Behavior from the Learning to Work Study

teacher behavior that LeCompte identified in her Learning to Work study.

Flow Charts. Flow charts permit the researcher to portray processes, or the flow of activities over time. They often are used to depict how events transpired or to assist groups in planning their activities. The research process diagram in Book 1, chapter 6 is such a flow chart, as is the research time line. The latter depicts the flow of activities planned for a research project, displayed over the three-year life span of the project. Flow charts can be organized in many different ways. Figure 11.2 presented earlier in this chapter is a flow chart created by Miles and Huberman (1984); Figure 11.8 presents the same material presented in Figure 11.2 but formatted differently.

Causal Networks. Causal network diagrams resemble flow charts, but they permit the researcher to order the events, concepts, behaviors, and other components of a cultural scene temporally so as to depict the direction of influences of one on the other. Causal networks portray a chain of events or influences in ways that the researcher expects, or predicts, they will occur or be related to one another. They are like summative models. Figures 11.9 and 11.10 illustrate two ways to display a chain of events or a set of causally related factors.

Sociograms. Sociograms depict the interaction patterns between individuals or groups of individuals within a particular social setting or context. They are used to show

Cross Reference: See Book 2 for a discussion on how to shift from formative to summative models that summarize triangulated data. Researchers do this to refine an initial theoretical position.

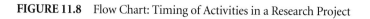

DATA COLLECTION PERIOD

|-----------------------------|

DATA REDUCTION

|---|---|

Anticipatory   During   Post

DATA DISPLAYS

|---|

During   Post

CONCLUSIONS DRAWING/VERIFICATION

|---|

During   Post

FIGURE 11.8   Flow Chart: Timing of Activities in a Research Project

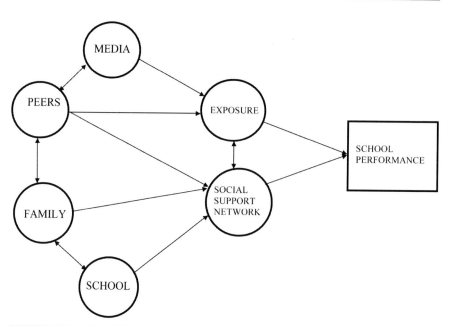

FIGURE 11.9   Causal Network: Factors Related to School Performance

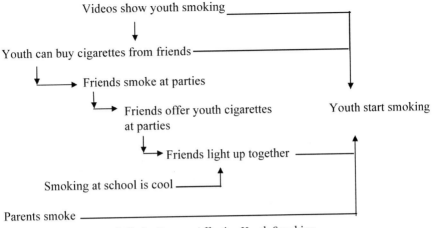

Videos show youth smoking

Youth can buy cigarettes from friends

Friends smoke at parties

Friends offer youth cigarettes at parties

Youth start smoking

Friends light up together

Smoking at school is cool

Parents smoke

FIGURE 11.10 Causal Chain: Factors Affecting Youth Smoking

who interacts with whom as well as the relative frequency of interaction among individuals within a group (Figure 11.11). Sociograms are frequently used in social network research.

In Figure 11.11, the large black circle represents the index person (the start point) who is providing the information about his network. The larger, lighter circles are his immediate male associates. The smaller, lighter circles are the close male friends of the index person's immediate associates. The darker circles on the outside upper right and left are "wifeys" or the girlfriends of the index person and of several of his closest male friends. The thinner lines connect associations among individuals in this network. The thicker lines represent drug sales/drug use networks. This sociogram portrays the relationship between the index person and his immediate personal relations. It provides a great deal of information on the pattern of relationships among individuals, the difference between friendship and drug networks, and the degree to which women partners are excluded in drug exchanges.

Cross Reference: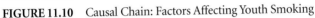
See Book 4, chapter 5 for details on social network research

Problems with Displays

As this discussion and exemplary figures demonstrate, the kinds of displays possible are limited only by the imagination of the researcher! Researchers should remember, however, that many readers are not visually oriented and

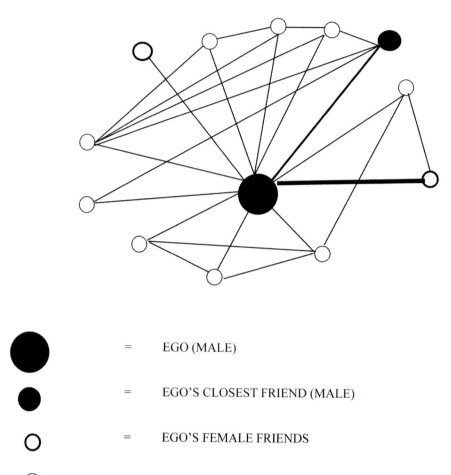

● (large)	=	EGO (MALE)
● (small)	=	EGO'S CLOSEST FRIEND (MALE)
○ (bold)	=	EGO'S FEMALE FRIENDS
○ (thin)	=	EGO'S MALE FRIENDS
▬	=	CLOSEST RELATIONSHIPS

FIGURE 11.11   Sociogram: Relationship between the Index Person and His Immediate Personal Relations

tend to skip over figures and diagrams. Thus, even the best diagrams and figures do not always speak completely for themselves. Researchers must include a narrative with figures to tell readers what the figure portrays, what they should notice within it, and what the researcher thinks is important about the figure or diagram.

Any of these display tactics can be converted to electronic or nontext formats and augmented with photographs, sound, and even documentary films. These methods allow researchers to display their work to larger groups. The simplest forms of visual presentation involve making printed paper handouts or using flip charts, large sheets of newsprint, or an overhead or LCD projector to display text-based material. Other formats that require more technical expertise and equipment are slide shows, computer-assisted displays such as PowerPoint or Prezi, or combinations of technology using visuals, motion, and sound. These techniques can make even the most arcane of presentations more interesting. However, we hold out several important cautions to researchers desiring to use these methods.

- Do not try to substitute sophistication of display or technical prowess for excellence of research results. Many researchers become so enamored with their PowerPoint or other computer software capabilities that they spend more time developing presentations than they do analyzing and interpreting data. Thus their presentations lack substance, even though they may be marvels of technical razzle-dazzle.
- Remember that equipment often fails. As we have noted in the previous chapters and books in this series, expected equipment may not be delivered, or if delivered may be broken. Bringing one's own equipment is not always sufficient; it, too, can malfunction. Power cords can be too short to reach outlets, outlets may be missing altogether, lightbulbs can burn out, tapes will stick or fail to record, and computers can refuse to interact with other necessary hardware or develop mysterious fatal ailments. The electricity can go out altogether, just when backup batteries go dead. This is why, although we have become dedicated advocates of high-tech presentations because they can be so effective, we also believe that researchers should have in reserve a foolproof backup at all times that requires no equipment of any kind for success.[2]

SUMMARY

In this chapter, we have discussed how researchers formulate their coded and analyzed qualitative data into meaningful stories they can tell and then organize those "stories" or compilations of data into displays that facilitate the understanding of the various audiences whom the ethnographer wants to reach. In the last chapter, we discuss interpretation of data, or how researchers go about making sense of the results they have obtained and translate that sense into reports, presentations, and documents that are meaningful to research participants, informants, partners, funding agencies, and other external constituencies.

NOTES

1. Another way of phrasing this might be, "If you can display it, you must really know it!"

2. The list of horror stories was compiled from actual situations in which the authors have found themselves.

12 —◆—◆—◆—

CREATING INTERPRETATIONS

INTRODUCTION: STRATEGIES FOR INITIATING INTERPRETATION OF RESEARCH RESULTS

Up to now, we have been talking about the process of trans-forming data into succinct reports on what the ethnographer found. We have outlined strategies ranging from using preexisting schemes for coding, enumerating, and interpreting data to recursive methods for "chunking" data and dividing the observed stream of experience into items, bits, and units that can be individually studied and then reassembling those pieces in ways that comport with how the research participants explain their world and illuminate how these explanations contribute to an entire cultural portrait. We also have talked about ways to start telling a story—and then how to present it to readers in comprehensible ways. This process creates research "results," but it does not constitute the end of the story.

All too often, researchers arriving at this point in the research process believe that their job is finished. *Mere "results," however, do not speak for themselves. Before they can be meaningful, research results must be interpreted.* This means researchers must tell the audience—often a number of different kinds of readers with multiple agendas and differing capacities for understanding and making use of research results—just what those results mean, beyond the simple facts of the case. What, for example, is the

Key point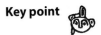

301

significance of the findings? How do they inform our understanding of this and similar phenomena? How do the findings fit into, modify, or contradict current understandings? Can they shed new light on theoretical understandings of human behavior and culture? Creating an interpretation can be challenging because it means taking leaps beyond the data or beyond what the crunched results actually portray and presenting the results in a broader context. Many researchers find it uncomfortable and even frightening to depart from results. But going beyond results is exactly what researchers are trained and hired to do.

While all researchers hope to find something that nobody else knows, much of what researchers do is to illuminate the obvious. Often enough, informants, research participants and partners, and even funding agencies greet the well-crafted report of an ethnographer with the statement, "Well, but everybody knows that!" In many ways, the job of the ethnographer is, in fact, to attribute meanings and importance to patterns and regularities that people otherwise take for granted in everyday life—until, that is, a researcher points them out, highlights them, and gives them broader significance by associating them with other experiences, situations, and literature.

However, while people in the site might have lay or folk beliefs about what "everybody knows," they are not likely to be able to step back from everyday knowledge to pinpoint the significance or implications of such knowledge for enhancing the human sciences, for future practice, or for program or policy innovation. Nor can they see clearly the relationships of their own group or institution with other groups or the meaning of the results for the overall survival of each. Finally, they cannot set the work in the context of other research on the same topic, showing how this particular study advances the field, contradicts other studies, or suggests a path to new research frontiers. This is because locals are focused on understanding local situations; they do not usually gain the external perspective that researchers have and are hired to provide as part of their presentation of results. Insiders also generally do not have the opportunity to read the research literature, see similar sites, or compare their situation with others unless a study is fully participatory. For example, although the teachers in the Arts Focus program appreciated the careful analytic descriptions of their practice that LeCompte and Holloway produced, they were not very surprised at the results. However, when fully interpreted beyond the mere results, the story being told helped everyone in the school understand the implications that the arts teachers' activities might have for the other teachers on the faculty of Centerline Middle School. They also provided insight as to what those results meant to other arts teachers in the school district and to teachers at Centerline Middle School in general, as Example 11.6 indicates. Interpretations in LeCompte's and Holloway's reports were useful to parents trying to choose an appropriate school for their children, and they also helped the school board make decisions about which programs to support and which to eliminate because of declining educational funds in the community. Similarly, Schensul and colleagues' work in Mauritius (Schensul et al. 1994) and Sri Lanka (Silva et al. 1997) placed research on sexuality and sex risk in the context of rapidly growing industrialization and AIDS risk in the Indian Ocean area (Schensul 1996) by demonstrating that the risk factors for promoting HIV infection were present, despite low HIV prevalence rates in both countries. At the same time, the research provided support for the importance of promoting national policies favoring sex education as a means to prevent AIDS risk in countries with deeply conservative religious and cultural ideas with regard to sexuality.

Although all of the above described constituencies were "local," the utility of most research projects do not have to be limited to the immediate community in which the study was done. Results and interpretations from the Arts Focus study, for example, could be of use to curriculum theorists and educational psychologists trying to develop more effective ways to teach children, as well as to museum directors, supporters of the arts, and artists trying to build more support for the arts in their communities. Similarly, research methods and results on sexuality and AIDS risk conducted in two countries in the Indian Ocean area were being disseminated by Stephen Schensul and colleagues throughout other Southeast Asian countries with the support of the World Health Organization and the

Rockefeller Foundation. Book 7 in this series is devoted to a discussion of the variety of ways in which ethnographic research can be used and disseminated in other settings, including policy formulation and promotion, intervention research, evaluation, administration, and museum and public programming settings.

Cross Reference:
Book 7

We argue that simply presenting results cannot provide the kind of guidance these types of constituencies need in order to make use of a study. The interpretation the researcher provides is crucial; it must be crafted carefully for a variety of potential users, whose needs must be identified in advance. The strength of the interpretation and any subsequent recommendations that might come from it lie in the skill and integrity with which ethnographers use their results to support the interpretation and the methods of delivery they devise for their presentation. Further, the methods of presentation should be chosen with reference to the audience the researcher wants to reach. As this discussion indicates, there are many possible audiences for LeCompte's and Holloway's single study of arts education or LeCompte's study of Native Americans, just as there are many for the studies of HIV risk exposure conducted in Mauritius or Sri Lanka. Put in a larger context, these studies have importance for policies and programs far beyond the simple case studies they seem to be. In the following box, we describe steps researchers can take to interpret their data and some of the central considerations and constraints that affect the direction of the interpretation.

STRATEGIES FOR INITIATING INTERPRETATION OF RESEARCH RESULTS

- Brainstorm and speculate with research partners.
- Review the research questions.
- Return to the formative ethnographic theory.
- Review the relevant theories in the field.
- Reanalyze the historical and sociopolitical context of the research findings.
- Evaluate the program.

- Present an "emic" (insider) interpretation and then contrast it with other, outsider interpretations.
- Repeat the same analytic processes used to generate results.
- Look for program relevance.
- Look for policy relevance.
- Consider the audience.

BRAINSTORM AND SPECULATE WITH RESEARCH PARTNERS

Throughout this book series, we have emphasized the importance of partnerships in research and of embedding research in the specific settings and communities where it has local meaning. Interpretation, like theory building, can be thought of as operating on two levels—local (with research partners) and general (in relation to other studies and the literature on the topic). While careful researchers often find it difficult to speculate about how their data might be used beyond the specific site, much less to speculate about the implications that the data might have for theory and practice, it is their job to do so. *An important first step in getting started is to enlist the help and support of research partners in considering the meaning of the research results to* **them.** Systematic review of research results with interested partners can have important implications. Partners gain deeper commitment to the results and their use in the process and may discover new ways of using the research for their own purposes. They also can provide important insights to the researchers. The brainstorming and thought that go into speculation, dreaming, and "playing with ideas" (LeCompte and Preissle 1993) with research partners and participants can generate some of the most valuable connections between a current project and those to come. In order to maximize the potential for good discussion with research partners, it is important to consider how best to present and represent research results. Some people relate better to diagrams, flow charts, and other visuals, some to numbers, and some to oral presentations. In feedback and discussion with the community of participants in a study of MDMA (the drug Ecstasy), for

Key point

example, researchers Jean Schensul and colleagues used a combination of PowerPoint presentations, a film based on in-depth interviews with Ecstasy users, and handouts to conduct "member checking." In this way, they determined whether the study had missed any important insights from different sectors. S. K. Singh, a researcher at the International Institute for Population Sciences, Mumbai, worked with artists who used as script material data from men interviewed on their drinking patterns and sexual relationships. These data represented important study implications; Singh and artists created street plays with them. The plays were performed in community settings where the study took place, and audiences were invited to discuss the implications of the performances and the meanings associated with messages about alcohol use and risky sex. Ideas such as these are detailed in a variety of texts and publications that can be helpful to researchers in thinking through how to represent results using visualization techniques to improve the likelihood of good reception by various audiences and to generate fruitful discussions. For further information, see Tufte 1990, 1992, and 1997.

REVIEW THE RESEARCH QUESTIONS

 Key point *A second step can involve reviewing the research questions to identify what initial hunches the researchers might have had about the significance of the study and its connection to existing bodies of research or knowledge.* Does the study enhance, confirm, modify, or disconfirm what is already known about the research questions asked, and in what ways? Do these confirmations, negations, modifications, or clarifications lead the researchers to revise and reformulate the original research questions? Were they the right questions at the right level of abstraction? Most research raises as many questions as it answers. In interpretation, researchers can reframe the original questions. In Jean Schensul's study of Latino children's activity outputs, the original question did not take into consideration gender differences. When she compared the findings of the study to the research literature on the topic, she noticed not only that there was no literature on Latino children, but that what literature on children did exist did not consider gender differences, either in children's activities or in their energy outputs (Schensul, Diaz, and Woolley 1996). The study question was then revised to consider gender differences in socialization practices and contextual factors playing a role in differential energy outputs. The results also pointed the way for future such studies of Latino children in general.

REVIEW THE FORMATIVE ETHNOGRAPHIC THEORY

Some studies based on prior field research begin with clearly formulated ethnographic theories; others construct theoretical frameworks in the process of analysis. These frameworks are based on some fairly specific hypotheses or hunches that are continually tested through preliminary analyses in the field and finalized in the study's analytic phase. The hypotheses or hunches usually are based both on the researcher's growing understanding of circumstances in the field and his or her knowledge of the research literature and comparable studies. ***In the end, it is important to return to the formative ethnographic theory guiding the study.*** If several iterations of the formative theoretical model have emerged during the course of the study, researchers can return to each one and examine the assumptions of each, review how the changes in the model occurred, and explain why the changes were made. Good iterative research not only strengthens and enhances models over time but continuously interprets and reinterprets the meaning of the data. Revising the history of the model as it grows is one way of reconstructing how researchers thought about the data throughout the history of the project. The explanations for why the changes have occurred contribute to interpretation of the meaning of the study. Data inventory matrices, such as those displayed in Figure 3.1 in this book, can facilitate this process by documenting how and why changes in the original research plans were made.

Key point

Cross Reference: See Book 2 for a full discussion of the relationship between initial theoretical models and the iterative path to refining and finalizing them at the study's end

REVIEW RELEVANT THEORIES

A study is generally based on one or more theoretical approaches or guiding frameworks. ***Researchers should begin their interpretation by reviewing relevant theories***

Key point

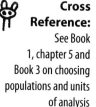

proposed by other researchers working on the same or related topics. In this way, researchers can identify the ways the study's findings confirm, disconfirm, modify, or clarify existing theories explaining what the researcher studied, and in what ways. Because there are many possible theories from which to select, returning to the unit of analysis is helpful here. If the study is about understanding the behavior or attitudes of individuals, for example, then psychosocial or structural theories that predict such behavior can be reviewed. If it is about groups or units within larger institutions, such as classrooms or clinics, small group or organizational theories can be reviewed. Perhaps the study compares socialization practices in a number of different communities. In this instance, theories about the topic at the community level might be useful to review at the start.

To explore how others have used these theoretical viewpoints, researchers can turn to other studies set within the paradigm(s) they originally selected to guide the study. They can also turn to what some have called "midrange theory" (Merton 1967; Pelto and Pelto 1978) or grounded or substantive theory (Glaser and Strauss 1967), which focuses specifically on explanations of local phenomena in the research site or that help to explain associations at the domain or structural level. Trotter and Schensul (1998) discuss some of the middle-range or substantive theories that social scientists use to explain behavior at the individual and cultural levels, especially in applied work. These include the following.

Cross Reference:
See Book 1, chapter 5 and Book 3 on choosing populations and units of analysis

Cross Reference:
See Book 1, chapter 3 for a discussion of research paradigms and Book 2 for a review of some ways to think about theory

MIDDLE-RANGE OR SUBSTANTIVE SOCIAL SCIENCE THEORIES

Individual Level: Sociocognitive Theories

- Cultural model theories
- Consensus theories
- Social construction theories
- Scripting theories
- Exchange theories
- Practice theories
- Sociocultural learning theories

Cultural Level: Sociocultural and Contexts Theories

- Social network theories
- Cultural ecological theories
- Critical theory

(Trotter and Schensul 1998)

Using these types of theories, researchers should ask whether comparisons have been made between their own study results and what others have found, and whether those comparisons led to conclusions about similar topics that confirm, negate, modify, or clarify the study's results. If so, people—even researchers—may have to change what they think about the topic under study. They also may have to borrow from other frameworks, not anticipated in the original study, to locate underlying reasons that explain what they have found. Sarah Staley and Candice Miller did this to find theories that explained why a glorious opportunity for improving race relations never happened, and why PhD students in one program were likely to graduate, while those in another program were not. Such modifications may even lead to the emergence of a new theoretical framework.

REPEAT THE ANALYTIC STRATEGIES THAT PRODUCED RESEARCH RESULTS

It sometimes helps the interpretive process to play with **Key point** *ideas and theorize with finished results in the same way researchers used to generate the initial results.* This involves engaging in the same analytic processes used in creating items, patterns, and structures, as well as variables and factors that help to explain the existence and organization of a domain. Researchers can compare and contrast the study's results with those of other studies; make connections or linkages between what was found in this study and results from similar studies; and try to find theories that explain the results more adequately than current theories. Metaphors, analogies, and similes can help users unfamiliar with the specifics of the research site or project to understand what was found and how it might connect with their own concerns. For example, in the 1970s, researchers who found that decision making in organizations did not follow what they assumed to be logical lines compared the decision-making process to a soccer or basketball game where decisions were made "on the fly" by assessing conditions from moment to moment. From there, they went on to develop a new theory of decision making in organizations and bureaucracies. Similar examples can be found in the examples cited in this book of medical research among Cambodian and Hmong populations (Fadiman 1997) and school reform studies (LeCompte and McLaughlin 1994).

PRESENT A CONTRASTED INSIDER AND OUTSIDER PERSPECTIVE

 Key point

Cross Reference: Distinctions between "insider" or "emic" and "outsider" or "etic" approaches or perspectives are defined in Books 1 and 2

Researchers can begin by describing the data as participants in the study interpret them, which constitutes an emic or insider's approach. They can then contrast this emic presentation with the way outsiders would view the same data (cf. Pelto and Pelto 1978, 54–65). Staley's study of two merged schools presented in Example 1.1 in this book used such a strategy.

LOOK FOR PROGRAM RELEVANCE

 Key point

Part of the interpretation also can address the extent to which a study's data and research questions were relevant to the group, program, or organization it studied. It is particularly important to look for program relevance when at least one component of the study involves an evaluation. Did the study enhance program objectives? If so, in what ways? If not, why? Were there unintended consequences or surprise results? If so, what might have accounted for them? Did the research provide data that program participants could use? Why or why not?

In general, the process of such an interpretation involves:

- describing the differences between the expected and the observed;

- explaining these differences both from an "emic perspective" and through comparison with other researchers' results for similar projects; and
- discussing implications for the project in question and for work in the field addressed by the program.

In Book 7, we discuss the ways in which ethnographic research can inform policies, programs, and interventions at the formative, implementation, and outcome stages.

Cross Reference: See Book 7

LOOK FOR POLICY RELEVANCE

Interpretations also can address policy relevance. Sometimes a study specifically focuses on a policy-related question. Examples of policy-related questions guiding research are the following: "What models of transitional housing for women are more likely to result in social and economic independence?" "Should the Houston Board of Education (or any other board of education) implement an arts and education program such as Arts Focus on a larger scale?" "Has the creation of charter schools resulted in improvements in educational outcomes among students in the Chicago Public Schools?" Other research may not be specifically policy oriented but may have implications for decisions under consideration by policy makers. Schensul's study of third- and fourth-grade children's activity outputs, for example, was never intended to be a policy research study. But in light of decisions made to increase physical education programs in the Hartford public schools, it had important implications for decisions regarding the types of programs needed for both girls and boys at that grade level.

Key point

Researchers should address specifically whatever light the study's results shed on current public or private policy governing the groups, programs, or organizations that were the target of the study. Making clear that interpretations do reflect on policy issues requires that researchers spend some time reading the appropriate literature, including newspapers, and talking with policy makers to know what policy decisions are current and how to frame results in order to ensure that they are recognized as important.

Cross Reference: See Book 7 on how to use ethnographic research to improve policy making

EVALUATE THE PROJECT

Key point Often, a study is commissioned as a straightforward evaluation. In such cases, *interpretation of data must address whether or not the project under study met its own objectives and if so (or if not), why.* Here interpretation rests on an explanation of these results. Evaluation also can ask whether or not those objectives were adequate or whether they were so narrowly construed that they did not really address the bigger goals of which the project was a part. Interpretation then can address the reasons for the disjuncture and focus readers on implications of the results for the project, for the context within which it is set, and for other projects like it. Some of the same considerations apply here as to interpretation for program relevance.

Evaluation is a politically charged activity that often involves making decisions about whether a program should be continued, changed, expanded, or discontinued. The preceding involves displays of power and influence; every program changed or discontinued has implications for people's jobs, value systems, friendship networks, and livelihoods. Insofar as it has the power to influence policies—and indeed sometimes it is commissioned specifically because it is intended to influence a policy regarding the program in question—ethnographic evaluation always may be considered to be policy research. Researchers should study the political context of the evaluation, both while they are conducting it and afterward, in order to know how to frame their results.

CONSIDER THE AUDIENCE

Key point *Interpretations also should take into consideration what audiences need to hear.* Audience issues address not only what significance or implications the data might have, but also what data to present and how to present them. To some extent, this means deciding at what level of specificity or abstractness the presentation should be. For example, an interpretation that focused on the positive impact of the arts program on teacher morale, student achievement, and school climate might be most useful to teachers; such a report could help them have the confidence to plan ways to integrate the arts throughout all content areas taught in the school. However, the principal might need an interpretation that focused on the value of the arts to children's cognition and success in school overall to convince a skeptical school board to provide sufficient funds for the program. Such an interpretation would still use the same data but organize it to make different key points. Arts administrators, by contrast, would be more interested in the extent to which such programs could be expanded to reach more children—future patrons and consumers of the arts—so as to convince them about the value of participation in the arts. As for policy makers, proper interpretation requires knowing enough about the different audiences for whom the research results are targeted to know how to organize and present those results so that they will be meaningful as well as heard.

SUMMARY

In this book, we have described strategies for interpreting a body of research results in ways that are meaningful both to the research community and to a variety of lay constituencies. These strategies are used in the last stage of the research process; they involve spelling out the significance of the findings for any number of users in the local community or organization sponsoring the research, for funding agencies, for the researcher's own professional and disciplinary peers, for policy-oriented agencies, and even for governmental bodies. Often, interpretations for differing audiences must address different segments of the research results or present them in different ways, since information needs for each group seldom will be identical.

In the remaining two books of the *Ethnographer's Toolkit*, we turn to issues that suffuse the entire research process. In Book 6, *Ethics in Ethnographic Research*, we present an analysis of the issues faced by researchers in general and ethnographers in particular, with respect to the ethical treatment of human subjects and community groups in research. Some of these issues involve managing the multiple sets of official regulations governing research with and on human beings; others involve the ethics of everyday life in the field and in interaction with research participants and their communities. Book 7, *Ethnography in Practice*, addresses team research and the construction of research partnerships, as well as the use of ethnographic research and results in a wide variety of programs, interventions, and policy interventions and approaches.

REFERENCES

Alleman, E. 2009. "Playing Soccer: Mexican-American Girls Honored and at Home on the Field." Course paper prepared for Advanced Qualitative Methods, Boulder, Colorado.

Altman, J., and W. P. Fogarty. 2010. "Indigenous Australians and 'No Gaps' Subjects." In *Closing the Gap in Education: Improving Outcomes in Southern World Societies*, edited by Ilana Snyder and John Nieuwenhuysen, 109–29. Clayton, Victoria, Australia: Monash University Publishing.

Apple, M. W. 1995. "The NCTM Standards as a Slogan System." *Journal of Research in Mathematics Education* 23: 412–13.

Babbie, E. 2007. *The Practice of Social Research.* 11th ed. Belmont, CA: Thomson Wadsworth.

———. 1995. *The Practice of Survey Research.* Belmont, CA: Wadsworth.

———. 1980. *Sociology: An Introduction.* Belmont CA: Wadsworth.

Berg, M. J. 1992. *Rapid Sociodemographic Assessment Project (RSA)* (11 monographs). Hartford, CT: Institute for Community Research.

Berg, M. J., E. Coman, and J. Schensul. 2009. "Youth Action Research for Prevention: A Multi-level Intervention Designed to Increase Efficacy and Empowerment among Urban Youth." *American Journal of Community Psychology* 43 (3/4): 345–59.

Berg, M. J., D. Kremelberg, P. Dwivedi, S. Verma, J. Schensul, K. Gupta, D. Chandran, and S. K. Singh. 2010 (August). "The Effects of Husband's Alcohol Consumption on Married Women in Three Low-Income Areas of Greater Mumbai." *AIDS and Behavior* 14: S1, S126–35. doi: 10.1007/s10461-010-9735-7.

Berg, M. J., and J. J. Schensul, eds. 2004. "Participatory Action Research with Youth." In "Approaches to Conducting Action Research with Youth," special issue, *Practicing Anthropology* 26 (2).

Berke, M. G. 2012. "A Comparison of Deaf Mothers Reading to Their Deaf Pre-schoolers to Hearing Mothers Reading to Their Hearing Pre-schoolers." PhD diss., Department of Speech, Language and Hearing Sciences, University of Colorado, Boulder.

Bernard, H. R. 1995. *Research Methods in Anthropology: Qualitative and Quantitative Approaches to Ethnographic Research.* Walnut Creek, CA: AltaMira.

Bernard, H. R. 2011. *Social Research Approaches: Qualitative and Quantitative Methods.* 2nd ed. Lanham, MD: AltaMira.

Bourdieu, P., and J. Passeron. 1977. *Reproduction in Education, Society and Culture.* London: Sage.

Bowen, E. S. [Laura Bohannon]. 1954. *Return to Laughter: An Anthropological Novel.* New York: Doubleday.

Broomhall, L. 1998. Field notes, "Interview 1 with Danny (pseudonym)." Hartford, CT: Institute for Community Research.

Brouillette, L. 1996. *A Geology of School Reform.* Albany: State University of New York Press.

Clifford, J. 1990. "Notes on (Field) Notes." In *Fieldnotes: The Making of Anthropology*, edited by R. Sanjek, 47–71. Ithaca, NY: Cornell University Press.

Cohen, J. 1968. "Weighed Kappa: Nominal Scale Agreement with Provision for Scaled Disagreement or Partial Credit." *Psychological Bulletin* 70 (4): 213–20. doi: 10.1037/h0026256. PMID 19673146.

Cohen, J., and P. Cohen. 1983. *Applied Multiple Regression/Correlation Analysis for the Behavioral Sciences.* Hillsdale, NJ: Erlbaum.

Council of Graduate Schools. *PhD Completion Project.* http://www.phdcompletion.org.

Denzin, N., and Y. Lincoln. 2003. "Introduction: The Discipline and Practice of Qualitative Research." In *The Landscape of Qualitative Research: Theories and Issues,* edited by N. Denzin and Y. Lincoln, 1-45. Thousand Oaks, CA: Sage.

Dewey, J. 1934. *Art as Experience.* New York: Penguin.

———. *Democracy and Education: An Introduction to the Philosophy of Education.* New York: Macmillan. First published 1944 by Collier Macmillan.

Deyhle, D. 2009. *Reflections in Place: Connected Lives of Navajo Women.* Tucson: University of Arizona Press.

Erickson, K., and D. Stull. 1998. "Doing Team Ethnography: Warnings and Advice." Sage University Paper #42. Thousand Oaks, CA: Sage.

Fadiman., A. 1997. *The Spirit Catches You and You Fall Down: A Hmong Child, Her American Doctors, and the Collision of Two Cultures.* New York: Farrar, Strauss & Giroux.

Fogarty, W. P. 2011. "Learning through Country: Competing Knowledge Systems and Place Based Pedagogy." PhD diss., Center for Aboriginal Economic Policy Research, Australian National University, Canberra.

Freire, P. 1970. *Pedagogy of the Oppressed.* New York: Continuum.

Friedenberg, E. Z. 1970. "Curriculum as Educational Process: The Middle Class against Itself." In *The Unstudied Curriculum: Its Impact on Children.* Overly, NV: ASCD Elementary Education Council, and Washington, DC: National Educational Association.

Geertz, C. 1973a. "Deep Play: Notes on the Balinese Cockfight." In *The Interpretation of Cultures,* 412–55. New York: Basic Books.

———. 1973b. "Thick Description: Toward an Interpretive Theory of Cultures." In *The Interpretation of Cultures,* 3–33. New York: Basic Books.

Gerstl-Pepin, C. I., and M. G. Gunzenhauser. 2002. "Collaborative Team Ethnography and the Paradoxes of Interpretation." *International Journal of Qualitative Studies in Education* 15 (2): 137–54.

Gilligan, C. 1982. *In a Different Voice: Psychological Theory and Women's Development.* Cambridge, MA: Harvard University Press.

Gilligan, C., N. P. Lyons, and T. J. Hanmer, eds. 1990. *Making Connections: The Relational Worlds of Adolescent Girls at Emma Willard School.* Cambridge, MA: Harvard University Press.

Gilligan, C., J. M. Taylor, and A. M. Sullivan. 1995. *Between Voice and Silence: Women and Girls, Race and Relationship.* Cambridge, MA: Harvard University Press.

Glaser, B. G., and A. I. Strauss. 1967. *The Discovery of Grounded Theory. Strategies for Qualitative Research.* Chicago: Aldine.

Goffman, E. 1961. *Asylums.* New York: Anchor Books.

———. 1959. *The Presentation of Self in Everyday Life.* New York: Anchor Books.

Golde, C., G. Walker, and Associates, eds. 2006. *Envisioning the Future of Doctoral Education: Preparing Stewards of the Discipline, Carnegie Essays on the Doctorate.* San Francisco: Jossey-Bass.

Greene, M. 1995. *Releasing the Imagination: Essays on Education, the Arts, and Social Change.* New York: Jossey-Bass Education.

Guest, G., and K. MacQueen. 2008. *Handbook for Team-Based Qualitative Research.* Lanham, MD: AltaMira.

Hawe, P., A. Shiell, and T. Riley. 2009. "Theorising Interventions as Events in Systems." *American Journal of Community Psychology* 43: 267–76. doi: 10.1007/s10464-009-9229-9.

Holley, F. M., and D. A. Doss. 1983. *Momma Got Tired of Takin' Care of My Baby.* Publication #82.44. Austin, TX: Office of Research and Evaluation, Austin Independent School District.

Holloway, D L., and M. D. LeCompte. 2001. "Becoming Somebody! How Arts Programs Support Positive Identity for Middle School Girls." In *The Arts, Urban Education and Social Change*, edited by B. Krensky and D. L. Holloway, theme issue, *Education and Urban Society* 33 (4): 388–408.

Hostetler, J. A., and Huntingdon, G. E. 1971. *Children in Amish Society: Socialization and Community Education*. New York: Holt, Rinehart & Winston.

Hunt, G. P., K. Joe-Laidler, and K. Evans. 2002. "The Meaning and Gendered Culture of Getting High: Gang Girls and Drug Use Issues." *Contemporary Drug Problems* 29 (2): 375.

Jackson, P. 1968. *Life in Classrooms*. New York: Holt, Rinehart & Winston.

Kostick, K., S. Schensul, K. Jadhav, R. Singh, A. Bavadekar, and N. Saggurti. 2010. "Treatment Seeking, Vaginal Discharge and Psychosocial Distress among Women in Urban Mumbai." *Culture, Medicine and Psychiatry* 34 (3): 529–47.

LeCompte, M. D. 1974. "Institutional Constraints on Teacher Styles and the Development of Student Work Norms." PhD diss., Department of Education and the Social Order, University of Chicago.

———. 1978. "Learning to Work." *Anthropology and Education Quarterly* 9: 22–37.

LeCompte, M. D., and D. Aguilera. 1996. *Year Three Final Product/Process Evaluation Report of the Phoenix Indian Learning Circle Program: A Partnership between the Osborne School District and the Phoenix Indian Center*. Phoenix, AZ: Phoenix Indian Center.

LeCompte, M. D., D. E. Aguilera, B. E. Fordemwalt, S. Wilks, and M. E. Wiertelak. 1996. *Final Report for The Learning Circle: A Partnership between the Osborne School District and the Phoenix Indian Center*. Phoenix, AZ: Osborne School District and Phoenix Indian Center.

LeCompte, M. D., and K. Bennett DeMarrais. 1992. "The Disempowering of Empowerment: Out of the Revolution and into the Classroom." *Educational Foundations* 6 (3): 5–33.

LeCompte, M. D., and A. G. Dworkin. 1991. *Giving Up on School: Teacher Burnout and Student Dropout*. Newbury Park, CA: Corwin Press.

LeCompte, M. D., and J. P. Goetz. 1982. "Problems of Reliability and Validity in Ethnographic Research." *Review of Educational Research* 52: 31–60.

LeCompte, M. D., and D. Holloway. 1997. "Evaluation Report for Arts Focus/Boulder School of the Arts at Base Line Middle School, September."

———. 1998. "Second Year Process Evaluation Report for Arts Focus/Boulder School of the Arts at Base Line Middle School."

LeCompte, M. D., and D. McLaughlin. 1994. "Witchcraft and Blessings, Science and Rationality: Discourses of Power and Silence in Collaborative Work with Navajo Schools." In *Power and Method: Political Activism and Educational Research*, edited by A. Gitlin, 147–65. New York: Routledge.

LeCompte, M. D., and J. Preissle with R. Tesch. 1993. *Ethnography and Qualitative Design in Educational Research*. 2nd ed. New York: Academic Press, 267–77.

LeCompte, M. D., and J. Schensul. 2010. *Designing and Conducting Ethnographic Research: A Mixed Methods Approach*. 2nd ed. Lanham, MD, AltaMira.

LeCompte, M. D., and M. E. Wiertelak. 1994 (September). 1993–1994 "Evaluation Report for the Learning Circle Program, Osborne School District, Phoeniz, AZ." Grant award SO61A20035.

Lee, M. 2009. "Children's Emerging Conceptions of Science." Paper prepared for the class Qualitative Methods 11, School of Education, University of Colorado, Boulder.

Lewins, A., and C. Silver. 2004. *Choosing CAQDAS Software*. University of Surrey, CADCAS Networking Project, http://caqdas.soc.surrey.ac.uk/.

Lofland, J. 1971. *Analyzing Social Settings: A Guide to Qualitative Observation and Analysis*. Belmont, CA: Wadsworth.

Lofland, J., and L. H. Lofland. 1984. *Analyzing Social Settings: A Guide to Qualitative Observations and Analysis*. 2nd ed. Belmont, CA: Wadsworth.

Lorde, A. G. 1984. *Sister Outsider: Essays and Speeches*. Berkeley, CA: Crossing Press.

Lovitts, B. E. 2007. *Making the Implicit Explicit: Creating Performance Expectations for the Dissertation*. Sterling, VA: Stylus.

Lutz, F. W. 1982. "Witches and Witchcraft in Educational Organizations." Paper presented at the annual meetings of the American Anthropological Association, Washington, DC.

Martinez, E. L. 1998. "Valuing Our Differences: Contextual Interaction Factors That Affect the Academic Achievement of Latino Immigrant Children in a K–5 Elementary School." PhD diss., School of Education, University of Colorado, Boulder.

Medina, B. M. 1998. "Dine K'ehgo Na'Nitin: Education in the Navajo Way." PhD diss., School of Education, University of Colorado, Boulder.

Merton, R. K. 1967. *Social Theory and Social Structure*. New York: Free Press.

Metz, M. H. 1978. *Classrooms and Corridors: The Crisis of Authority in Desegregated Schools*. Berkeley: University of California Press.

Miles, Matthew, and A. H. Huberman. 1984. *Qualitative Data Analysis: A Sourcebook of New Methods*. Beverly Hills: Sage.

Miller, C. 2009. "Doctoral Success? Negotiating a Field of Practice." PhD diss., Department of Educational Leadership, University of Colorado, Denver.

Minh-ha, T. T. 1989. *Woman, Native, Other: Writing Postcoloniality and Feminism*. Indianapolis: Indiana University Press.

Mishler, E. 1986. *Research Interviewing: Context and Narrative*. Cambridge, MA: Harvard University Press.

Moonzwe, L., J. Schensul, and K. Kostick. 2011. "The Role of MDMA (Ecstasy) in Coping with Negative Life Situations among Urban Young Adults." *Journal of Psychoactive Drugs* 43 (3): 199–201.

Murdock, George P. 1971. *Outline of Cultural Materials*. 4th rev. ed., 5th printing, with modifications. New Haven, CT: Human Relations Area Files.

Nastasi, B., J. J. Schensul, A. DeSilva, K. Varjas, P. Ratnayake, and S. Schensul. 1998/1999. "Community-Based Sexual Risk Prevention Program for Sri Lankan Youth: Influencing Sexual-Risk Decision Making." *International Quarterly of Community Health Education* 18 (1): 139–55.

Patton, M. Q. 1990. *Qualitative Evaluation and Research Methods*. 2nd ed. Newbury Park, CA: Sage.

———. 2002. *Qualitative Research and Evaluation Methods*. Thousand Oaks, CA: Sage.

Pelto, P., and G. Pelto. 1978. *Anthropological Research: The Structure of Inquiry*. New York: Cambridge University Press, 54–65.

Radda, K., J. Schensul, S. Clair, and M. Weeks. 1998. "Social Security: High Risk Sites and the Context of Illicit Drug Use among Older Adults." Paper presented at the annual meetings of the America Anthropological Association, Philadelphia, PA.

Rogoff, B. 1990. *Apprenticeship in Thinking: Cognitive Development in Social Context*. Oxford: Oxford University Press.

———. 2003. *The Cultural Nature of Human Development*. Oxford: Oxford University Press.

Romagnano, L. 1991. "Managing the Dilemmas of Change: A Case Study of Two Ninth Grade General Mathematics Teachers." PhD diss., School of Education, University of Colorado, Boulder.

Romero, M., and M. J. Berg. 1997. "Indicators and Precursors of Alcohol Use in Preadolescent Girls: A Preliminary Analysis." Paper presented at the Annual Evaluation Conference of the Center for Substance Abuse Prevention.

Said, E. W. 1978. *Orientalism*. New York: Vintage.

Sanders, D. W. 2011. "Mathematical Views within a Lakota Community: Towards Mathematics for Tribal Self-Determination." PhD diss., School of Education, University of Colorado, Boulder.

Sanjek, R. 1990. *Fieldnotes: The Making of Anthropology*. New York: Cornell University Press.

Schensul, J. 1996. "AIDS in the Indian Ocean Area." Paper presented in an invited session on AIDS in the world, organized by Douglas Feldman. American Anthropological Association Annual Meeting, Washington, DC.

———. 1998. "Community Based Risk Prevention with Urban Youth." In *School Psychology Review*, special issue, *Mental Health Programming in Schools and Communities*, edited by B. Nastasi, 27 (2): 233–46.

———. 1998/1999. "Learning about Sexual Decision-Making from Urban Youth." Special issue, *International Quarterly of Community Health Education: Cross Cultural Perspectives of Women's Sexual Decisionmaking: Implications for Sexual Health Protection at the Community Level*, edited by M. I. Torres and M. Weeks, 18 (1): 29–48.

———. 2009. "Community, Culture and Sustainability in Multilevel Dynamic Systems Intervention Science." *American Journal of Community Psychology* 43 (3–4): 241–56.

———. 2010. Schensul, J. "Engaged Universities, Community Based Research Organizations and Third Sector Science in a Global System." *Human Organization* 69(4): 308–20

Schensul, J., D. Chandran, S. K. Singh, M. Berg, S. Singh, and K. Gupta. 2010. "The Use of Qualitative Comparative Analysis for Critical Event Research in Alcohol and HIV in Mumbai, India." *AIDS and Behavior* 14 (S1): S113–S125.

Schensul, J., N. Diaz, and S. Woolley. 1996. "Measuring Activity Levels of Puerto Rican Children." Paper presented in a symposium on the health of Puerto Rican children. Second Annual Conference of the National Puerto Rican Studies Association, San Juan.

Schensul, J., S. Nair, S. Bilgi, E. Cromley, V. Kadam, S. D'mello, and B. Donta. 2012. "Availability, Accessibility and Promotion of Smokeless Tobacco in a Low Income Area of Mumbai." *Tobacco Control*, March 12 e-publication. doi: 10.1136/tobaccocontrol-2011-050148.

Schensul, J., and E. Trickett. 2009. "Introduction to Multi-Level Community Based Culturally Situated Interventions." *American Journal of Community Psychology* 43: 232–40. doi: 10.1007/s10464-009-9238-8.

Schensul, S. L., M. Borrero, V. Barrera, J. Backstrand, and P. Guarnaccia. 1982. "A Model of Fertility Control in a Puerto Rican Community." *Urban Anthropology* 11 (1): 81–99.

Schensul, S., M. Munoz-Laboy, and M. Bojko. 1998 (December). "Using National Data Sets to Guide Ethnographic Research on Children and Youth." Paper presented at the annual meetings of the American Anthropological Association, Philadelphia.

Schensul, S., G. Oodit, J. Schensul, S. Seebuluck, U. Bhowon, J. P. Aukhojee, S. Rogobur, B. L. Koye Kwat, and S. Affock. 1995. *Young Women, Work and AIDS-Related Risk Behavior in Mauritius.* Women and AIDS Research Program, Research Report Series, No. 2. Washington, DC: International Center for Research on Women.

Schensul, S., N. Saggurti, J. Burleson, and R. Singh. 2010. "Community-Level HIV/STI Interventions and Their Impact on Alcohol Use in Urban Poor Populations in India." *AIDS and Behavior* 14 (S1): S158–S167.

Schensul, S., J. Schensul, G. Oodit, U. Bhowon, and S. Ragobur. 1994. "Sexual Intimacy and Changing Lifestyles in the Era of AIDS: Young Women Workers in Mauritius. *Reproductive Health Matters* 3: 83–93.

Schensul, S., R. K. Verma, B. K. Nastasi, N. Saggurti, and A. A. Mekki-Berrada. 2009. "Sexual Risk Reduction among Married Women and Men in Urban India: An Anthropological Intervention." In *Anthropology and Public Health: Bridging Differences in Culture and Society*, 2nd ed., edited by M. Inhorn. and R. Hahn. New York: Oxford University Press.

Silva, K. T., S. Schensul, J. Schensul, B. Nastasi, M. W. A. de Silva, C. Sivayoganathan, P. Ratnayake, P. Wedisinghe, J. Lewis, M. Eisenberg, and H. Aponso. 1997. *Youth and Sexual Risk in Sri Lanka.* Women and AIDS Research Program, Phase II Research Report Series, No. 3. Washington, DC: International Center for Research on Women.

Spivak, G. C. 1988. "Subaltern Studies: Deconstruction Historiography." In *In Other Worlds*, edited by G. C. Spivak. London: Routledge & Kegan Paul.

Spradley, J. P. 1979. *The Ethnographic Interview*. New York: Holt, Rinehart & Winston.

Staley, S. 2010. "Transforming Identities, Communities and Spaces: What Could Have Been But Wasn't." Paper presented at the American Educational Research Association, Denver, CO.

Trickett, E. 2009. "Multilevel Community-Based Culturally Situated Interventions and Community Impact: An Ecological Perspective." *American Journal of Community Psychology* 43: 257–66. doi: 10.1007/s10464-009-9227-y.

Trotter, R., and J. Schensul. 1998. "Research Methods in Applied Anthropology." In *Handbook of Methods in Cultural Anthropology*, edited by H. R. Bernard, 691–736. Walnut Creek, CA: AltaMira.

Tufte, Edward R. 1990. *Envisioning Information*. Cheshire, CT: Graphics Press.

———. 1992. *The Visual Display of Quantitative Information*. Cheshire, CT: Graphics Press.

———. 1997. *Visual Explanations: Images and Quantities, Evidence and Narrative*. Cheshire, CT: Graphics Press.

Vadeboncoeur, J. A. 1998. "Emancipatory Knowledge Construction in Teacher Education: Developing Critically Conscious Roles through Metaphor and Service Learning." PhD diss., School of Education, University of Colorado, Boulder.

Van Maanen, J. 1988. *Tales from the Field: On Writing Ethnography*. Chicago: University of Chicago Press.

Von Gunten, K. 1999. "Ways of Learning and Knowing in Lakota Oral Stories." PhD diss., School of Education, University of Colorado, Boulder.

Vygotsky, L. 1978. *Thought and Language*. Cambridge, MA: MIT Press.

Weitzman, E., and M. Miles. 1995. *Computer Programs for Qualitative Data Analysis*. Thousand Oaks, CA: Sage.

Weller, S. C., and A. K. Romney. 1988. *Systematic Data Collection*. Newbury Park, CA: Sage.

Wengraf, T. 2004. *Qualitative Research Interviewing: Biographic Narrative and Semi-structured Methods*. 3rd ed. Thousand Oaks, CA: Sage.

Wolcott, H. F. 1990. *Writing Up Ethnographic Research*. Newbury Park, CA: Sage.

Yoshida, B., P. Pelto, and J. Schensul. 1978. "The Principal and Special Education Placement." *National Elementary Principal* 8: 1–7.

Znaniecki, F. 1930. *The Polish Peasant in America and the Old World*. New York: Farrar and Rinehart.

INDEX

ABOUT THE AUTHORS
AND ARTISTS

Margaret LeCompte received her BA from Northwestern University in political science, and after serving as a civil rights worker in Mississippi and a Peace Corps volunteer in the Somali Republic, she earned her MA and PhD from the University of Chicago. She then taught at the universities of Houston and Cincinnati, with visiting appointments at the University of North Dakota and the Universidad de Monterrey, Mexico, before moving to the School of Education at the University of Colorado-Boulder in 1990. She also served for five years as executive director for research and evaluation for the Houston Independent School District. She is internationally known as a pioneer in the use of qualitative and ethnographic research and evaluation in education. Fluent in Spanish, she has consulted throughout Latin America on educational research issues. Her publications include many articles and book chapters on research methods in the social sciences, as well as her cowritten (with Judith Preissle) *Ethnography and Qualitative Design in Educational Research* (1984; 1993) and coedited (with Wendy Millroy and Judith Preissle) *The Handbook of Qualitative Research in Education* (1992), the first textbook and handbook published on ethnographic and qualitative methods in education. Her collaborative work in research methodology continues with this second edition of the *Ethnographer's Toolkit*. Dr. LeCompte is deeply interested in the educational success of linguistically and culturally different students from kindergarten through university, as well as reform initiatives for schools and communities serving such students. Her books in these areas include *The Way Schools Work: A Sociological Analysis of Education* (1990, 1995, and 1999) with Kathleen Bennett deMarrais and *Giving Up on School: Student Dropouts and Teacher Burnouts* (1991) with Anthony Gary Dworkin. Her diverse interests as a researcher, evaluator, and consultant to school districts, museums, communities, and universities have led to publications on dropouts, artistic and gifted students, school

335

reform efforts, schools serving Native American students, and the impact of strip mining on the social environment of rural communities. Her most recent research involves explorations in the politics and finance of public universities. A Fellow of the American Educational Research Association, the American Anthropological Association, and the Society for Applied Anthropology, she also was awarded the Spindler Prize for advances in the field of anthropology and education by the Council on Anthropology and Education of the American Anthropology Association, an organization that she also served as president. She has been editor of the journals *Review of Educational Research* and *Youth and Society*. A founding member and the first president of the University of Colorado-Boulder chapter of the American Association of University Professors (AAUP), she also served as vice president of the Colorado Conference of the AAUP and was active in faculty governance at the University of Colorado. As professor emerita, she continues to use action research strategies in the service of improving the intellectual life in higher education.

Jean J. Schensul, founding director and now full-time senior scientist, Institute for Community Research, Hartford, is an interdisciplinary medical/educational anthropologist. Born in Canada, she completed her BA in archeology at the University of Manitoba and her MA and PhD in anthropology at the University of Minnesota. From 1978 to 1987, as deputy director and cofounder of the Hispanic Health Council in Hartford, Connecticut, she built its research and training infrastructure. In 1987, she became the founding director of the Institute for Community Research, an innovative, multimillion-dollar community research organization, conducting collaborative applied research in education, cultural studies and folklore, participatory action research, and community intervention research in the United States, China, and India. Dr. Schensul's research cuts across the developmental spectrum, addressing contributions of ethnography to disparities and structural inequities in early childhood development, adolescent and young adult substance use and sexual risk, reproductive health, and chronic diseases of older adulthood. She is the recipient of more than twenty National Institutes of Health research grants, as well as other federal, state, and foundation grants. In addition to conferences, workshops, over eighty peer-reviewed journal articles, many edited substantive special issues of journals including *Anthropology and Education Quarterly, AIDS and Behavior, American Behavioral Scientist*, and the *American Journal of Community Psychiatry*, her collaborative work in research methodology is reflected in a book (with Don Stull) titled

Collaborative Research and Social Change, the widely celebrated seven-volume series, the *Ethnographers' Toolkit*, with Margaret LeCompte, and in other articles and book chapters on ethnography and advocacy, community building, and sustainability of interventions. She has served as president of the Society for Applied Anthropology and the Council on Anthropology and Education and is an elected board member of the American Anthropological Association. In recognition of her work as a scholar-activist she has been awarded two senior anthropology awards, the Solon T. Kimball Award for anthropology and policy (with Stephen Schensul) and the Malinowski Award for lifetime contribution to the use of anthropology for the solution of human problems. Dr. Schensul holds adjunct faculty positions in the departments of Anthropology and Community Medicine, University of Connecticut, and she is codirector of Qualitative Research and Ethnography, Interdisciplinary Research Methods Core, Yale Center for Interdisciplinary Research on AIDS.

A fiber artist, quilter, teacher, curator, and lecturer, **Ed Johnetta Fowler-Miller** is acknowledged to be one of the most creative and colorful improvisational quiltmakers in the United States. Widely exhibited in the United States and internationally, her quilts can be found in many important museums, corporate and private collections including The National Gallery of the Smithsonian Institution in Washington, D.C.; Nelson Mandela's National Museum in Cape Town, South Africa; Wadsworth Atheneum Museum of Art in Hartford, Connecticut; and the Rocky Mountain Quilt Museum in Golden, Colorado. Her home state of Connecticut awarded her its most prestigious artistic award, The Governor's Art Award, as well as the Wadsworth Atheneum Museum of Arts first Presidents Award; Leadership of Greater Hartford's Arts and Cultural Award, Vision Award for Arts; and Cultural and Capital Community College Heritage Award. The Home and Garden Station featured Ed Johnetta on the Modern Masters series; she appeared on Debbie Allen's series *Cool Women*, Public TV, Tokyo, Japan; and her woven creations were worn by actress Phylicia Rashad on *The Cosby Show*. The Sunday *New York Times* featured her in the Best of the Best series, and most recently, she appeared on HGTV's *Simply Quilts*. In 2009 Ed Johnetta represented the United States and the Women of Color Quilters Network at the largest quilt festival in the world in Yokohama, Japan, and in 2010 she represented the United States in Costa Rica, where she lectured and taught workshops. She has exhibited her work across the United States and lectures and offers workshops in New England, elsewhere in the United States, and worldwide. More information can be found at http://www.edjohnetta.com.

Graciela Quiñones-Rodríguez is a gourd carver/lutier/ multimedia artisan/performer and Master Teaching Artist. She draws most of her inspiration from indigenous and traditional Puerto Rican imagery and symbols to create *higüeras* (gourds), clay/wood figures, and folk string instruments (*cuatros*, *tiples*, and *bordonuas*). She has been a resident artist in numerous schools and libraries throughout Massachusetts, Connecticut, and New York. She has received fellowships and awards from the Commission on the Arts, the New England Foundation for the Arts, and the National Endowment for the Arts. Her works have been on exhibit in Puerto Rico, the Smithsonian Institution, University of Massachusetts, Wisconsin, New York, and several exhibit sites throughout Connecticut. She is a member of Urban Artists Initiative and the Connecticut Cultural Heritage Arts Program. Graciela Quiñones-Rodríguez is a licensed clinical social worker, currently working at the Storrs campus of the University of Connecticut.